LANGUAGE AND LITERACY SERIES
Dorothy S. Strickland and Celia Genishi, SERIES EDITORS

NONFICTION FOR THE CLASSROOM

Milton Meltzer
on Writing,
History,
and Social Responsibility

Edited and with an Introduction by
E. Wendy Saul

International
Reading
Association

Teachers College
Columbia University
New York and London

Published simultaneously by Teachers College Press, 1234 Amsterdam Ave., New York, NY 10027 and The International Reading Association, 800 Barksdale Rd., Newark, DE 19714

Library of Congress Cataloging-in-Publication Data

Meltzer, Milton, 1915–
    Nonfiction for the classroom : Milton Meltzer on writing, history, and social responsibility / edited and with an introduction by E. Wendy Saul.
      p.   cm.
    Includes bibliographical references and index.
    ISBN 0-8077-3378-4 (acid-free paper). — ISBN 0-8077-3377-6 (pbk.: acid-free paper)
    1. United States—Historiography. 2. Historiography. 3. United States—History—Study and teaching. I. Saul, Wendy. II. Title.
E175.M45   1994
973'.072—dc20   94-25084

ISBN 0-8077-3377-6 (paper)
ISBN 0-8077-3378-4 (cloth)
IRA Inventory Number 154

Printed on acid-free paper

Manufactured in the United States of America

01 00 99 98 97 96 95 94   8 7 6 5 4 3 2 1

Contents

Part III: Intriguing People

For teachers who know the value of humane detours, and students who seek new paths.

Acknowledgments

I gratefully acknowledge the help of friends and colleagues in putting and pulling this book together. First, I wish to thank both Milton and Hilda Meltzer whose generous hospitality made long conversations not only possible, but truly enjoyable. I feel fortunate to count them as friends.

Appreciation is also extended to Heidi Grant, a meticulous researcher, for her careful work in tracing down numerous and often obscure references for this volume.

Debbie Louis, a colleague in Maryland, was especially helpful in the early stages of this project. She assisted with the initial organization of the material and made a daunting task seem possible. William Johnson—historian, editor, teacher, friend—helped in all the really tough editorial decisions. His appreciation of both history and graceful prose made his advice particularly valuable. Both he and Debbie also served as appreciative readers, sharing with me a deep enthusiasm for Meltzer's books and essays.

My debt to Margie Forsyth, administrative assistant, typist, reader, and critic, is enormous. Her perseverance, attention to detail, constancy, and support are felt in a daily way, but particularly on this project.

Finally, I wish to thank my family, my children Matthew and Eliza, and my husband Alan Newman, for their support on this book and for their ability to sometimes laugh at the chaos I bring to their lives.

E. W. S.

Editor's Note

Privately I call this collection, "Illuminating Shadows." The shadows I refer to are in one sense the historical past, and Milton Meltzer, through his work, surely illuminates that which has gone before. But for me the shadow metaphor does more. While certain events and characters are enlivened through our standard histories, others remain as shadows. Meltzer not only enables us to see the figures and events casting these shadows, but also enables these shadows to illuminate, that is, clarify, less inclusive versions of history.

The essays in this volume have been collected, and in many cases reconfigured, from over 150 original speeches and papers. Meltzer, like all lecturers, tends to repeat or restate important ideas. Although he often rearranges material, elaborates on ideas, or refocuses remarks, a reader of an unedited collection would find it, in many ways, repetitious.

In looking at the original material, I noted that some essays, for instance, the biographical pieces on Dorothea Lange or Lydia Maria Child, because of the subject focus, did not include information presented elsewhere. I grouped these biographical pieces together and edited them lightly. They are found in Part III.

Other works, primarily the pieces on social issues and ethnicity, were relatively easy to sort out. By creating folders called racism, terrorism, antisemitism, and so forth, and cutting and pasting relevant passages from several originals, I was able to fit the pieces together well and make sense of them. These essays are found in Part II.

The major editing problem arose with the material now reconfigured as Part I. The conceptual underpinnings of Meltzer's books—his ideas about how nonfiction works, about its status, about his implied audience, about what drives him as a writer—were woven through virtually every essay, though rarely repeated verbatim. Here I, as editor, made many decisions. Although the phrases are all Meltzer's, the organization of these pieces is largely my own. In other words, I suspect that people who listened to Meltzer's speech on Dorothea Lange in the Oakland Museum (California) in 1978 will recognize the essay published here as the lecture they heard then. No one, on the other hand, was there to hear the essay entitled "On Teaching and Learning History," although it may well sound familiar to many who have attended a Meltzer talk.

Introduction

For well over 200 years British and American writers have created books for youngsters that focus on real people, places, and events. Some have laced the truths they seek to share with the rhetoric of inspiration. Others have attempted to disguise fact by wrapping it in the garb of fiction. Still others have sought to draw in youthful readers through a "gee whiz" gathering of surprising data and astounding photographs. Milton Meltzer, arguably the best writer of social history for children and adolescents ever, has crafted his books on a different loom, with threads as familiar to adults as to young people. Exacting and energetic in his research, lyrical but unflinching in his prose, and always true to the moral vision that gives meaning to fact, Meltzer has offered his readers the kind of history people who *do* history value.

Any student of Meltzer's more than 80 books is treated to the pleasure of consuming artful fact. Through his presentations we have learned about many aspects of the past, from American Presidents and the Great Depression to the experiences of traditionally underrepresented populations. The essays gathered in this volume, however, were conceived and have been collected for another reason, not to teach history, but rather to offer a behind-the-scenes view of what it has meant for Meltzer to *write* history. These pieces, individually and in the aggregate, help answer questions that naturally arise as one tries to understand more about the process of assembling and interpreting information: Who is the author? What drives him? Why has he chosen the subjects he has? What decisions does he make as one schooled in particular academic traditions? As a writer for young people? An artist? How does he judge the success of his efforts?

This introductory essay has yet a different purpose. First, I wish to introduce readers to Milton Meltzer, the modest and unassuming man I so much admire. Second, my goal is to think publicly about the view of history that undergirds Meltzer's work. For devotees of children's and adolescent literature, such information about a noteworthy author is always of interest. My hope, however, is that Meltzer's ideas will also benefit educators who wish to think more systematically and critically about what it means to teach social studies or to teach literature in elementary and secondary classrooms. In other words, in this introduction I suggest that those of us concerned with classroom life have much to learn from what Meltzer has modeled in his literary works.

INTRODUCING MILTON MELTZER

In 1988 Milton Meltzer published a book-length memoir entitled *Starting from Home: A Writer's Beginnings.* In many ways this volume is about what it meant to come of age in the 1920s and 1930s; what it felt like to be the child of working-class, immigrant Jews living in Worcester, Massachusetts; what it was like to discover and fall in love with Thoreau and Blake and Whitman. Where other writers might dwell on the nuances of family and social life that made them different from their brothers, their neighbors, their friends, Meltzer tends to focus on those elements that are easily recognized by others growing up in that era.

Still, tucked into this robust tale one can find early signs of the personal predispositions and habits that mark the writer Meltzer is today. These roots are particularly apparent in the author's descriptions of his parents.

> [Ma] had no notion that some kinds of work were for women only, and that men should not be expected to do them. I made my bed, dusted the furniture, and dry-mopped the floors every single day. She was maniacal in her insistence on cleanliness, neatness, order and regularity. . . .
>
> Ma found it hard to forgive human error. Perfection was her natural standard. It even extended to sleep. I remember I slept on my back when young, and never seemed to move in the night, so that when I woke in the morning the sheet was smooth and flat, without a wrinkle. Maybe I was trying to show Ma I didn't mess things up even while asleep. As for how long you slept, she had fixed ideas there, too. To stay abed more than eight hours was a gross offense. "Lazy good-for-nothing!" she'd exclaim, usually routing me out of bed only minutes past the allotted time. (1988c, pp. 49–50)

The habits Mary Richter Meltzer sought to establish in her children are still apparent in her middle son. He rises early and, after a workout in a nearby gym, is usually at his desk by 7:00 a.m. On shelves behind and next to his desk sit the books from which he draws information about the subject of his next book. Each bibliographic source is coded, and notes taken from these works are handwritten on 3 × 5 slips of paper and arranged in a mottled cardboard box, usually in chronological order. Except for the resource books that move on and off the "work shelves" with each text-in-progress, I suspect that his methods and tools have changed little in the 40 years that he has made his living as an author. The yellow legal pad on which the first draft is written, the manual typewriter used for a second draft, the cup filled with pens and pencils and boxes that hold horizontal stacks of 3×5 notes, all are surely as familiar to and controlled by Milton Meltzer as were the washboard and baking pans his mother used in the first half of this century.

Benjamin Meltzer, Milton's father, was a window washer by trade. In one poignant scene Milton describes seeing Pa coming home from work.

> That winter had dragged on without any of the thaws that sometimes eased the harsh New England weather. One snow on top of another, huge drifts, and when it seemed the sun must break through, a fresh fall to renew the white nightmare. I boarded a street car that was worming its way slowly through the icy snow. I was deep in my book when I heard a harsh cough, then another and another, coming from a passenger several seats down from me. I glanced up from the page, and saw that it was my father, racked by his chain smoker's cough. He was almost asleep, his head nodding, his legs slumped into the aisle, his shoulders shaking now and then as the cough persisted.
>
> I studied him as though he were a stranger. The long years of work in all weathers had etched his skin like acid. His leathery face had two deep crevices running from the corners of his mouth upward. His hands were almost black, his fingers and palms crisscrossed with cuts and cracks made by water, wind, ice, snow, and freezing cold. Never lifting his eyes, he didn't notice me. When our stop came at the corner of Providence and Dorchester, he got up to leave, going past me but still not seeing me. I rose after him, walking behind him to the exit, suddenly aware how bent his back had become, his spine curved by the endless hours of labor in that position. As I got down from the trolley, I called out "Pa!" He turned, waited for me to catch up. Then he reached out and stroked my cheek, a rare gesture for him. His fingers felt like sandpaper on my face. (1988c, pp. 57–58)

This passage illustrates perfectly the perspective that character-izes Milton Meltzer's work. Like a videographer he pans the entire scene, goes in for a "close up" and then, surprisingly, puts down the camera and walks, side by side, with his subject. That ability to stand back from those one loves and to describe the scars of experience has led to what Meltzer recognizes as his affinity for "the underdog." Men like Ben Meltzer had few advocates. They spoke and expected little, found pride in supporting their families and having no debts. How does one give back to such a parent? Perhaps by championing rights and causes that serve the silent masses? Perhaps by making vivid the stories of those who dared to fight back? Perhaps by seeking to understand what really differentiates those in power, those with confidence, from those whose energy and ambition are consumed in the process of living.

Parents mark children with both biological and environmental tokens. No less profound may be the effects of gifts young people find for themselves. Again, in *Starting from Home* Meltzer describes the moment when he entered, by chance, a tall building of dark red stone, the library.

> I climbed the high steps and walked into a world I would never leave. Off the main hallways were the treasures I was hunting for. Dozens, hundreds, thousands of books packed into shelves running along the wall, reaching from the floor far higher than my eager fingertips could stretch.
>
> Hungry for the printed word, my appetite was insatiable. I started at one wall of the children's room and worked my way around to the last. . . . At first the librarian would suggest a title or an author to me. But she soon realized that mine was a fundamental hunger. I was like some insect nibbling words to appease an instinctive craving. (1988c, pp. 33–34)

That same drive and approach to books seems as alive in Meltzer today as it did more than 6 decades ago. After working until 12:00 or 1:00 p.m., he takes a break for lunch and exercise, then, for relaxation, sits in a comfortable chair in his sunny living room and reads. He reads the *New York Times* and keeps up with several periodicals. He reads widely about the figure who may become the subject of his next book. He especially enjoys published letters and diaries. He reads about the figures he has chronicled. He reads about the locale of his next Elderhostel (study trip). He reads quickly. His memory for detail is astounding.

It seems to me no accident that Milton Meltzer derives such pleasure from the act of writing for young people. It was through books that he found his way past the tedium his father must have endured. It was in books that he realized the perfection his mother longed for. By entering books he could, and still can, make the curiosities and obsessions, talents and temptations of others his own. As an author he offers this same access to another generation of young people. This is not just engaging work, but indeed a gift.

To say that I am a teacher, a mother, a scholar is to describe a life of competing, sometimes tortured choices. However, in thinking about Milton Meltzer the historian, the writer, the husband, father, and grandfather, I have no sense of such tensions. He is steady, like a patient outfielder waiting for a high fly ball; his books land gracefully, firmly in his glove. This is not to suggest that any life can be lived without tensions, but rather that Milton Meltzer has found great pleasure in the people he loves, the places where he has lived, and the work that he performs. His is an unpretentious self-satisfaction, regularly punctuated with books—the books he writes, the books he and his wife read together and discuss, the bookstores and libraries he frequents.

It is no accident that *Starting from Home* is dedicated to Anna Shaughnessy, Meltzer's brilliant high school teacher who introduced him to the writers who still matter so much. At one point, Meltzer recounts going back to Thoreau's *Walden* when "deeply troubled by the course [his own] life was taking" (1988c, p. 81)—to the passage that describes a bug emerging from an old applewood table, which for 60 years stood in a farmer's kitchen. Thoreau concludes:

> Who knows what beautiful and winged life, whose egg has been buried for ages under many concentric layers of woodenness in the dead dry life of society, deposited at first in the laburnum of the green and living tree, which has gradually been converted into the semblance of a well-seasoned tomb—heard perchance gnawing out now for years by an astonished family of man, as they sat around the festive board—may unexpectedly come forth from amidst society's most trivial and handselled furniture, to enjoy its summer life at last! (quoted in Krutch, 1989, p. 350)

There is a kind of energy that writers give to readers, sometimes, oftentimes, delivered by a teacher, which enables those who are touched by it to go on, to grope their way through the darkness. Milton Meltzer knows the power of that gift.

> As I finished reading [Thoreau's] lines, I began to sob. The image of the bug emerging into life after all those years in its wooded tomb touched something deep in me. The tears poured out in relief. Feelings that had been frozen so long, melted in a rush. My wife, who had come running at the sound of crying, looked at me in amazement, then put her arms around me. I felt like one reborn. (1988c, p. 82)

Contributing to and spending a life immersed in that writerly life, must, to a man so touched by art and history and the possibility of finding hope in the most desolate of places, seem like a blessing. How is that sense of possibility passed on to another generation? How do books contribute to a young person's vision of him- or herself as a powerful and responsible and caring agent of change?

HISTORY AS INQUIRY

It was my first semester in college, my first real history course, the first exam of the year. After hours of study, I was ready. In response to an essay question, I not only fired back every fact that our instructor had tossed our way, but was also able to quote, almost verbatim, each example and analogy used by both the professor and the author of our Western Civilization text. A week later our exams were returned. I got a B, and a comment that seemed absolutely shocking at the time: "Learn to be more discriminating."

The question of how to teach interpretation, how to help students value the choice and arrangement of information rather than the rudimentary amassing of fact, is of critical importance to educators. Before working with the essays in this volume, I had always focused my search for interpretive strategies on the word *story* embedded in *history*. "Help students see that they were telling a story," I said to myself. "Practice by telling stories from the more recent past, stories that we can all recognize and critique," I told the soon-to-be teachers with whom I work. But my emphasis on story, if not a false connection, was a case of mistaken etymology.

Milton Meltzer, a master of historical storytelling, knows to begin any discussion of history not with story, but with inquiry. The ancient Greek Herodotus, referred to as the father of history because he sought to do more than simply preserve from decay remembrances of what men had done, founded a tradition of scholars who gathered information from multiple sources and who recognized the importance of ordering fact, understanding context, and positing explanation. Where those before him sought mainly to record the actions of the Greeks and the barbarians, Herodotus, and those who follow in his footsteps, provide a sense of the long sweep, and connect, compare, contrast: They turn an event around until it makes sense in context. This attention to connections is absolutely central to all that historians do. Meltzer seems continually aware of and makes clear the connections between action and thought, between minor and major goals and achievements.

In thinking about Meltzer's books (or any successful historical endeavors) as inquiries, the articulation of questions and the cognizance of bias become key factors in researching and presenting fact. The best professional historians teach students to reflect on issues such as these:

"What is worth knowing?" "Who is a reliable source?" "What facts in a given document are emphasized or ignored?" "Whose sense of 'normal' is evident in the description or recreation of events—whose values?" "Whose perceptions of time?" "Whose perception of pleasure or pain?"

Meltzer not only is conscious of his own answers to these and similar questions, but is also skilled at helping readers become aware of their own biases as consumers and potential writers of, as well as actors in, history. Although this is surely a laudable objective, I would argue that in so doing Meltzer achieves an even more important goal: His work invites young people to become more vital and thoughtful makers of history by linking action and inquiry. "When the historians tell us that Columbus 'discovered' America, what do they mean?" asks Meltzer (1990a) in the first chapter of *Columbus and the World Around Him*. "Surely not that no one knew America was there. . . . It was Columbus who didn't know where he was" (p. 9). Look at the situation from another point of view, he tells readers. Question that which has always appeared obvious. Recognize who in a given interpretation of events is made to seem powerful or stupid, treacherous or decent.

In his biography of the photographer Dorothea Lange, Meltzer (1978) quotes from a speech given by Charles R. Van Hise, one of America's leading geologists. Van Hise's comments are, I suspect, as significant for the historian as they were for the photographer.

> Good descriptive work is discriminative. Good descriptive work picks out certain of the facts as of great value; others of subordinate value; and others of no value for the purposes under consideration. How then can this discrimination be made? How can the facts be selected which are of service? Only by an insight into the causes which have produced the phenomena. Without this insight to some extent at least a description is absolutely valueless. (p. 89)

How does one learn to inquire and shape an argument and how can Meltzer's work be used to teach inquiry to others? Ironically, in order to answer these questions, I believe that we need to return to the seemingly less sophisticated notion of history that predates Herodotus— history as memory.

HISTORY AS MEMORY

The south end of the Meltzers' living room wall is lined with books. As Meltzer describes his own move from journalist to author of children's books, he walks to the shelves that hold his more than 80 volumes and remarks, "When I was nearing 40 I wrote my first book. . . . A book, I felt, would be so much more permanent than the other things I had written." As a creator and custodian of the public memory, Meltzer has taken on an obligation: "A civilization without memory is no longer civilized. It loses its identity. If it doesn't know what it is and where it comes from, it has no purpose. Without purpose, it withers and dies" (1987b, p. 93). For Meltzer, memory implies the clarification and the contextualizing of incident. He is critical of treatments that "deflate heros and launder villains"; versions of experience that falsify memory.

A metaphor borrowed from psychology may prove helpful here. Imagine a man who, as a child, had been beaten and abused by his parents. His tendency, the patterns of behavior to which he almost automatically returns in raising his own children, are like those exhibited by his parents. When he gets angry, both his behavior (taking out a belt) and his justifications for this behavior ("I turned out all right, didn't I?" or "You insulting my old man?") are the direct result of an unexamined life. To help the adult in this position, as well as his children, one must churn up, give voice to, and explore the memories that serve as the template for this father's actions. Once those memories are identified and owned, one can begin the process of sorting, identifying patterns, looking for confirmation, and, finally, seeking ways to make changes. Both memory and inquiry enable us to ask; both memory and inquiry allow us to restore. Sometimes one leads, sometimes the other, but eventually both are essential to real progress.

Meltzer knows much about the relationship between inquiry and memory. More than 35 years ago, after successfully collaborating with Langston Hughes on a pictorial history of African American culture (1956), Meltzer got an inkling of an idea. He steeled his nerves and asked Hughes, who had already written an autobiography, if he, Meltzer, might try his hand at a young person's biography of the life of the artist. Hughes consented. As Meltzer was wrapping up the interviews, Hughes unexpectedly died. Meltzer the friend and admirer was devastated. Meltzer the writer simply put away his notes, unable to look with artistic and historical detachment at the conversations and documents he had collected. In order to construct the Hughes biography, Meltzer had to learn to situate deep sentiment in context, how to locate caring in the detached and unbending chronological record. This skill, finally mastered, became Meltzer's signature as an author. *Langston Hughes: A Biography* (1968), a book animated by affection and admiration, was nominated for a National Book Award.

Although certain of Meltzer's biographies are clearly born out of a regard or fondness (which sometimes becomes more intense as he comes to know the subject in question—he admits falling in love with Lydia Maria Child), in no case is the biographer sentimental. Nor does he turn from those unpleasant defects of character that mark a human being. Even when a less than admirable character like Columbus is taken on, faults are always played against the background of what men with similar urges, pressures, and ambitions did during this period of time. Although we might find other connections between and among the biographies. Invariably, Meltzer chooses subjects that help his readers better understand power—how it works and how people respond to it.

Meltzer writes about characters he believes young people should remember because they were extraordinarily forthright in their call for justice and equality. He writes about presidents and political figures who were powerful and examines the sources of their commitments and energy. He writes about and asks us to remember the dangers of leading a life where nothing but wealth and power matters. It is not by accident or an act of advertising might, for example, that Meltzer's biographies of the presidents have sold more copies than his brilliant life stories of Langston Hughes or Lydia Maria Child, both of which met with major critical acclaim.

Milton Meltzer has chosen to spend a good part of his life writing about people whose words and deeds have gone untended and been washed from the landscape of the historical record. In re-establishing those gardens, searching, editing, and introducing these men and women to young people, he has produced books, permanent tributes to the everyday bravery of African Americans, Hispanic Americans, Chinese Americans, and Jewish Americans. In looking at the edifice of American history he notices and calls attention to the mortar as well as the brick, studying the relationship between the two. Because of his books, the voices of Civil War soldiers and civil rights recruits continue to be heard. Through his books young people learn about the slow trauma the Great Depression leveled against their grandparents and the acts of bravery that offered hope even in the darkest days of the Holocaust. The garden of inquiry is built from, is planted with, memories.

In this sense Meltzer's books are extraordinarily hopeful. Predicated on the assumption that every person's history counts, he encourages readers to think critically, energetically, and passionately about a world that could be. By celebrating the achievements and documenting the injustices that befall people not traditionally mentioned in books for young readers, by looking at the quirky or difficult decisions undertaken by political figures, by asking us to look again, this time more carefully, at the myths that dominate our culture, Meltzer invites outsiders and skeptics to take part in this America. In *Thaddeus Stevens and the Fight for Negro Rights* (1967), for instance, he prompts his readers to look again—the record is there to be re-examined.

> Wicked ... wretched ... evil ... hard ... malignant ... vindictive ... domineering ... revengeful ... unforgiving ... implacable ... cunning ... mad ...
> Thaddeus Stevens has been called all these names, and more. He can lay claim to being one of the best-hated men in our past. ... The harsh judgments his enemies made in his lifetime still echo in the textbooks students use now.
> What did the man do to deserve this?
> He fought to establish free public schools.
> He defended fugitive slaves in the courts.
> He championed the right of free speech for dissenters.
> He spoke up for unpopular minorities: Indians, Mormons, Jews, and Negroes.
> He led the political struggle to free the slaves and to protect their rights through the passage of the thirteenth, fourteenth, and fifteenth amendments to the Constitution.
> And he tried to reconstruct the defeated South on the foundation of justice for all and a democracy of true equality.
> If this is what he stood for, why do so many Americans detest him? Why, for that matter, is Robert E. Lee—who led armies in a bloody war to preserve slavery—called a saint, while Thaddeus Stevens—who warred against slavery—is called a devil? (pp. xi–xii)

Each of Meltzer's books seeks to pursuade young readers that they can draw from and build on the past through inquiry, that it is by questioning that one really comes to know the meaning of freedom.

But I believe there is more. For Milton Meltzer, the relationship of personal memory to inquiry is the relationship of art to fact. To say that Meltzer recognizes that for history to become meaningful it must touch the psyche as well as the mind, is not accurate, for such a statement suggests a bifurcation of head and heart. What art does, what good writing does, is forge a link, create and make real the connection between what we know and what we feel. Barbara Hardy (1987) in her essay "The Nature of Narrative" puts it this way.

> We dream in narrative, day-dream in narrative, remember, anticipate, hope, despair, believe, doubt, plan, revise, criticize, construct, gossip,

learn, hate, love by narrative. In order really to live, we make up stories about ourselves and others, about the personal as well as the social past and future. (p. 1)

Or as Meltzer (1987b) notes in the final chapter of *The Landscape of Memory,* entitled "Art Shapes Remembrance,"

> The artist serves a special function when he can shatter the amnesia or culture he is part of. . . . Writers understand the power of memory and also how vulnerable it is to pressure. When a society's past comes to be seen as politically mad or personally embarrassing, the temptation by the rulers to blot it out is great. (pp. 113–115)

In thinking about the roots of Meltzer's writing I am drawn back to an image elaborated in *Starting from Home* (1988c). More than a half century later the author remembers himself as a child, the little "Americansher" rambling past the dirt streets of Worcester, past open meadows to a rock planted deep in the earth. Carved on its face was the "thrilling news" that Jonas Rice, the first permanent settler of the town, had "built his log cabin right there on my street!" Meltzer goes on:

> Sitting on Jonas' rock, I could imagine the wolves howling in the night and hearing the bloodcurdling shrieks of the bands of Nipmuck Indians who burned cabins and attacked settlements which threatened their hunting and camping grounds. . . . Old Jonas' rock was in an empty lot. With a pointed stick, I dug here and there beneath the long grass, looking for signs of a disappeared people. But never did I find a stone tool, an arrowhead, a tomahawk, or even a bit of broken pottery. Then one day it dawned on me that echoes of Indian voices were all around me. The place names I had taken for granted—Quinsigamond, Tatnuck, Packachoag, Wachuset, Asnebumskit—were the beautiful names Indians gave to the lakes, streams, and hills they loved so much. (p. 23)

I find in this image so much of what has come to define Meltzer's work—a thrill in locating fact and information, a desire to connect with people and places of another era, the urge to dig for that which lies underneath the obvious marker, a fascination with the unrecorded voices (it was on Jonas's rock that Meltzer learned to listen for the voices of Native peoples), and the ability to make all of that come alive through narration. There is also the unspoken fact that Meltzer was a young child, whose genealogical roots had been effectively severed, searching for roots in America. It is not by chance, I would argue, that the image of roots and the call to look at the "underside of history" appear frequently in these essays.

It would be inaccurate, however, to suggest that Meltzer the author is particularly conscious of either his motives or his particular place in the canon of children's literature. For example, he tells the story of an editor, familiar with his books on African Americans, who suggested in 1973 that he take on a book about the Jews. "Why me?" Meltzer replied. Her answers made sense: "First, because you are Jewish, and second, because you have worked with both blacks and Jews, you will deal sensitively with the tensions that dominate relations between the groups at this moment." Meltzer thought about her points and took on the project, writing another award-winning volume, *Remember the Days: A Short History of the Jewish American* (1974b). Was his initial reaction to the project denial or naivete?

Meltzer's lack of self-consciousness is evident in other ways as well. He confesses, somewhat sheepishly, that a curator for a new Dorothea Lange retrospective recently came to visit him for advice. Just 2 months before, he had decided to clean the storage bin in the basement of his apartment building and had simply tossed out all the notes collected for his brilliant autobiography of the photographer. I can imagine no one more thorough and uncluttered in his approach.

INQUIRY, MEMORY, AND THE SCHOOLS

Somvathey, a sixth-grade student originally from Laos, wrote to his teacher, Miss Blackwood, about a new book he was reading called *Voices from the Civil War* by Milton Meltzer (1989). Miss Blackwood, who encourages readers to both feel and think as they respond to literature, suggested that Somvathey frame his response as a letter to Mr. Meltzer. He wrote:

> I like how you discribe the events with letters and diary entry, because when I was reading your book I felt like I was in the storys and I'm experiencing the event myself. I think that the letters and diary discribe the event more correctly than any other source. I like reading the letters because they have so many great lines that come out and grab your heart and touch it in a special way. (unedited personal communication, October 14, 1992)

The discovery that history can in fact touch your heart, and the analysis of how and why it is able to touch any heart, is central to the teaching of both social studies and the humanities. But until history has sparked a question, made the pain of another human being palpable, or caused a student to reflect on his or her daily experiences in terms of the past, social studies are viewed as dried leaves—memories swept helter skelter by the wind or gathered and disposed of in plastic bags with little thought of where they come from or where they go.

It is interesting to note that the term *inquiry* is most often associated in the schools with science, not social studies. Science educators have sought to engage students in authentic, hands-on problem solving and have developed inquiry-based lessons by working with practicing scientists and engineers to create lessons that mimic the processes used by adult professionals in the field. Other science educators have chosen to focus on young people's own questions. In both cases the curriculum is identified with authentic queries and insists on the importance of teaching the act of analysis or interpretation.

Similarly, teachers of writing know the value of helping students learn from the lives of real writers; we value authentic accounts of the ways authors we emulate go about their work. My hope is that many of these Meltzer essays, in part or in whole, can be shared with young readers. When I think of the "hooks" or the "entry points" to historical study suggested by these essays, several appear obvious: personal caring, nurtured curiosity, and an interest in argument for the purpose of effecting social change.

It is sometimes helpful to think of a book as an invitation, and the reader's reaction to the work as a response to that invitation. When I receive an invitation to a fund-raising event in the mail, an invitation that I know went out to thousands of people whose names were purchased from a list, almost automatically I toss the piece of "junk mail" in the trash. I know that it was not really intended for me. Conversely, if a hand-addressed card comes from Aunt Shirley, I know that it is my obligation to respond. Even if I cannot attend the particular event, I am aware of a real person sitting home waiting to see if she should order up another helping of rock cornish hen. Another kind of invitation to which I will respond comes from a party who represents an idea I embrace or wish to identify with. For example, if I have supported a presidential candidate and an invitation to the Inaugural Ball arrives, I will try to RSVP before all the places are given away.

These same sorts of relationships exist between author and reader. If a student is given a textbook written by committee for a cast of thousands, a textbook that seeks to be evenhanded and passionless, the tendency is to toss it in the mental waste basket. A less harsh treatment might be rendered by a student who has an identified or particularized interest. For instance, a reader with a fascination for World War II may go to the index and see what the author's line is on that subject or to see if there is more to learn from this particular treatment of the event. The caring, in this instance, springs completely from the reader's experiences outside the textbook. Although the textbook can nurture a hunger generated elsewhere, it is rarely able to "whet the appetite."

Competent teachers, working with students not yet "hooked" on history, seek to make the issues under consideration come alive. Often they use their own knowledge to generate involvement or introduce young people to "real life" players, people whose emotional connections with the material at hand make concrete the problems under review. The hope, in either case, is to motivate students to go back and look brick by brick at the structure that has been erected in the standard texts. Ideally, such an approach might cause young people to examine not only these bricks, but also other building materials helpful in constructing historical interpretations. Good teachers model the pleasure of historical study and promote personalized and expanded interest on the part of their students. They know that internalized motivation is more potent and enduring than good grades or high test scores.

The problem, of course, with relying only on teacher knowledge or firsthand accounts is obvious—the lively historical details each teacher or "historical player" has available is limited. Meltzer's works add immeasurably to the sources both children and their intellectual guardians have on hand. His eye and ear are experienced in locating documents from the past that resonate in the present. His books are rich in details that bring readers close to the historical subject and help young people question what they might have done in similar circumstances. Through understatement and a wide-eyed detachment, Meltzer reports on startling events without preaching, giving the reader room to move in on the characters and events depicted. In short, his books help create a vision of social studies that builds on student caring. His is a history that thinks *and* feels.

While the act of caring provides one entry into and is ultimately important in doing social studies, it is not the only way to capture the intellectual imagination of young people. For some the very act of inquiring, questioning, turning the puzzle upside-down and sideways can inspire and stimulate intense study. Although teachers can model this sort of curiosity, students are also well-served by looking at what professional historians do. The essays in Part I on Meltzer the writer are intended to give teachers and students an overview of the concerns a good historian brings to the subject, while the pieces in Parts II and III will serve as important models for those seeking to write about thorny topical issues or to fashion biographies from raw data. In the Epilogue Meltzer writes about the economics of being an author and, in so doing, asks readers to consider what our society values.

Another force driving both novice and experienced historians is an interest in change. The questions of continuing interest to young people concerned about a more just and hopeful tomorrow are played out again and again in stories from the past. The past is the field test for a new and better world. The past contains the record of heroes and heroines, some famous, some nearly forgotten, who worked for a better and more decent world. The past shapes our vision of who and what we can be.

Milton Meltzer is perhaps the only and certainly the most prolific and competent writer for young people who invites a critical reading on matters of political and social importance. In his book entitled *Crime in America* (1990b), for instance, he prods readers to examine the comparative hurt caused by white collar criminals and petty thieves seeking bread for the table. It is the kind of argument future citizens see as immediate and important. With his books readers practice authentic problem solving and rigorous thinking.

A colleague in bilingual education and I frequently discuss books such as E. D. Hirsch's *Cultural Literacy* (1988), or the standardized catalog of names and dates students use to prepare for Regents exams. My colleague sees value in such lists, asserting that they "level the playing field," that they put cultural outsiders on an equal footing with insiders. When I am not attacking the content of the lists *per se*, my argument focuses on the narrow, utilitarian vision of history such lists promote. Without narrative, facts can be memorized, but they will not be memorable. Such activity is akin to collecting evidence without knowing the position of either prosecution or defense. Isolated bits of information connected neither to inquiry nor to memory are feeble, they do no work.

What must we as readers and teachers do to reconfigure scattered factoids into powerful thoughts? What attitudes undergird and make possible the inquiring historical mind? In reading through these essays I notice two unstated assumptions that seem to shape all that Meltzer thinks and writes about. The first is that skepticism is never viewed as kin to cynicism. On the contrary, skilled doubting proffers hope. Healthy skeptics, when they build, actively search for solid ground; they test their structures to ensure their strength. Hope born and maintained in the tough light of skepticism is more likely to be sustained than ideas constructed from a flaking optimism.

A second attitude shaping these essays as well as Meltzer's books might be characterized as a faith in the power of students to reason, a trust in their ability to think hard and act fairly. Unlike writers of textbooks, for instance, who begin by telling students the conclusion they are expected to reach, Meltzer trusts young people to put the puzzle pieces together once they are laid out on the table. In his books he talks with, rather than at, his audience. He assumes that his readers have questions, that they feel, that they have an urgent need to make sense of their world. This trust also reflects the tough optimism referred to earlier.

Meltzer's trust can serve as a powerful model for all of us who work with young people. It is based not on Constitutional cheerleading, but rather on a thoughtful recognition that it is in the interest of students to care. There are vital lessons for those of us in education to learn from these essays. If we see our students as individuals who face important decisions, decisions that will affect the world in which we and our children and our children's children live, then we and the young people we teach become cohorts struggling together. We need to recognize that we all have such moments, such opportunities and challenges in our lives. Meltzer's books help us celebrate people who approach such moments with intelligence, decency, and courage.

Part I

MELTZER ON WRITING

The essays in this part are especially useful for teachers of writing and/or history. They suggest, individually and collectively, that there is a connection between what writers have to say and the way they say it, that good expository or narrative prose is born of deep investment and passion. As a colleague said to me after reading these essays, "We need more writers who get mad when they see the world burn."

Participants in writing conferences are often asked to specify what they want readers to listen for: Did this introduction grab you? Did you find this piece convincing? Meltzer encourages us to put other issues on the table—What did this piece cause you to value? How? Does this piece give you courage or does it weary you? Does it make you want to know more? About what? Does it invite you to re-examine other aspects of history?

Moreover, these essays, both individually and collectively, sketch out a special role for young people in the struggle to make this world a better place for everyone. "Is Meltzer's faith in young people appropriate or misplaced?" I would ask my students. Other, sometimes thorny, cross-curricular issues, such as what constitutes a "good" question or a "productive" question, can also be informed by essays in this section.

For those interested in helping students develop and internalize criteria for evaluating their own work or the writing of other historians, these essays are a gold mine. A teacher might explore a given piece with the class to model the process of locating criteria, after which individuals or small groups might work on several different pieces. The power of building an evaluation rubric from the essays of a well-respected author, and the conversation of a class around the issues he raises, is at once intellectually sound and empowering.

An alternative approach might involve first asking students to read from Meltzer's primary works, noting the rhetorical strategies and values that mark them. Introducing the essays at this point, to see how the books themselves exemplify the values the essays champion, may add a poignancy to the critical works. Students might also be encouraged to write their own essays on what matters to them as writers and/or historians.

Some classroom-based activities that spring from essays in this section might be more closely tied to one subject area or another. For instance, the piece entitled "Where Have All the Prizes Gone?" serves as an excellent springboard for a debate on how literary prizes should be organized and allotted. Others, such as "On Teaching and Learning History," can surely help focus a discussion about the purposes of studying social studies. This, coupled with "The Book as Revelation" and "History as Sausage: Richly Textured and a Bit Spicy," would surely inform a discussion of excellent teaching as well as writing practices.

The final essay in this section, entitled "Imagination, Invention, and Information," is taken from the Afterword written for the second edition of *Underground Man* (1990c), Meltzer's only work of fiction. This essay talks in important ways about the boundaries between fiction and nonfiction, about how fact can both inspire and confine, and about the contribution of imagination to historical interpretation.

I know of no other essays that so effectively invite teachers and their students to explore what it means to be a writer of history. The pieces in this part provide the theoretical bases for a series of lively discussions. More important, perhaps, they serve as powerful examples. In these pieces we come to understand how a passion for justice drives and disciplines research, and, finally, how intelligence informs the heart.

CHAPTER 1

Seeding Vision, Energy, and Hope: Writing and Social Responsibility

We are in deep trouble. As citizens, as writers, as readers. And the nature of that trouble has to do with the failure to place human needs above financial gain. "Nice guys finish last." You hear it everywhere. It is a deeply rooted conviction. Yet it betrays our best values and it breaks the human connection. It represents a moral blindness that endangers us all.

I think such aspects of American life ought not to be neglected in children's literature. My own work is confined to nonfiction, to what is commonly called "information" books. A limiting phrase, unless you ask, information about what? The young reader needs to be informed not only about how houses are built, how trucks run, how flowers grow, how birds fly, how weather is formed, how physical handicaps are overcome, but about how character is shaped and how the world works. The disasters of nature—hurricanes, floods, droughts—are worthy of attention, but so are the disasters of human society. I mean Vietnam. I mean the Holocaust. I mean poverty. Disasters created by human beings, disasters suffered by human victims. All children will encounter fundamental problems of race and class and tyranny in their lifetime. To create an awareness of such issues early on is a fitting responsibility for us writers. We can trace the origins of American democracy in our work and help create pride in the struggle to extend and deepen our civil and human rights. At the same time we cannot close our eyes to both the open and secret ways America's decision-making power has been concentrated in what some call the power elite or the military-industrial complex. The more clearly we see our nation and others in the light of their historical development, the more apparent it becomes that all institutions have been made and could be altered by us, the people. I hope books holding out the vision of a genuinely democratic and equitable society will excite the imagination of young readers and stretch their minds.

Hearing this, you may ask, what about objectivity? Isn't the historian supposed to be neutral? Cool? No, I take sides. And I don't believe anyone who writes is neutral. If they were, they would not be human; they'd be dead souls. Writers need to be honest, to spit the truth out, to tell what they know, what they think. It isn't their job to make the reader feel good, although there are some editors who believe that it is. If the world is burning, you cry "Fire!" You don't smile, you get mad!

What I write comes out of the values I'm committed to. That's true of any writer. Adolf Hitler wrote *Mein Kampf.* His values—if that's the right word!—stink on every page of that horror. Thoreau, Mark Twain, Dickens, Tolstoy—their vastly different values permeate their pages. No writer is neutral, no matter how much he or she may claim to be. The direction our work takes comes out of the values we are committed to. The question is, *what* values does the writer have?

I feel that a prime obligation of the writer is to combat the cynical and defeatist view of human nature that dismisses any attempt to make society more just, more fair, more decent. In writing biography, whether of the famous or the obscure, I want to give young readers vision, hope, energy. And to do it honestly, without concealing the weaknesses, the false starts, or the wrong turns of my heroes and heroines. Even those who try their best not to live by selfish attempts to outsmart their fellows can make tragic mistakes. Still, I write about them because they share a deep respect for the rights, the dignity, the value of every human being. They stand against exorbitant wealth and power for the few, and poverty and powerlessness for the many.

There have not been many victories for such people. In the books I write I do not want simply to tell the stories of past failures. Yet neither do I want to let us forget or deny the past. What I do want to bring out are new possibilities by emphasizing those times or events in the past that reveal people's ability to resist injustice, to join together, even, sometimes, to win. That kind of history, I believe, is creative.

All of us—not only writers, but editors and teachers and librarians and parents—all of us, I think, are joined in the collective effort to shape a world where every child may grow in the spirit of a community that fulfills the best in us.

How best to meet that standard? Every writer will have his or her own way. Mine is to shape a human approach to American life, past and present. Through original sources—letters, diaries, memoirs, journals, interviews, eyewitness accounts, speeches, and songs of the day—the reader discovers how it felt to confront the redcoats at Lexington, to lose one's husband at Gettysburg, to defy the terror of the Ku Klux Klan, to toil alongside one's mother in a Lower East Side sweatshop, or to live in a West Virginia coal town where everything is owned by the company.

My aim is to challenge young Americans to examine the past as they move into their future. And you cannot do that without stirring their feelings so that they live the history of others as though it were their own personal experience. The question of who gains and holds power, and how that power is exercised, is vital to an understanding of the great abuses of power that Vietnam and Watergate and the Iran-Contra affair typify. A concern for history from the bottom up, the story of common humanity, ought not to skip over the operations of those who have power and sometimes or always abuse it. We look to the young to question and inquire and agitate and push us forward against the resistance of the powerful.

Honest books can serve that end. They can help the young reader to see that while stupidity and criminality and folly and injustice are all manifest in the world, the people have won some hard-fought victories over them. I try to tell the truth in all my books. By truth I do not mean that I write simply to convey facts. The books are, I hope, works of revelation as well as information. Books to help young readers understand the world as it is, and to realize that we need not accept that world as it is given to us. Is it possible to achieve a more just society? Can we break free of the notion that human fulfillment comes from piling up material goods and private privileges? With little concern for what happens to other members of the human race?

Books make their greatest mark when they reach readers in their growing years. The young look everywhere for that ground of truth on which they can stand before they commit the power of their body and mind to the world as it is, or as they might wish to remake it.

A writer whose work is meant for young readers tries to find some pattern of meaning in the struggle to realize his own humanity. The direction his work takes comes out of the values he is committed to. No writer is disinterested, no matter how much he may claim to be. The question is, what interests does he have? Whatever he writes has some effect. It is possible for writing to turn young readers in a new direction, give them courage, pride, confidence. Just how this happens I don't pretend to know. I only remember that a number of books I read when young did have a memorable influence on me.

What I hope my books do—what I'd like every book to do—is to raise questions in the minds of young readers. Teach them not so much facts and dates or formulas but the art and necessity of asking questions. Why do things come out this way? Do they have to be this way? Could they be changed? Should they be changed? How do people go about changing their lives or the world they live in? Change is always taking place, whether we wish it or not. But shouldn't we, as thinking, feeling beings, grow conscious of it and try to shape change to more human ends? If we are not to repeat our Watergates and Iran-Contra disasters again and again, then some moral sense, some critical spirit, must be imparted somehow to young people. A society is in great danger when its leaders lie because they do not want the people to know, and when its people fear to ask questions, or have forgotten how.

I write about people and events that are meaningful to me, and try my best to make something of what I feel come through to the reader. For some years I wrote without any great self-consciousness about the subjects I chose. Then one day a reviewer described me as a writer known for his interest in the underdog. A pattern had become obvious. It was not a choice deliberately made, but this is how it has gone, 80 or more books—histories and biographies dealing with human aspiration and struggle. They include the African American's fight for freedom and equality; the worker's attempts to organize; the desperate battles of the hungry and dispossessed to survive the Great Depression; and the ethnic histories—of the Native Americans, the Jewish Americans, the Hispanic Americans, the Chinese Americans.

As for my biographies, they deal with the lives of people who appealed to me for many different reasons. But what links them all is the fact that each one fought for unpopular causes—Margaret Sanger, Langston Hughes, Lydia Maria Child, Henry David Thoreau, Mark Twain, Thaddeus Stevens, Dorothea Lange, Mary McLeod Bethune, Betty Friedan. Whatever subject I choose to write about, the desire to make this a better, more peaceful, more fulfilling life for the many who do not share in such an existence, animates what I do.

Almost everything I write has to do with social change—how it comes about, the forces that advance it and the forces that resist it, the moral issues that beset men and women seeking to realize their humanity. Commitment to a certain set of values, almost without my realizing it at first, has shaped the course of my work. I found myself writing about those aspects of history that had been neglected, obscured, or distorted. The scales in our world have long been weighted in favor of the rich, the white-skinned, the powerful. I have not been neutral; I see nothing wrong in the historian who feels a commitment to humane concerns—to the ending of war, of poverty, of racism. We cannot be neutral even if we want to be. Whatever we write has some effect. Writing of one kind may make the young reader feel cynical, passive, hopeless. Another kind of writing may turn him in a new direction and give him courage, pride, and confidence.

How this happens it is very hard to find out. Each of us is different, and what moves us to change is incredibly complex. But that sometimes we *do* change, all of us know. Who cannot remember what one teacher said to us at a critical moment? Or what one book revealed? Something we heard, something we read, led us to look at life and ourselves differently. It is not always a dramatic, direct, personal experience that reshapes us. Many abolitionists who had never been in the South became persuaded by what they read that slavery was wrong and that they must help to overthrow it. We are more than what our own sensory system feeds into us. What others feel to the greatest intensity when they suffer grief or pain or hunger, we can feel in at least some degree and can perhaps act on that feeling. Without that capacity we are hardly human.

So writing history, I think, can be useful if it makes young people more aware, deepens their feelings, broadens their experience, enlarges their understanding—and perhaps even moves them to action. This is the kind of historical writing that is worth doing, and the more of us who try, the better.

CHAPTER 2

Where Have All the Prizes Gone?

Nonfiction writers have struggled long and hard to break down the stereotype that plagues our work. The books we write are still, in many places, by many people, dismissed as "fact" books. But are they merely "informational?" Not if they are any good. To their creation the same quality of imagination is as essential as it is in the writing of fiction. For history has to be imagined before it can be written. Yes, the historian relies first of all on documents and other sources. But the events and personalities have to be reconstructed by the imagination. This prejudice is most clearly reflected in criticism of children's nonfiction, or rather the general lack of it.

Every year since 1922 the Newbery Medal has been awarded to some author for the most distinguished contribution to American literature for children. Of the 53 Newbery winners to date, how many have been nonfiction? Only four. Van Loon's *The Story of Mankind*, the very first, in 1922; Meigs's *Invincible Louisa*, in 1934; Daugherty's *Daniel Boone*, in 1940; Russell Freedman's *Lincoln: A Photobiography*, in 1987. Two other winners are fictionalized biography (Yates's *Amos Fortune, Free Man*, 1951, and Latham's *Carry on, Mr. Bowditch*, 1956). One other calls itself a biographical novel (de Trevino's *I, Juan de Pareja*, 1966).

What about The Boston Globe–Horn Book Awards? Or the National Book Award that used to be given for children's literature? Is the picture different? It wasn't, for a long time. Nor for most of the other children's book prizes designed to honor the best literary work. The laurels crown the storytellers. Librarians, teachers, reviewers—the three groups who usually administer the awards or serve as judges—have seemed reluctant to consider nonfiction literature.

But what is Henry David Thoreau's *Walden*? What is Boswell's *The Life of Samuel Johnson*? What is Tom Paine's *Common Sense*? Not one of them literature? All merely nonfiction? Let's go to the dictionary. "Literature," says the one at my elbow (the *American Heritage Dictionary of the English Language*, 1976), "is imaginative or creative writing."

What about art? Can such works as those I have named be considered artistic? To the dictionary again: It defines art as "the activity of
creating beautiful things." Does Thoreau's *Walden* satisfy that?

Literary art has, I think, two related aspects: its *subject*, what a
book is about, and the *means* the writer uses to convey that material,
the *craft*. The craft is the making, shaping, forming, selecting. And
what the reader gets from the exercise of the writer's craft upon a subject is an experience. If the subject is significant, and the artist is up to
it, then the book can enlarge, it can deepen, it can intensify the reader's
experience of life.

Imagination, invention, selection, language, form. . . . these are
just as important to the making of a good book of biography, history,
or science as to the making of a piece of fiction. Yet in Sheila Egoff's
huge collection of pieces on children's literature, *Only Connect* (1969),
there is scarcely a single reference to nonfiction. Of the score of contrib-
utors, only two refer to nonfiction, each mentioning but one example
considered of literary value. John R. Townsend (1968), the British critic,
ignores nonfiction entirely in his piece, "The Present State of English
Children's Literature." Perhaps the fact that he writes children's novels
explains his bias? Egoff herself, who uses that catch-all definition of
literature as "the best that has been thought and written," never men-
tions nonfiction in her piece (1969, p. 443).

I looked again at Isabelle Jan's book, *On Children's Literature* (1973).
She deals primarily with French and English literature, but talks too
about the writers of many other countries. And again, nothing about
nonfiction. Yet at the very end of her closing chapter, she has this to
say:

> Why indeed should a certain form of artistic expression be judged supe-
> rior to another, considered to be the only one worthy of being called "lit-
> erature," and established as the norm, when all that really counts is that
> human expression should have the widest possible range, no matter from
> where it springs or what form it adopts? What is important is man's abil-
> ity to create. (p. 147)

I agree. Then why, I wonder, did she exclude nonfiction from her
own book?

The very name "nonfiction" is so curiously negative, but I can
think of only a few critics who have given serious attention to nonfiction. One is England's Margery Fisher. In her own review journal,
Growing Point, she has always discussed both nonfiction and fiction
with the same care and acuteness of vision. Several years ago she published in America a 500-page evaluation of nonfiction called *Matters of
Fact: Aspects of Non-fiction for Children* (1972). As a writer and occasional

reviewer I find it as useful and stimulating as her monthly magazine. What I like especially about Fisher is that she does not treat each new book, whether it be a realistic novel, science fiction, a life of Lincoln, or a study of cowboys, as though nothing had ever been written on it before. There is constant comparison and evaluation, drawing upon her rich knowledge of the whole body of children's literature. Often Fisher summons up works long past to inform us that something better in this respect or that is available. I treasure her critical essays on books, grouped by theme or genre, not only for the specific assessment of each title but for the general principles to be deduced from the comparative analysis.

Fisher (1972) points out that "the writers of non-fiction for children are not universally thought of as writers in the same way as authors of junior novels. . . . Because of an unexpressed feeling that information books are not 'creative,' they are far more often reviewed for their content than for their total literary value" (introduction).

A children's book editor of *The New York Times* was heard to dismiss works of nonfiction categorically as "non-books." Perhaps he was irritated by the assembly-line information books some publishers have unloaded on schools and libraries. Such mass-produced books are often perfunctory, tasteless, unreadable, although in a feeble defense it is said they fill some educational need. The editor could not conceive of such books making any contribution to literature. But in his distaste he went to the extreme of rarely opening his pages to the discussion of nonfiction for children. He did take picture books and novels quite seriously.

In the specialized children's review media there is a somewhat better balance between space given to fiction and to nonfiction. Still, *The Horn Book Magazine* issues I have tested in scattered samples show a heavy weight on one side; that is, picture books and fiction taken together get far more than double the space of nonfiction. Often more than 20 novels will be reviewed while only one biography or one history book is singled out for attention. Science books are treated in intelligent roundups, with helpful comparisons drawn. If space is at a premium, why not try this method sometimes with history or biography?

School Library Journal attempts to review every one of the 2,000-odd children's trade books published annually. *Kirkus* claims to review about three out of four. I would guess *The Horn Book Magazine* reviews perhaps 300 a year in its six issues. The policy of both *The Horn Book Magazine* and the American Library Association's *Book List* is to cover only books they can recommend, subject to qualifications. *The New York Times* on Sundays says it reviews about 350 children's books a year, but most of these are only touched on briefly in its special seasonal issues.

Where reviews of nonfiction are published, most of the time the reviewer limits him or herself to asking, How much information does the book contain? And how accurate or up-to-date is it? Infrequently a reviewer will compare the book with others on the same subject. But again, only as to factual content. Rarely will he or she ask what more there is to the book than the mere facts. I would want to ask, How well is it organized? What principle of selection animated the writer? What is the writer's point of view? Does the writer grant admission to other opinions of value?

And then, beyond all this, what literary distinction, if any, does the book have? And here I do not mean the striking choice of word or image, but the personal style revealed. I ask whether the writer's personal voice is heard in the book. In the writer who cares there is a pressure of feeling that emerges in the rhythm of the sentences, the choice of details, the color of the language. Style in this sense is not a trick of rhetoric or a decorative daub; it is "a quality of vision." It cannot be separated from the author's character because the tone of voice in which the book is written expresses how a human being thinks and feels. If the writer is indifferent, bored, stupid, mechanical, it will show in the work. The kind of man or woman the writer is, is what counts.

Style in any art is *both* form and content. They are woven together. The historian Peter Gay (1976), who cared enough about this question to give a whole book to *Style in History*, shows how in all the classic historians—Gibbon, Burckhardt, Macaulay, Ranke—style shaped, and in turn was shaped by, substance.

To go back to one of my prize examples, Thoreau: What literary work is more crammed with factual substance than his? His interest in the particular and minute is what makes many of his best pages. But, he said in his *Journal*, there was something more than facts that he wished to set down.

> Facts should only be as the frame to my pictures; they should be material to the mythology which I am writing; not facts to assist men to make money, farmers to farm profitably, in any common sense; facts to tell who I am, and where I have been or what I have thought: as now the bell rings for evening meeting, and its volumes of sound, like smoke which rises from where a cannon is fired, make the tent in which I dwell. My facts shall be falsehoods to the common sense. I would so state facts that they shall be significant, shall be myths or mythologic. Facts which the mind perceived, thoughts which the body thought,—with these I deal. (quoted in Meltzer & Harding, 1962, p. 70)

Please don't misunderstand me. I make no claim that every piece of nonfiction written for children—or adults, for that matter—has literary merit. Only some, a few. A great many books are only mediocre, and a number should never have been published. But the same is true for novels. Who will remember 90% of them 5 years later? One year? Tomorrow? Still, to go back to the Newbery Awards, I would guess that some of the novels given the prize in the past might easily have been matched or surpassed in literary quality by works of nonfiction, if only the judges had not swallowed the nonsense that fiction alone can be literature.

I have often wondered what goes on in the rooms where the judges meet to decide on literary awards. One librarian who served for a time on the Newbery Award committee told me that fiction is everything. Nonfiction is given short shrift in the debates over the final contestants. Many committee members simply do not believe that nonfiction can have any more literary value than a mail-order catalog or the telephone directory.

But I found one judge who had the courage to publish her opinions and confess to her prejudices. It was the children's novelist Jane Langton (1972), who told all in *Publishers Weekly*. Langton served as one of the two judges for the Book World Children's Spring Book Festival Awards. Her three-page article dealt honestly with the problems of the judge drowned in scores of entries. She was dead certain she could tell a good novel from a bad novel without any academic set of standards to go by. One sniff, and she knew. But she was all at sea in judging the nonfiction entries. Finally, after much rummaging through the stacks of books and thinking about her responses, some standards emerged for the nonfiction. To be in the running a book had to "exude some kind of passion or love or caring" (p. 89). If the author didn't care, why should she? It had to have literary quality. She, the judge, had to like it. And she had to feel the book could make a mark on the young person reading it, change him or her in some way. Which meant, as well, that the young reader too had to like it.

Good! Those standards appeal to me. But what happened when it came time to apply them? Langton and the other judge, a librarian, conferred feverishly on their favorites by mail and phone in order to arrive at the final list of five. In that last moment over the phone, Langton said, "Now don't you think we've got to have at least *one* nonfiction book? What about. . . . " and she named one title. "Yes," said the librarian, "I think that's the best one" (p. 90).

So that's how winners are made.

Was it fair? Langton asked that herself. No, she answered; they chose only one nonfiction book among the five winners out of—(and here I quote)—"sheer naked prejudice and personal bias in favor of fiction" (p. 90).

Recognizing this bias, this prejudice (which I have tried to demonstrate is almost universal), Langton urged that fiction and nonfiction should be given separate awards and be judged by separate judges.

CHAPTER 3

On Teaching and Learning History

Young people don't appear on the scene with a built-in appreciation of history. I think of the day I was riding a Manhattan bus down Broadway. Sitting behind me were two boys, about 12 years old. I couldn't help overhearing their talk. One boy groaned that he had put off doing his history assignment and now had to read the whole book this weekend and write a report. "Don't be crazy," said his sophisticated friend. "You don't have to read the whole book! Just read the first chapter and the last chapter, and then the middle page of the other chapters. But be sure you don't copy out of the last chapter because that's what most of the kids do, and the teacher can always spot it."

What a formula for getting by! But what does it imply about the teaching of history and the textbooks used to that end? Dull, dull, dull. With all too few exceptions. Considering that gloomy fact, we might almost welcome the news that the study of history is no longer required in many high schools. And in many states even the teachers of history have little or no serious training in that subject.

What is the historian? The historian is the creator and custodian of the memory of civilizations. A civilization without memory is no longer civilized. It loses its identity. If it doesn't know what it is and where it comes from, it has no purpose. Without purpose it withers and dies.

To the historian we entrust the care of the public memory, of ourselves as a nation. The historian constructs history out of the facts he finds and his understanding of the meaning of those facts. What we think of our government is shaped by what the historian has told us as much as by our experience of the way that government functions. We look to our government for certain things—justice, equality, freedom; we have certain expectations of it when it comes to protecting and improving the material welfare of our lives, because of our sense of what it has done in the past and what it stands for. What the government does now, or fails to do, to meet our expectations, may fulfill those hopes or disappoint them. The result is sometimes a new view of the outcome or direction of history.

What I am saying is that Washington is not some given thing, an object, or a cluster of institutions that exists outside time, independent of anything else. It is an ever-changing structure of government, molded by the conflict of forces and people in the past and influenced by those same elements today. Our understanding of it, our attitude towards it, is shaped by the memory of the past, memory transmitted by the historian.

But how is history taught in the schools—if it *is* taught? It is often done with the help of textbooks that treat the past very gingerly. When Frances Fitzgerald (1979) analyzed American history textbooks some years ago, she found controversial ideas were often left out. Liberal and radical figures and trends were shunned. The textbooks tiptoed around all ideas, in fact, including those of the nation's heroes. What Thomas Jefferson or Martin Luther King thought and did was either ignored or so watered down as to be meaningless. So too were the ideas and actions of people like Senator Joseph McCarthy or Adolf Hitler. The heroes were deflated and the villains laundered. All with an eye to being politically safe, beyond criticism or reproach. Such versions of our collective memory confuse basic issues and values. History is made mush.

Stirred into the mush is dishonesty and deception and, yes, even betrayal. This kind of falsification of memory, of the past, is done almost everywhere, in different degrees and with varying effect. In antidemocratic societies history is always rewritten to suit the government's latest position. It happens even in democratic countries.

Take our role in Cambodia, that tragic country in southeast Asia. After the truce of 1973 in the Vietnam War, a huge fleet of American planes, under President Nixon's orders, bombed Cambodia, causing terrible destruction of life and property. United States officials tried to keep the world from knowing what had happened. Then in 1975 a communist party called the Khmer Rouge took over the wreckage in Cambodia and made fanaticism king. The young revolutionaries drove the entire population of the cities and towns into the countryside, to clear jungle and scrub. Over one million people were killed by execution and enforced hardship. Everyone suspected of being educated or a professional was murdered; the country was enslaved.

In 1984 a movie was made about that terrible modern history. Called "The Killing Fields," it was based upon the book of a *New York Times* reporter in Cambodia, Sidney Schanberg (1985). When an audience of college students and professors in Boston was asked, after watching the film, how many of them had known these things had happened, one-third said they had never heard about the American bombing of Cambodia or about the nightmare years of mass murder under the Khmer Rouge that followed. Blank pages in their history books; silence in their classrooms.

Out of his own country's bitter experience as a communist state, the Czech historian Milan Hubl wrote that erasing a people's memory is the first step to crushing the people themselves. You do it by destroying its books, its culture, and then its history. Soon that nation will forget what it is and what it was.

Or take Japan, a country whose past and present are closely linked with our own. In Japan, forgetfulness of the historical past has been commonplace. Only recently have Japanese tourists vacationing in Hawaii come to visit the monument at Pearl Harbor. There lie the remains of the battleship Arizona, sunk that long-ago day of December 7, 1941. Pearl Harbor and the other Japanese actions in the war are not held firmly in mind by the Japanese. The schools teach only the chronology of the war, without any comment or judgment. Not until the 1990s did the textbooks and teachers' guides begin to encourage discussion about the lessons of the war, although they have stressed the need for peace.

For Japan, the horror of Hiroshima and Nagasaki are far more overwhelming than Pearl Harbor. But a Japanese professor of history, Kiyoko Takeda, thinks it harmful for the nation not to confront the symbolic importance of Pearl Harbor and Japan's role as an aggressor. "In general," he says, "Japanese tend to forget the past, thinking that it can be washed away. But I always tell my students that recognizing what we have done in the past is a recognition of ourselves. By conducting a dialogue with our past, we are searching how to go forward" (quoted in Meltzer, 1987b, pp. 97–98).

It is not only children who are left defenseless without historical memory. In 1985, during the fortieth anniversary of the Nazi surrender at the end of World War II, President Ronald Reagan blundered into the Bitburg cemetery of Germany with the best of intentions and the hope of "reconciliation." German soldiers, he said, suffered as much under Nazi tyranny as did the men, women, and children in the concentration camps. He could not have made this colossal mistake unless he was ignorant of the tragic facts of that war. Like a number of our presidents, and many of our schools, he neglected history. By laying a wreath on a German military cemetery, he honored the graves of SS men, an elite group of Nazi fanatics trained to consider themselves as the "super race." They became Hitler's most merciless instrument of terror, torturing and murdering countless victims. To honor such men was profoundly offensive to anyone with a memory, anyone with the smallest grasp of what the Nazis meant in history.

To do what Reagan did at Bitburg was to distort memory and increase misunderstanding. How could Mr. Reagan not know that? He was himself in his thirties during that war, but to judge by his remarks and his conduct, the whole horror—the pivotal event of the twentieth century—made no deep or lasting impression on him.

What I have been trying to stress by these examples of history ignored, or distorted, is the importance of reading it, studying it, and discussing it. *When* events happened, *how* they happened, and *why* they happened—to answer these questions is to make sense out of a tangle of events that was not designed as a pattern. Writing history, just like writing historical fiction, is an exercise in imagination. In the historian's case, however, the exercise is restrained by the limits of our knowledge.

But besides the many books that we classify as history, there is another resource teachers can draw upon to help bring history alive for their students. I mean, of course, literature. And in my mind literature is not narrowly confined to poetry and fiction.

One summer while in England, in Yorkshire, where D. H. Lawrence was raised, I was studying his novels. We were lucky to be able to visit Eastwood, a mining town, to see his working-class home, to listen to the daughter of a mining family describe what their life was like, to walk around the slag heaps of coal that poisoned the rural atmosphere. My professor was a woman from these industrial towns who managed to earn a university degree while married to a miner. She could talk to us about Lawrence's development as a writer from an historical point of view—out of the harsh experience of living a life not too different from his, though 100 years later.

When Lawrence brought home the published copy of his first book, my professor related, and showed it to his father, his father remarked: "And they gave you that many guineas for *this*! You who never did a real day's work in your life?" She too, when she came home and told *her* father that she had just been appointed to a lecturer's position in the university, heard him say, "And you get *paid* that much just for sitting behind a desk a few hours a day?"

I think picking up such insights helps you to understand literature and the life it springs from. Understanding includes a sense of time and place, an appreciation of past and present, a grasp of the differences between "then" and "now." It means being able to deal with the complexities of cause and consequence. The younger the students are, the simpler must be the ways of helping them to gain such understanding.

It's natural for students to ask, Why am I told to study history? What am I supposed to be getting out of it? What does the past have to do with me now? If these questions are not answered well, then it is almost certain that young readers will come to believe history is dull and boring. Better to be doing anything else than cracking the tedious textbook.

In considering what a great deal of classroom attention would be given to the Bicentennial of the U.S. Constitution, I wrote a biography for young readers of the man who presided over the Constitutional Convention in Philadelphia—George Washington. Hearing that name, many will shrink back. A book about George Washington? That monument? Those statues? That face on the dollar bill? That head carved on Mount Rushmore?

No, I answer, not that—but the man. The real man, the man who lived so long ago it's hard to remember he was human. But he was. He wasn't GEORGE WASHINGTON in capital letters, carved in marble when he was born. He was an infant, given a name like any other name that meant nothing to anyone but the family. And then he grew up. And near the end of a life rich in great experiences, he was turned into a monument after whom Americans would name a thousand sons, and things, and places.

The human being becomes lost when that happens. The truth lies buried beneath the fairy tales and the falsehoods. What the man was really like I've tried to convey in my book. He was just as individual as you or I. Different from others in some ways, yet the same in other ways. Just as hard to understand, yet just as easy to like or to love when you got to know him, with all his strengths and failings, his humor and anger, his doubts and certainties.

George Washington was the dominant figure in that glorious cluster of Founding Fathers. But what about the rank and file? What about his ragged, hungry, freezing soldiers at Valley Forge? What about the blacksmiths and carpenters and seamen and farmers who peopled the villages and towns of the colonies? What about the slaves who tilled the fields of Washington and Jefferson? What about the women? ("Remember the Ladies," as Abigail Adams admonished her husband John.)

They all played their part in the developing American Revolution. Yet who has heard their voices? To help young people understand the Revolutionary era as a human experience, I wrote another book, *The*

American Revolutionaries: A History in Their Own Words (1987a). It brings to the reader the living experience of these forgotten ones. Some students may have at least a vague notion of the major events of the Revolution. But this book brings home to them a sense of the individual people who made those events. Their needs, their feelings, their hopes, their frustrations, and their fulfillment come alive in the letters, diaries, speeches, testimonies, and memoirs of the period from 1750 to 1800. Surely this kind of book adds another—and highly readable—dimension to the study of the Revolution and its aftermath.

Why can't an imaginative teacher pick a selection from such a book and read it aloud to her class? It doesn't have to be a history teacher. A reading teacher, an English teacher could choose a passage and let students hear the true voice of a Massachusetts farmer, a soldier from South Carolina, a woman in New York whose house has been occupied by British Redcoats. Those students will find out that history is people, people in trouble, people reaching out for something better in life, people struggling against odds, people with fears and doubts and hopes and passions—people like *themselves.*

And with the help of a sensitive teacher, they'll learn too that literature isn't created only by the so-called professional author. The qualities of literature can often be found in the untutored, but deeply felt, words of the ordinary man and woman and child.

Children's literature is now frequently the focus of reading programs for beginners. Since I am not a professional in that field, I learned about this movement through an article by Bernice Cullinan (1986) in *Horn Book Magazine.* She told how such programs grew from work done in New Zealand and achieved "tremendous rates of success" (p. 108). Central to such projects is that the reading material embrace the rich stimulating language of the best children's literature. Young children are drawn into the pleasure of reading by books with rhythmic language, engaging plots, and vivid characters.

Now is there any reason why another kind of writing cannot be introduced a bit later on in school, so that children will enjoy discovering their own past? As a people? As a nation? As citizens of the world? Must the teaching of history in the fifth or eleventh or whatever grade be confined to the boring and emasculated textbooks I mentioned earlier?

I'm sure many people have come across the delightful picture books of leaders of the American Revolution written by Jean Fritz. The titles alone will entice readers of any age: *Why Don't You Get a Horse, Sam Adams?* (1982b) or *What's the Big Idea, Ben Franklin?* (1982a) or *Will You Sign Here, John Hancock?* (1982c). Fritz's books are a refreshingly irreverent portrayal of the Founding Fathers. She makes mortals out of that pantheon of immortals, but without violating her concern for historical accuracy. Ferdinand Monjo's picture books about people of the early American era are just as much fun to read and learn from.

For children of the 7 to 11 age group, Viking publishes many biographies in a series called *Women of Our Time.* Author and illustrator combine strengths in a 64-page format that offers a wide range of personalities from the athlete Martina Navratilova or the entertainer Diana Ross to voices for women's rights, such as Betty Friedan, or the needs of the poor (Mother Teresa). Whether the subject is a popular celebrity or a political figure, the same scrupulous concern is shown for historical accuracy and for the complexity of personality. There is no fictionalizing and no glorification. These are women of achievement, but they are revealed, warts and all.

The challenge of honest fictional portrayal of the past is also being met by some novelists young people enjoy. James Lincoln Collier has written some books by himself, and others with his brother Christopher. Set in the Revolutionary period are such excellent books as *Who Is Carrie?* (1987), *My Brother Sam Is Dead* (1974), *The Winter Hero* (1985), and *War Comes to Willy Freeman* (1992). Of course there is Scott O'Dell's *Sarah Bishop* (1980) and the classic *Johnny Tremain* (1944) by Esther Forbes. These are stories that challenge stereotypes and are not afraid of controversy.

For readers in the middle and upper grades there are nonfiction books that convey the experience and the actions of women struggling for equal rights, of blacks fighting for civil rights, or Native Americans resisting the destruction of their civilization, of immigrant groups clashing with other cultures as they try to make a home in America.

Such books are not to be dismissed by that damning phrase, "information books." The facts are there, yes, but with sensitive concern for atmosphere, for setting, for pace, for character, for dramatic impact. Quality nonfiction has earned more attention in recent years than it once received, but it still needs the active interest and support of people who care for the best in writing, whatever form it may take.

CHAPTER 4

The Book as Revelation

When I started my research into the lives of the Jews of Eastern Europe, from whom most of today's American Jews are descended, it struck me how often they spoke of a book that had come as a revelation to them when they were growing up. Again and again the angry young men of Czarist Russia mention Chernyshevsky's *What Is to Be Done?* (1986). The novel's utopian vision of a socialist society became Holy Scripture for the radical intelligentsia of the 1860s and 1870s. Others refer to Lilionblum's autobiography, *The Sins of Youth* (1842). It was widely read because of its frank picture of the conflict between rigid orthodoxy and rationalism, which so many young Jews in Eastern Europe were agonizing over.

Such books make their greatest mark when they reach the reader in his or her adolescent years; that is the time when each young person must forge for him- or herself a sense of identity. Of course it isn't books alone that play a part in the young person's quest for self-actualization. There is upbringing in family and community, schooling, and, now, films and television. Young people look everywhere for that ground of truth on which they can stand before they commit the power of body and mind to the world as it is, or as they may wish to remake it. It is not always direct, personal experience that reshapes us. Many whites who had never been to the South became persuaded simply by what they read—that slavery was wrong and that they must help to overthrow it. The life of Lydia Maria Child furnishes examples of the power of both the personal and the literary experience. A successful young American novelist of the early nineteenth century, she heard William Lloyd Garrison, the abolitionist, make a speech in Boston one day. That speech changed the whole pattern of her life. She said, "It is of no use to imagine what might have been, if I had never met him. Old dreams vanished, old associates departed, and all things became new" (quoted in Meltzer & Holland, 1982, p. 558).

Lydia Maria Child decided to study slavery, to trace its roots and causes, to understand its consequences. She wrote a book about it, making an attack upon racial prejudice her central theme. The book, which originally came out in 1833, was called *An Appeal in Favor of That Class of Americans Called Africans* (1968). It was the first book attacking slavery to be published in the United States. It is equally distinguished as one of the early arguments against racism. It proved to be the most influential book of its kind until the arrival, 20 years later, of *Uncle Tom's Cabin* (Stowe, 1852/1981). It had a profound effect upon many individual readers, whose lives were changed by the power of her thought and feeling. William Ellery Channing, Wendell Phillips, Thomas Wentworth Higginson—such giants of the antislavery cause publicly declared that it was Lydia Maria Child's book that converted them to abolitionism. Reading the *Appeal* made people ask questions about themselves and their world.

What about writers whose work is meant for young readers? They too are trying to find some pattern or meaning in the struggle to realize their own humanity. Sometimes I think I know the answers before I start work on a book. The act of writing often teaches me better. If I am lucky, I may find out what the true questions are. And while I'm at it, if the book is any good, it may suggest some useful questions to readers and help them find their own answers.

One of our most distinguished scholars, Carl Becker, said that what the concerned historian chooses to investigate in the past is shaped by what is going on in the life of the present. The investigator looks for what will answer to today's concerns. Becker believed the search for knowledge should be purposeful, should help us to solve the problems of human existence.

To show what I mean, let's look at some of my own books, as examples of intention and method. It's up to the reader and critic to decide whether the work is good or bad. I know that books written with the best intentions can be terrible. Even those that have had a recognizably profound effect upon masses of readers can be adjudged a literary mess. *Uncle Tom's Cabin*, for example, until Edmund Wilson rediscovered merits in it that generations of critics had ignored, was considered by many an unbelievably bad novel.

Many of my books have had something to say about minorities in American life. They deal with that question which is at the heart of our history—racism. More and more of us are now coming to see the centrality of racism in the United States. Only recently has any atten- tion been paid to those institutional practices that give advantage to the white and penalize the black. Few of these institutions in America are openly racist any longer. Civil rights measures have deprived much institutional racism of any status in law. But institutional practices re- main covertly racist nevertheless. Built into them are attitudes, traditions, habits, assumptions that have great power to reward and penalize.

As a white writer concerned with racism, I think my main job is to combat racism within the white community. It should be obvious that we cannot deal with the black experience without talking about the white experience. And vice versa. Each has shaped the course of the other.

In thinking of how to write about racism, I decided not to use the traditional approach of the historian, who usually looks at past societies from the top. This, the historian tells us, is what the king, the president, the general, the men who ruled, did. But what about the people on the bottom? How did the strange new land look to kidnapped Africans carried in chains across the Atlantic? What was life like for the slave picking cotton or cutting cane? For the despised free black living on the fringe of a slave society? For the preacher plotting an uprising in the piney woods? For the mother standing with her child on the auction block? For the fugitive hiding in the swamps?

I dug into letters, speeches, memoirs, diaries, journals, slave narratives, newspapers, court records, public hearings, interviews, affidavits, eyewitness accounts. In them I found more than enough traces of the past to edit a documentary history of black Americans. Called *The Black Americans: A History in Their Own Words* (1984), it appeared in three volumes. My aim was twofold: to help the reader understand what African Americans felt, thought, and did, and to make whites see themselves in the light blacks had seen them, down through the centuries of racism.

Later, working toward the same goal, but taking a different tack, I narrowed the historical focus to just one of the 11 southern states involved in the important Reconstruction era, running from the Civil War to 1877. I chose Mississippi because today we identify it as one of the poorest and most backward states of our South. Yet, in contrast, back in Reconstruction times Mississippi made the greatest advance toward democracy. By offering a close-up of what Reconstruction was really like in Mississippi, I tried to shatter the myth, about what most whites, in the North and South, thought Reconstruction was.

My reason for choosing Reconstruction to write about was the desire to recover for the young reader those times in our past that have shown the possibility of a better way of life, a more humane, a more decent existence. During Reconstruction the black freedpeople tasted democracy for the first time. They voted at last, they built the South's first public school system, some farmed their own land, and some were elected to public office on every level of government.

That book tried to provide insight on racism through sharp focus on a single episode in history, Reconstruction. I've also tried the panoramic approach in the hope of making slavery itself meaningful to young readers. Americans have only a hazy notion of the slavery our country tolerated for 250 years. The textbooks, until recently, have treated slavery gingerly and often falsely. For generations our fiction and films romanticized the plantation life in the South. Most people find it hard to feel in their bones the nature of slavery as an institution that degrades man to a thing. And few know that slavery has never died out. Millions of men, women, and children, according to United Nations findings, are still held in slavery in many countries (Meltzer, 1971a). Yet what life is like from the slave's point of view has rarely been described outside of the scholarly literature. I went back more than 10,000 years to the lands of the Middle East—Sumer, Babylon, Egypt, Assyria, Israel—to trace the origins of slavery and its development in the widespread worlds of Greece and Rome. Because of the racism rampant in our own time, I was particularly concerned with the question of color as a factor in slavery. It has not been of the same importance throughout the past. In the ancient world color was not a dividing line: Whites enslaved whites, by the millions.

Not long ago, when blacks tried to break free of the stifling Chicago ghetto to find homes in the suburbs, the children of Slavic immigrants took to the streets against what they called an invasion, yelling "Niggers are nothing but slaves!" They never knew that the word *slave* comes from the time when the Germans supplied the slave markets of Europe with so many captured Slavs that the name came to mean "slave."

Racism and slavery were at the heart of the American Civil War, of course. But they were also crucial elements of other American wars. Young people have been told little about them. Realizing what parallels there were between the War in Vietnam and the Mexican War of the 1840s, I wrote a book about the earlier conflict. You see the war from the standpoint of the men who joined up in a patriotic fever to do the fighting. You hear about the handful of people back home who opposed the war as a ruthless land grab, as a means to expand slave territory and strengthen the power of the slaveholders in the national government. And you look at the war through the eyes of the Mexicans, too. How does an American war feel to the victims on the other side? What do the Mexicans think when invaders come killing and burning their way into the Mexican homeland, piously declaring they are doing it for the enemy's own sake, to introduce an inferior people, largely Indian, to a higher, Anglo-Saxon civilization?

You see too how a President manipulates a Congress into war.

How Congressmen twist and turn between what their conscience tells them is right and what political ambition tells them is "necessary." How politicians influence military decisions no matter what the terrible consequences for the other side or for their own soldiers. And how, when people come to see a war as unnecessary, unjust, and evil, they can mount a tidal wave of opposition to end it.

The other war whose issues I think are significant for today was the Seminole War of 1835–42. It was the longest, bloodiest, and most costly of all the Indian wars in our history. It was fought in Florida by two minorities—the Seminole Indians and the blacks—joined as allies against the dominant white majority. The whites were greedy for the Indians' land and wanted to recapture the escaped black slaves who were being hidden by the Indians. The Indians fought to protect their homeland and the runaway slaves to whom they had given shelter. The blacks were fighting for their freedom. A ragged, starving guerilla force, the Indians and blacks defied the power of an invading army ten times their number. In the end, 4,000 Seminole Indians were driven into exile by a mighty nation that boasted of its justice, its honor, and its love of liberty. But America paid a heavy price for its racism, a price we still pay in many ways. What conquering the Indians did to us as a people and a nation we are only beginning to understand.

The question of means and ends is always deeply troubling. Many times during the 1960s I was struck by the parallel between the decisions faced by the young civil rights activists in the South and the choices confronting the abolitionists of more than 100 years earlier.

One of those abolitionists captured my imagination in the 1950s, when I first began to do research in the history of slavery. His name was Calvin Fairbank. He was born in 1816 in Pike, a frontier village of upstate New York. There are fleeting references to Fairbank in many studies of slavery and the abolition movement. He moves in and out of the pages of the antislavery press, in news items or in letters by him or about him. It was clear he was a significant, a symbolic figure in the antislavery movement. But not because he exercised direct leadership. He didn't—he was rather a loner, doing what he had to do by himself. He was obscure, shadowy, hard to pin down. I pursued him through heaps of old newspapers, through court records, journals, diaries, biographies, and autobiographies. But I never felt I had sufficient information to be able to write his biography, even when I found the memoirs he had written in 1890, when he was old and sick and destitute, and hoped this cheaply printed book would bring in the few dollars he needed to stay alive. Fairbank's book is fascinating in its account of his almost unbelievable adventures. But it is too fragmentary. There are too many holes in it, and it is rarely self-analytical. He said his original draft had been many times longer, but friends—those well-meaning souls—had counseled him to cut it savagely on the ground that no one cared any longer about the abolition days and no one would take the trouble to read a big book about Calvin Fairbank. I hoped that the original draft might still be hidden in some attic, but when I tried to trace Fairbank's descendants the line petered out in the 1930s. I came up against a blank wall and finally had to give it up.

It was then that I decided to find out the truth about Fairbank by making up his story and writing a novel about him, *Underground Man* (1990c), starting from the facts I had been able to gather and then moving—Lord knows where—down whatever path my own experience and imagination might take me.

In essence, what I did know about Calvin Fairbank was this: Howling wolves and circuit-riding preachers were the chief diversions of his frontier childhood. His mother, a devout Methodist, gave him, he said, a sense of justice without regard to race, class, or sex. From a boyhood of farming he turned to the church for his life's work, but soon began to feel preaching Christ's precepts wasn't enough. He had to try to realize the Lord's will in action. He had seen a little of slavery when he rafted his father's lumber down the Ohio to Cincinnati. He decided slavery violated God's law. Unlike most well-meaning whites who had come to the same conclusion, but who contented themselves with antislavery prayers and petitions from the sanctuary of the North, Fairbank moved to the South, into the devil's stronghold. For years he lived underground, guiding 47 slaves out of Virginia and Kentucky and into freedom. He worked mostly by night, piloting the fugitives through the forests. In all sorts of disguises they moved on foot or on horse, in buggy, carriage, or wagon, in or under loads of hay, furniture, boxes, bags. They crossed the slave's Jordan—the Ohio—swimming or wading, on boats, skiffs, rafts, logs.

He never let one slave be captured. But he himself was taken. Twice caught and twice convicted, he spent a total of 17 years and 4 months in the Kentucky state prison, suffering brutal beatings almost daily. For he was the most notorious "nigger-stealer" in the South and was penned up in a place where everyone hated what he stood for, from the warden and the guards to the "poor white trash" who were his fellow prisoners. What made him take such risks? Such men may seem saints to people who believe in their cause, but surely they have weaknesses as well as strengths, for they are human beings too. They must know vanity and fear and hatred and doubt as well as humility and courage and love and certainty. I knew from my reading of that era what moral issues troubled the abolitionists, especially those who risked what Calvin Fairbank did. And it seemed to me that those questions were the same ones that trouble today's young people. When, if ever, is one justified in deliberately breaking the law? Is it right to use violence in achieving a moral goal? Should one tell lies before a court of justice if it may mean going free to continue the good work? What course do you take when your obligations to your family clash with your responsibility to the cause? What happens when you are so wearied by an unending struggle for justice that you want to lay your burden down?

The character of such a man is explored by showing him in action. He was what he did. He did what he was. And he acted with and against other human beings. Many of these were black. Since I did not—could not—feel as at home with the black characters in the story as with the white, I relied on the autobiographical material of numerous slave narratives as well as the experience of slaves who survived long enough to have their recollections taken down in the 1930s. I made use of slave songs, of advertisements for runaway slaves, of eyewitness reports of slave auctions, of casual news items dealing with blacks. All the episodes in the slave rescue sections are based upon actual events. Other historical figures in the novel who appear under their own names are adapted from their own accounts.

The outer experiences of the central character are patterned on Calvin Fairbank's life story, but with certain changes to suit my purpose. But his inner life, of course, is something else. His motives, his doubts, his confidence, his despair—they are my imagining of what it would be like to live such a life. How true, how real the character I tried to create, is for the reader to judge.

CHAPTER 5

History as Sausage: Richly Textured and a Bit Spicy

I have not taught in the classroom except for a brief training period in my college days when I thought I would like to be a teacher and then decided I would rather be a writer. I will, however, risk saying something about the teaching of history, speaking not as a teacher, but as a writer and editor of books many schools use, as the friend of many teachers, and as the father of children who have gone through the school system.

What is happening in the school today is unbelievably different from my own school days. Looking back at the school I attended in a Massachusetts city, I see schools as a kind of totalitarian society— benevolent, but nonetheless totalitarian. The principal and his teachers ran things; the only responsibility we students had was to come to class and do our assignments. I don't remember that any of us protested having little responsibility and no authority. We expected to be treated as children. It was no surprise that we were.

Nothing much changed in the conduct of the schools for a great many years. By the late 1960s, however, a great wave of unrest began washing through the schools. Many principals reported some form of active protest in their schools, and others who noted no protest said they expected it in the near future. The spread of underground newspapers was another form the protest movement took. Their number in the high schools alone was estimated to be at least 1,000 by 1969.

The serious disorders—strikes, sit-ins, demonstrations, riots— were not just big-city events. They happened in small towns and middle-sized cities everywhere in the country. In the major cities, racial conflicts were the chief cause of disruption. But elsewhere the central issue, according to private and governmental studies, was the growing effort toward more student freedom and involvement in school policy.

The issues the high school students were concerned with were first of all political, including the war in Vietnam. Then came dress regulations and disciplinary rules. And finally, there was pressure from the students for reforms in education itself.

All this, deeply disturbing though it was, could also be taken as a healthy sign of change. Some students, at least, were asking questions. They were taking less and less for granted. They wanted to know why and what for. It had long been the fashion to praise "critical thinking" and "personal independence" as worthy educational objectives. If the protest actions evidenced such qualities—and I know they arose out of other sources as well—then the schools had not killed the best that is in our children.

But I question how much the classroom has contributed to the shaping of inquiring, flexible, and creative minds, and how much comes from the great world outside. In too many classrooms curiosity had been murdered. What students have learned is how to con the teacher and beat the system.

Yet what we have long said we want the schools to teach is "the art and science of asking questions." Real questions, questions about things kids care about, questions that can often embarrass or threaten us. Why are things this way? Do they have to be this way? Can't they be changed? How do we go about making change? If institutions have become rigidly resistant to change, is violence justifiable to bring about change? What is the cost of change? Who loses and who gains by change?

I don't know to what extent we can expect the school or the teachers to answer such subversive questions. Our own society, like all others, often represses dissent at some point considered to be dangerous. The school's function is to prepare young people to take full membership in that society. Education gives the young a sense of the culture, practices, and values of the society, and presumably teaches the skills needed for a productive role in that society.

Those values and mores were assumed to be stable, unalterable. But change is so pervasive in the world now that the old cultural stabilities can no longer be taken for granted. There are new possibilities for human action. The options open to us are different. New technology has broadened the range of what we can do. What we choose to do with the new possibilities depends upon the values we are committed to.

And this brings me to history. True history is not the myth making that so many of our textbooks are ridden with. It does not bear witness to the lives of saints. It asks questions, it stimulates reflection, it tries to bring us closer to understanding. The questions it raises about the record of past generations helps us think more clearly about the future we are trying to shape. As for the ferment we are plunged into, history, better than any other discipline, helps us to understand what it is all about. Without an understanding of the forces moving the world we live in, we are likely to be their victim.

This is not to say that there is only one plot in history, and the events of every era merely repeat it. But there are patterns discernible in the continuous flow of the past. And although we cannot predict the future by it, history offers a useful guide to what is to come. It helps us to identify possible future events or situations and to assess their likelihood. Inseparable from this process is the matter of changing values, both personal and social. And here—as an aside—I think young people are much more aware than their parents of the need to restructure values that are a product of the new technology. Technological change is making previously unattainable goals possible and is at the same time making it relatively easier to realize other values. Our children have been born into a world in which tremendously rapid change is pervasive. They do not operate on the assumption that stability is typical of this world. Nor should our schools. To expect change and to be ready to deal with it—that is the hallmark of wise administrators and good teachers.

It is discouraging to learn that so many students hate history. History to them is a packaged product, a long piece of stale bologna, sliced thin and served up cold. It is some inert body of facts put down on paper, facts that have little interest and no point. In school they find history courses dull, boring, mechanical, repetitious. And meaningless—that above all. For the textbooks and the instruction are all too often scrubbed clean of controversy.

Yet history as the story of human society is explosive with energy and genius. It is the story of evil as well as good, of failure as well as success, of frustration as well as achievement, of hate as well as love. America's history is not a bland record of steady and inevitable progress toward perfection. It should never be presented reverently. Yet this is what the textbook and teacher so often do, to the boredom and disbelief, if not the disgust, of the student.

How can a national history full of wonderful figures and careers and violent events be made dull? Think of Franklin, Jackson, Thoreau, John Brown, Douglass, Lincoln, Vanderbilt, Jay Gould, Altgeld, Carnegie, Debs, Emma Goldman, DuBois, any Roosevelt of your choice. Call them heroes or villains—sometimes they were both at once—you cannot contest the abundant variety and complexity of their lives, their influence, their individuality and yet typicality at the same time.

But you *can* make their stories dull. Dull when you leave out the doubts and hesitancies, the lies and compromises, the betrayals and denials. The danger in writing for young readers is superficiality. It grows out of the injunction to "keep it short." To keep it short you need to simplify. When you overdo that, when you compress too much, you provide crude and shallow explanations for subtle and complex events and people. In other words, you falsify. And that leads your readers to think of contemporary events and problems in the same oversimplified way and to expect pat solutions to a Vietnam or the crisis of the cities.

This doesn't mean that books for young people cannot be honest and truthful. Writers of conscience struggle with their material—and themselves!—to move closer and closer to that goal. Sometimes the struggle is with the publisher, too. But many editors are ready and eager now for books that deal with crucial issues, both past and present. Fiction for children has been far more realistic in recent years, and nonfiction doesn't hesitate to touch any part of society. There is much greater freedom of subject matter and language. The young have always been interested in everything that goes on. It is we who took so long to recognize that and respond to it.

In what ways are writers and publishers responding? I cannot pretend to speak for anyone but myself, for the work I am directly or indirectly responsible for as a writer and editor. I am too pressed by my own obligations to keep up with what everyone else is doing in the field of history. Still, I try to see samples of other people's work and I read enough of the trade and professional journals to gain some notion of developments in the field at large.

I do believe several good things have been done to provide better materials in history. I'd like to point out some of these projects. In the 1960s, Harvard and the U. S. Office of Education sponsored an experimental Social Studies Project out of which came a variety of materials tested and evaluated in the junior and senior high schools. Talented teachers in the schools and universities worked closely together to develop what was called the Public Issues Series, put out by American Education Publications.

Central to each unit in the series was a small paperback book designed to help students talk sense to each other about the persisting problems or dilemmas that are at the root of many public issues, past and present. Subjects included African Americans, municipal problems, rights of the accused, community change, Communist China, twentieth-century Russia, Nazi Germany, the New Deal, colonial Kenya, the rise of organized labor, the railroad era, the American Revolution, and religious freedom.

The editors believed the ability to discuss such issues in a meaningful way is a prime function of citizenship. They had in view high
school students of average ability. They hoped to teach them how to
clarify and justify their positions on public issues. The books helped
the students to do this by presenting dramatic case studies that focused on real persons in crucial situations.

Then there were sequences of challenging questions about values
and facts. Every technique and device was used that might help students to understand what the discussion process itself is. The case
studies were usually investigations of single institutions, decisions, situations, or individuals. By zeroing in on a limited incident rather than
a sweeping set of events, it is possible to go deeper, to gather more
detailed information, and thereby to avoid the superficial and dis-
torting approach I spoke of earlier. Take such questions as these: How
does a corporation grow? What went into the decision to drop the
atomic bomb? What are the living conditions of a black family in an
urban slum? How does a politician seeking election behave? Out of
the examination of such probing questions can come conclusions that
are applicable to a more general class of incidents. The historical topics
this series chose took in questions of value that persist throughout
history and across cultures. Skillful teachers can make use of the parallels between human dilemmas in other times and places and the present issues of our own society.

I found the Public Issues Series fresh, vital, provocative. Events
that would seem relatively distant to a student were made challenging
and important. The booklets used many different techniques to catch
the student's interest. Events were presented in the style of a good
historical novelist, or as the eyewitness account of a reporter. Documents and raw data were used, too, as well as interpretive essays. The
teacher could choose a variety of means to make the material work in
the classroom. I liked the stress on the open-ended inductive approach,
for these public issues can be viewed in many lights. The project didn't
tell the teacher which was the "best" or "right" way.

I felt that in the hands of a teacher who cares, the Public Issues
Series could involve students, could show them the significance and
importance of public issues. Take such a basic question as the use of
violence at that time: the violence erupting in the schools, the colleges,
the ghettoes—and in Vietnam. In these booklets the problem of violence was explained in several different contexts—in the American
Revolution, in the British sailors' mutiny during the war against France
in 1798, in the labor struggles of the 1930s for the right to organize, in
the battle of young Richard Wright to survive within the black code of
his native Mississippi.

No matter what the setting, the issues are similar, the conflicts of values are the same. Presented in such a framework, the important factual information is more likely to be mastered, and the student is so much readier to learn what it means to analyze and understand a social issue. Consensus in the class is not the goal. Work in the subject may be stopped with many doubts remaining in the student's mind. But hopefully, some will have come to understand that facts alone do not resolve issues. There are the ultimate questions of value and meaning.

In one area of our history the facts themselves were long suppressed. Doubleday, through its Zenith Series, was one of the first publishers to recognize its responsibility for lighting up what has been called the "underside" of American history. The Zenith books were written to a sixth-grade reading level but the content paralleled social studies programs from the sixth to the twelfth grades. Many of the titles dealt with black history. They revealed the black heritage and participation in American life that previously were denied or ignored.

Such books were designed for both white and black readers. And it is vital that the white student read the same books the black reads, or he or she will continue to have the impression many textbooks helped create, that American history is strictly white history.

By stressing the necessity for all students to study black history, I do not mean patching in to the traditional texts a few thumbnail biographies of outstanding blacks or a few paragraphs on the valor of black troops in our many wars. I think more and more historians have come to see the centrality of the African American, of the South, and of racism in the development of American life. Not that every aspect of American history has turned upon this misnamed "Negro question." But much of our past has been powerfully influenced by the problem of slavery and of the freedpeople. Our Constitution and our political parties—were they not molded by issues concerning blacks? The new nation's commerce and industrial growth—didn't these rest on the South's slave economy? Our territorial expansion South and West—was it not a direct product of slavery? And our imperial expansion later in the nineteenth and twentieth centuries—was it not conditioned by racism? As for the Civil War and the politics and economics out of which it exploded—was it not all linked to slavery? In the 1930s President Roosevelt called the South the nation's number one economic problem—didn't that problem's roots go back into slavery and the position of the African Americans afterward? And what about the great struggles in the 1950s and 1960s to bring about some basic change in the lives of most African Americans? Did it not demonstrate how powerful a hold racism has on our society?

I think it is clear from this that African American history should not be segregated from basic American history. Since it is central to our history, the black vision and experience should be linked with it so that a vital new version of American history is written. It will be a history that not only helps blacks to see themselves, but lets whites see themselves honestly, too.

If a whole people were lost from the mainstream of our history, they need now to be restored. Not for their sake alone, but for the health and sanity of all of us. A people systematically blotted out of history have demanded re-entry into history, demanded respect for their dignity and their humanity. This is no new fight they are waging. It began long ago and has gone on for many generations. But today it has reached a dynamic and a power never attained before. After years of neglect, the colleges and universities began to develop black history and black studies programs to meet the enormous pressure. Many mistakes were made under the circumstances. But it is all to the good that at last a start was made. Out of the work in higher education should come the knowledge and trained staff to effect deep changes in the elementary and secondary schools where it is most urgent to develop good programs.

We should not expect too much from black studies. They are not some form of group therapy or legend making. They need to be taught as an intellectual discipline, like any other subject. And they are certainly no substitute for learning individual skills or acquiring technological or professional training. Alhough black history may be no panacea, it is a necessary medicine, a kind of truth serum, if you will, that is indispensable if we are to make any progress toward building a healthy society.

CHAPTER 6

Imagination, Invention, and Information

Readers often ask how a historical novel is created. How much of it is fact and how much fiction? How are they linked? Or they may ask, what is "true" and what is "untrue"? I would answer by saying that if a novel is good, the truth of it exists quite apart from verifiable facts—which doesn't mean, at least in the case of my *Underground Man* (1990c), that most of the story isn't taken from history.

Sometimes I've been asked, Why did you choose to make a white rather than a black the hero of your novel? At the time I began the book, there were in print several biographies for young people of black abolitionists—people like Harriet Tubman, Frederick Douglass, Sojourner Truth. There were very few about white abolitionists, however, even such prominent ones as William Lloyd Garrison or Wendell Phillips, and none at all about lesser known white abolitionists, such as Calvin Fairbank, who dared go into the South to rescue slaves. Surely they deserved to have their stories told? Especially since the white rescuers were few indeed compared with the number of whites who either openly favored slavery or may have disliked it but kept silent and did nothing. Most slaves who escaped had only themselves and their fellow blacks to thank.

I find a kind of parallel between telling stories such as Fairbank's and telling the story of the very small minority of Christians who risked their lives to rescue Jews during the Nazi era. In my book *Rescue: The Story of How Gentiles Saved Jews in the Holocaust* (1988b), I said: "Against the immense darkness of the Holocaust, the light shone by the rescuers is only a tiny flicker" (p. 156). But those few, like Calvin Fairbank or my fictional hero, Josh Bowen, were men and women whose lives were witness to the truth that there is an alternative to the passive acceptance of evil. It was Fairbank's—or Josh's—ability to respond to the evil of slavery that made his attempts at rescue possible. He felt compassion for the suffering of others, strangers though they were, and so he acted, bound in the oneness of humanity.

Underground Man (1990c) was my first work of fiction. It came after 20 years of writing nonfiction, chiefly history and biography. And it didn't begin as a novel, but as a biography of Calvin Fairbank (see also Chapter 4). I had run across his name in several books about the antislavery movement. Brief as the references to his courage and daring were, they intrigued me. What had he been like? Where did he come from? What forces had shaped his character and led him south to rescue black men, women, and children from slavery?

To answer these questions I set out to write his biography. But because my research failed to unearth enough evidence to do justice to his story, I decided reluctantly to give it up. Then my editor suggested that I write a novel about the man instead. After all, I had written many books about African American history and the antislavery movement; couldn't I use that experience to create a fictional image of Fairbank?

Challenged by the prospect of trying a new form of writing, I agreed. I soon discovered that because I had begun by using Fairbank's real name, I felt blocked in my efforts to imagine characters, events, and dialogue that were not strictly according to the actual facts. In short, it was my training as an historian that inhibited me. Then one night, waking from sleep, I saw the solution as though written in the air before me. Why not change the hero's name? And so he became Joshua Bowen, instead of Calvin Fairbank, which removed the barrier to invention. Josh was my creation. I could put ideas in his head, words in his mouth, and feelings in his heart that sprang from my own understanding of such a man's character and temperament.

My venture into fiction was not at the expense of history, however. Almost everything in the novel is solidly rooted in fact. I collected data like an investigative reporter (which is one aspect of the historian's job). On my shelves were rows of books about African American history and the abolition movement, gathered in the course of research for previous projects. My desk was piled high with notes when a lucky find occurred. In a secondhand bookstore (I am always prowling them for such treasures), I found a blue-covered book, cheaply printed and now almost in tatters, dated 1890. The title page read *Rev. Calvin Fairbank During Slavery Times* and, below it, "Edited from the manuscript." A brief preface by Fairbank stated that he had written a 1,200-page manuscript, but that everyone considered it too long. He had then cut it to the bone.

It was a great break, although I raged against those well-meaning friends—probably tired of hearing Fairbank's tales of adventure—who had made him throw away much of the bigger part of the story.

Fairbank writes in a plain style, simple, direct, and with a fierce hatred of slavery sizzling just below the surface. Sometimes he recalls conversations and provides character sketches of the people he encountered in his struggle to liberate slaves. But there are holes in the story, gaps any reader would want to have filled in. "And then what happened?" is always in the reader's mind when pursuing an adventure story. I also wanted to know more about the places his adventures took him to, about the people who tried to help him or hurt him, and about the experience of being imprisoned for long years.

Because I was writing for young readers, I changed the time sequence of the story, thereby making my hero about 10 years younger than he actually was at the time of these events. I thought by doing that I would enable my readers to identify more readily with the hero. But except for that change, almost everything in the book is true. The people he encounters are derived from the people Fairbank knew; they bear their actual names. Although some of the dialogue is adapted from Fairbank's own account, more of it is invented by me—consistent, I hope, with how people in that time saw themselves and understood the issues.

Fairbank's autobiography dismisses his childhood in a few pages. We learn very little about his family, his parents, their feelings for one another. (These may have been given much more attention in the original draft.) What I decided to do, then, was to conjure up a family life for him, to imagine relationships and interests that might influence the development of a boy born in the wilderness of upstate New York in the early nineteenth century.

Because I particularly wanted a dramatic opening to hook the reader and at the same time express the tension between a father and his son, I hit upon the bear hunt in Chapter 1. Jacob Axley, a fictional character, is based on what I'd read of circuit preachers on the frontier—their goals, their duties, the hardships of their ministry, the rewards of their work. Gradually Josh finds himself moving toward preaching. His need for a new birth in Christ comes from Fairbank's own book, in which he mourns his youthful alienation from God and from time to time promises himself resignation to His will. Fairbank wrote that often, alone in the forest, he would imagine himself with an audience before him, "pointing them to the lamb of God" (quoted in Meltzer, 1990c, p. 250).

In Chapter 4, the description of the revival meeting in the campground is derived from many books I read about the Great Awakening that seized America in that time. The classic source for the connection between religious revival and antislavery is Gilbert H. Barnes's *The An-*

tislavery Impulse, 1830–1844 (1933). God, the preachers said, insisted that the saved perform benevolent deeds, that they take a personal responsibility for improving society. Out of such a spirit sprang the crusade against slavery. Young people like Fairbank began to see social activism as a way of life. Some became circuit riders, abolition agents, editors of radical papers burning to aid in America's regeneration.

When I write about Jacob Axley preaching to the vast crowd, his words are taken from reports I read about other preachers. The books in the saddlebags that form Josh's schooling were actually read by schoolchildren at the time. I took special pleasure in putting in Lydia Maria Child's abolitionist book, *An Appeal in Favor of That Class of Americans Called Africans* (1833/1968). I had just written a biography of Mrs. Child and was very fond of this feisty woman who fought so hard against slavery and for women's rights (Meltzer, 1965).

The episode of Josh's encounter with the runaway slave Sam, which takes up most of Chapters 5 and 6, runs less than two pages in the Fairbank book. But it was enough to get me going, to give me a chance to re-create Sam's life as a slave on a Kentucky farm as he tells it to Josh. The details of his story I took in part from the many authentic narratives of fugitive slaves published in the pre-Civil War years to win support for the abolitionist cause. I took passages from Solomon Northup's *Twelve Years a Slave* (1853) and from *Narrative of the Life of Frederick Douglass* (1845), as well as from other slave tales, for my documentary works, *The Black Americans: A History in Their Own Words* (1984). The narratives were powerful portraits of slave life, of physical abuse and privation, of separation from loved ones, of emotional distress. They gave northern whites a vivid picture of the slaves' humanity, their cultural vitality, and their accomplishments, thus undermining current racial myths. In my novel, the effect of his meeting with Sam is to waken in Josh the determination to identify himself with the people "that are in bonds, as bound with them" (Meltzer, 1990c, p. 252).

In Chapter 7, Josh crosses the Ohio river to Kentucky to start his new and dangerous life as an agent of the Underground Railroad. It was in this slave state that most of Fairbank's daring rescues took place. To build my knowledge of the conditions of slavery there, of the attitudes of both whites and blacks, I read several books about the Kentucky of that day. Most useful was J. Winston Coleman's *Slavery Times in Kentucky* (1940). I had used it earlier while researching other books but now found it enormously helpful for both details and insights. It contains many references to Fairbank himself. Some of what Fairbank's own book tells us is supplemented and enriched by fresh information Coleman gathered from contemporary newspapers and court records. Coleman's bibliography steered me to other books and pamphlets about the state's slave conditions as well as to biographies of Kentuckians.

The personality of Reverend Billy Shaw and the description of the miserable farm he operates near Maysville (Chapter 7) are both taken from the accounts of travelers in the South. Many Europeans visited the slave states and, returning home, published their impressions. Americans from the free states did the same. One of the most valued accounts is by the New Englander Frederick Law Olmsted, who made two lengthy trips south between 1852 and 1854, reporting his day-to-day observations for a New York newspaper. The assignment resulted in three volumes that appeared in 1861 as *The Cotton Kingdom*. The same Olmsted became the nation's foremost landscape architect, designing New York City's Central Park and many other parks and gardens.

Shaw's slave Annie is depicted partly out of imagination and partly from vignettes of tough-minded women who never let a master enslave their spirit. The elements of Shaw's sermon to the slave congregation came from travelers' accounts of sermons they sat through while visiting plantations.

The Quaker Levi Coffin, introduced into the story in Chapter 8, is a major historical figure with whom Fairbank worked early on. In his role as "president" of the Underground Railroad, Coffin helped thousands of slaves to freedom. The Society of Friends, also known as Quakers, was the first religious institution in this country to condemn slavery as morally evil and the first to require all its members to free their slaves. They helped to found antislavery organizations and did much to advance the restriction on or ending of slavery. Many Quakers probably would have quietly aided fugitives who came to their doors, but some, like Coffin, became organizers of rescue attempts.

I found much useful material in histories of the rescue movement. They included Lary Gara, *The Liberty Line: The Legend of the Underground Railroad* (1961); Wilbur H. Siebert, *The Underground Railroad from Slavery to Freedom* (1898); and William Still, *The Underground Rail Road* (1872). Still, a free black was leader of underground railroad operations in Pennsylvania from 1849 to 1861 and was involved in many of the most famous rescue cases. His is the source closest to actual history.

Josh's talk with Levi Coffin expresses the views of most Quakers, considered moderates by such abolitionists as William Lloyd Garrison, who advocated immediate emancipation and denounced the Constitution as a slave document. When Coffin convinces Josh to attend the school in New York for the training of antislavery agents, it gives me the chance to show what this intense form of special education devoted to a cause was like. (There were similar schools in the 1960s, to train college students to go south and help in the civil rights movement.) All the people brought into the story here are historical figures: Theodore Weld, William Lloyd Garrison, the Grimke sisters, Amos Dresser—about whom or by whom much has been written. Benjamin Thomas's biography, *Theodore Weld, Crusader for Freedom* (1950), describes the school.

Fairbank did not attend the New York school, but he did study at Oberlin College, an Ohio school considered radical because it offered, for the first time in the history of higher education, equal instruction regardless of race or gender. Fairbank must have met antislavery students and teachers there.

The tactics antislavery agents used—entering churches and, without permission, standing up and speaking boldly against slavery, and often against the church itself for its silence on the issue—are dramatized in Chapter 9. My knowledge of these tactics comes from the memoirs of such men as Henry C. Wright, Stephen Foster, and Parker Pillsbury, as well as from reports of their actions in the *Liberator*, Garrison's newspaper. They were called "come-outers" because they advocated separation from their slaveholding brethren. They were tossed out, beaten, and nearly lynched for the uproar they caused in church. Quotes from press clippings and the placards reproduced in the book are all authentic. After exposure to a series of these, Josh decides that his work must be in the South itself. He can't wait for emancipation. He must act now to help free slaves. He thinks not in abstract numbers— millions of people in bondage—but of individuals, of real men and women and children. The conversation he has with Levi Coffin, considering whether to go disguised as a peddler (a common front) or as the circuit rider he himself was, is based on the tactics men like him used.

The story of William Minnis (Chapter 9) is given by Fairbank in considerable detail; Emily Ward's and the Rhoads' stories, much less so. Helen Payne occupies only a paragraph in Fairbank's book, but I saw the opportunity to enrich her story with an attempt to get at her thinking. Kentucky's pressure on Ohio to stop interfering with slave property is in the official records of both states. I introduce other rescue efforts, such as Julie's story (Chapter 10), to illustrate how masters sexually exploited their female slaves, even those as young as Julie. The horrifying outcome of Julie's attempt to escape demonstrates the great risk of flight.

The last part of Chapter 10 and all of Chapter 11 focus on the story of Eliza (whose name I changed to Talitha because I invented a few of the details) and the slave question. It was the "most extraordinary incident" in Fairbank's life, he says in his book (quoted in Meltzer, 1990c, p. 257). He gives about eight pages to it. Coleman's history of Kentucky devotes four pages to the Eliza auction; I found it took me 20 pages to tell it the way I wished. The Noah Tyler episode is purely fictional but based on accounts of slave auctions in the newspapers of the period.

Salmon P. Chase and Nicholas Longworth, who played important roles in backing Talitha's—or Eliza's—purchase, were important historical figures. Chase, an abolitionist lawyer, later became a senator from Ohio, governor of the state, Lincoln's Secretary of the Treasury, and Chief Justice of the U. S. Supreme Court. Longworth was a noted horticulturist.

Josh's encounter with Deborah Walker (Chapter 12) is based on the connection between Fairbank and a Vermont woman, Delia A. Webster, the head of a school for girls in Lexington, Kentucky. I changed her name and some of the circumstances to suit my plot, but the basic story is true. Coleman's history tells us much more about it than Fairbank does, with many of his details taken from reports in the Kentucky press and from court records.

The rescue of the Lloyd Hawkins family by Deborah and Josh stands upon the actual rescue by Webster and Fairbank of Lewis Hayden, his wife, and their son. The family ultimately reached Boston, where Hayden became one of the busiest station-keepers on the Underground Railroad, helping runaways and gaining considerable influence in Boston as a leader in the black community. The John Rankin who takes over the protection of the Hawkins family on the free side of the Ohio was a well-known white abolitionist originally from the South.

The arrest of Josh and Deborah is exactly as it happened. My account of the trial is taken from the press, court records, and a pamphlet published by Webster herself, which contains some of the documents I quote from. The differences between their positions gave me a chance to probe the crisis of conscience both people faced as they decided on a course of action. Josh's speech to the court before sentencing I made up out of my sense of what abolitionists felt and how they reasoned. Fairbank provides only a few sentences about it in his memoir.

Life in the Kentucky prison (Chapters 14–17) is touched on only briefly by Fairbank. But starting from the elementary facts, I was able to enlarge on them after much research. I found that Dorothea Dix, the social reformer who crusaded for more humane treatment of the mentally ill and the imprisoned, had visited the prison during the years Fairbank was there. Her long report of neglect and abuse, of what the cells looked like, how the prisoners were treated, and the work they were made to do, was invaluable.

But how to reconstruct the mental and emotional state of Josh in prison? What was it like for a notorious abolitionist to be thrown among prisoners, most of whom hated what he stood for? I thought of other prisoners whose dissident points of view must have alienated them from their fellow inmates. I remembered reading the prison memoirs of Alexander Berkman, the anarchist who spent 20 years in a Pennsylvania penitentiary for his attempt to kill Henry Clay Frick, the manager of the Carnegie steelworks, because of Frick's brutality to the workers during the Homestead strike of 1892. Rereading his book and looking up the memoirs of other political prisoners helped me to put myself in Josh's place.

The details about the weaving of hemp in prison came from Fairbank's book. He was actually allowed to conduct Sunday school classes and to preach in prison. I invented his use of newspaper stories that recorded aspects of southern life, but the clippings themselves are all real. A cholera epidemic did strike Kentucky at the time and spread to the prison, but Fairbank gives it only a paragraph. I built it up to dramatize the compassionate side of Josh's character and to bring his recovery of faith and hope to a climax.

Fairbank's father really did come to Kentucky to carry petitions for his son's release and was struck down by the plague and buried among strangers. I used Josh's meeting in prison with his father and their reconciliation to bring on the final resolution of the conflict between the two that set the story going in my opening chapter.

Fairbank, like Josh, was pardoned after nearly 5 years in prison. And, like Fairbank, Josh goes on a tour (Chapter 18), speaking at antislavery meetings. And again like Fairbank, Josh, while in Indiana, responds to an appeal to rescue Tamar, a slave about to be sold on the auction block. The rescue accomplished, Fairbank was kidnapped on free soil and forced back into Kentucky, where he was convicted for violation of the slave code. Fairbank was sentenced to 15 years of hard labor.

My story ends with the slamming of the prison door behind Josh. I wrote this note to let readers know that the story of Josh was fundamentally true. Fairbank himself stayed in that prison until the Civil War, when Union troops entered Kentucky and freed him. Adding up both his terms in prison, Fairbank spent 17 years behind bars.

Part II

TOUCH THE HEART AND OPEN THE MIND

Despite whole language and writing workshops, despite cooperative learning and teacher development opportunities, much of what we remember about schools has remained the same. Reading over the essays in this part, I find myself pulled back in time. In my schools certain people were highly visible—they were elected to the student council and the National Honor Society, they laughed comfortably in the cafeteria, and teachers chatted easily with them before and after class. There were, of course, others who came to school regularly, who had a circle of friends, who did their work, but from an "insider's" perspective, these students remained essentially invisible. When they were recognized, whether for academic or extracurricular achievement, their names evoked a slightly startled remembering—oh yes, him.

From the outsider's point of view, however, there is no forgetting about insiders. The insiders are the players, the outsiders the audience. The insiders set the standard, the outsiders are measured against that standard. My initial interest in teaching sprang, in part, from a personal commitment to change the formula, the balance between insiders and outsiders. As a teacher, graduate student, faculty member, and writer, that impulse to make schools different has guided my work.

Teachers who are motivated to encourage all students to take risks, to reveal themselves, to make school a place where the insider/outsider distinction is fluid, even dynamic, will find the essays in this part helpful. By describing the obstacles confronted by ordinary people—African Americans, Jews, Pacifists—Meltzer helps all of us, insiders and outsiders, understand what it means to be washed from the pages of history.

The first essay in this part focuses on history from the "bottom

59

up." The American Revolution, the Civil War, the Ku Klux Klan, the Great Depression, the civil rights movement—none would exist without the people who stuffed a sandwich in their pocket and went out to demonstrate their beliefs. We are moved by mothers and teachers with the courage to take a stand. History, according to Meltzer, gives coherence to the stories of people like ourselves, not just the architects, but the masons and bricklayers. He talks in this piece about the importance of telling stories in people's own words. I can think of no better introduction to an oral history project or a writing project in which students are asked to create a history of their own town or city. Here, the tension and balance between the personal and the political is formally addressed.

The second essay, "On Ethnic Stereotyping," squarely faces the issue of prejudice. Sometimes people remain outside circles of power because they choose not to be involved. In other instances they are kept away not because of their beliefs, but because of their skin color, their parentage, their place of birth. Meltzer hits hard at tokenism as a solution. The issues he writes about are timely. As the demographics of public schools change, students need a chance to be actively informed about and engaged in making this a more humane and caring world.

The next essay, "Writing About the Jews," is revealing not only as a chronicle of anti-Semitism, but as a personal essay about how difficult it is to identify oneself as the victim. This chapter may well serve as a model for students wishing to examine their own histories, their own reflections, their own internalization of difference.

The piece entitled "On Racism" may similarly serve those who do not identify as members of a minority group, but who do feel the mighty pull of justice. "As a white, I am part of the problem," begins this essay. Rather than a self-indulgent dwelling on the author's role as a white man, Meltzer chides his readers: ". . . none of us is really alone, and each of us has the power to speak up, to protest, to organize for change. We are all part of the lives of others." Meltzer then goes on to examine what we can do to eliminate racism. Again, this piece serves as an excellent model for a similar kind of self-examination.

The final two pieces in this part describe groups of people— pacifists and terrorists—whose minority status and identity formed in reaction to the times. I watch young people struggle between a search for meaning and the crass consumerism of the "me generation." My hope is that these essays will help them to think about what it is they do stand for, what situations they find intolerable, what might support them in their attempts to overcome peer pressure and external rewards.

Whereas many authors, in writing about such matters, would sound didactic or shrill, Meltzer helps us through the insecurities that make prejudice feel somehow justified. Carolyn Coman, author of adolescent fiction, crystallizes this point when she writes:

> Isn't diversity, after all, a giant relief, a gift that in the giving makes room enough for us all? I count on the differences that make other lives seem inspiring and wondrous, outrageous and heart-breaking. I count as well—perhaps even more—on the connections that enable us to understand other lives. (Coman & Dater, 1988, pp. 7–8)

CHAPTER 7

Ordinary People: In Their Own Words

Much of my work has to do with letting people of the past speak in their own voices. As much as possible, to tell their stories through what the scholars call "primary evidence." You can see how I've done it in books dealing with the history of African Americans, Chinese Americans, Hispanic Americans, Jewish Americans, Native Americans. Some of these books are documentary histories. Others are narrative histories into which I've woven many passages taken from primary sources. I do this for two reasons. One is because of my belief in the value of presenting history from the bottom up. I want readers to understand the part ordinary people play in making our history. The other reason is to catch the attention of readers and transport them into the past, to induce in them that leap of imagination that gets them out of present-mindedness, the narrow view that nothing before their own time matters much.

I've used this method in dealing not only with minority groups but with other aspects of history and with social issues: terrorism, human rights, labor struggles, the Great Depression, the Ku Klux Klan, the Civil War, the American Revolution, and so on.

Many teachers have probably had the experience of working in a town where a major event occurred in the past, for instance, a strike, in a time before the local students were born. Yet the boys and girls know nothing about it. It is not discussed or even mentioned in their schools. That part of the community's life has been hidden from history.

Why? Because the history of so-called ordinary people is not thought to be important. Schools downplay the actions of working people or the poor when they challenge social injustice. It is that neglect which has led many scholars in recent years to search the "history from below." For workers, women, ethnic and racial minorities, immigrants—all have a history that should be uncovered and made known.

It isn't only historians who are interested in the past. Which students in a classroom are not interested in who they are and where they came from? Interested in the story of their family, their community, their organizations? They need only to be shown examples of how fascinating and how significant their personal and family histories are to change the all-too-common impression that history is a bore and a waste of time.

After all, what is history but the coherent story of the lives of people of the past? And not just of the empire builders, but of people very much like themselves. And thus, in the kind of history I try to write, young readers find those timeless constants that all persons and societies share: sorrow and happiness, success and defeat, effort and reward, effort and failure, love and hatred, guilt, shame, pride, compassion, cruelty, justice, injustice, birth, death. Everywhere we look, no matter what the time or place, we find these great fixed elements. We cannot imagine that life in the future will ever be without them.

When young people, or adults for that matter, read this kind of history—the original documents left behind by the people of the times, woven into a narrative—they are helped to locate their individual lives in the chain of generations. They can find common bonds with people far off in time and space, recognizing in them our common humanity while understanding the differences that may separate us. Such history provides a way of understanding one's background, of finding roots that grow not only out of the family, but out of the workplace, the community, the region, the nation.

To examine the past by reading what people said of it in their own words is to gain a new perspective on the world around us. Exposed to such living testimony, readers find out not only what people did, but how they felt and thought about what they lived through. They see how things have changed; they develop a sense of perspective that makes their world of today more understandable.

I think too that this kind of history helps students to see they are not outsiders, living on the fringes of great events, just looking on as the world turns and changes. History written on the grand scale, sweeping over great issues and crises, dealing only with the powerful few, can make students feel insignificant. What do they have to do with all that? But reading the personal record, told by the players themselves, returns readers to the face-to-face world of everyday life. It connects them to life as people experienced it *then*—whether in their parents' generation or 100 or 500 years ago.

My emphasis on the experience of ordinary people does not mean that I think power and power-holders should not be investigated in the telling of the story. We are filled with disgust over the grave abuses of power the nation suffered from in the 1960s and 1970s and 1980s, when Vietnam and Watergate and the Iran-Contra scandal and the savings and loan disaster happened. The best defense against their recurrence is to acquire an understanding of the institutions, and the actors in whom power is invested, and through whom power operates. Our best values make us feel concern for the people without power. But they cannot act in their own defense unless they understand the powerful and learn how those with power seek to control affairs. My interest has always been in providing books that let the people who shaped our history tell the story themselves. The traditional approach of the historian is to look at past societies from the top, to note what the men who *ruled* did and said. The history I've tried to write gives us examples of real men and women trying to meet the issues of their day, just as we here and now are called upon to solve the issues of our own time. Honest writing will point to the value, and to the necessity as well, of human efforts to make the world move closer to our highest ideals.

But what about the people on the bottom? How did the world look to them? How did their beliefs and actions affect their world? We can't understand America only by examining the lives of the Nixons and the Rockefellers. When we look at our country solely from the view of the small minority at the top, we inevitably get a very distorted picture.

Of course, it isn't easy to get a view of the past from the bottom up. After all, it is the men on top whose accomplishments were carved in stone, revered in palaces and monuments, recorded in state documents, blazoned in the press, while the people on the bottom were ignored. Who asked what they thought? And when they acted, as soldiers in an army or rebels in a cause, the rank and file disappeared into the anonymous mass. They were the voiceless ones.

Attempting to correct this many years ago, I tried to look for the testimony of the many as well as the few when I edited my three-volume documentary series of African American history, called *The Black Americans: A History in Their Own Words* (1984). I also tried to use this approach in pioneering a Knopf series called the Living History Library. The book that launched it was my *Bread—and Roses: The Struggle of American Labor, 1865–1915* (1991a), the story of working-class life in America from the Civil War to World War I—the 50 bloodiest years in labor's struggle for equality. Then I worked on *Brother, Can You Spare a Dime? The Great Depression, 1929–1933* (1991b), told from the point of view of the dispossessed farmers, the sharecroppers, the

youngsters riding the freightcars and living in hobo jungles, the migratory workers in the West, the blacks in the ghettoes, the jobless teachers
and engineers, the declassed small businesspeople and professionals
forced onto welfare.

My third volume for this series was called *Bound for the Rio Grande*
(1974a), which deals with the Mexican War of the 1840s. You see the
war from the perspective of those gripped by a patriotic fever to do
the fighting, from the view of the people back home who opposed the
war as a ruthless land grab, or as a means to expand slave territory
and strengthen the power of the slaveholders in the national government, and also through the eyes of the Mexicans. How did that American war feel to the victims on the *other* side? What did the Mexicans
think when invaders came killing and burning their way into a foreign
land, piously declaring they were doing it for the Mexicans' own sake,
to introduce them to a higher, Anglo-Saxon civilization? Using their
own words, I tried to show how a President manipulated a Congress
into war, how those Congressmen twisted and turned between what
their conscience told them was right and what political ambition told
them was necessary, how politicians influenced military decisions no
matter what the terrible consequences for the other side or for their
own soldiers, and how public opinion swung finally into a tidal wave
of opposition to a war most people came to see as unnecessary, unjust,
and evil.

What does it take to make a difference?

What quality did all these people share whose voices we have just
listened to? In time of trouble they never said there was nothing they
could do about it. If you believe there is nothing you can do, then how
are you likely to behave? You're resigned, you're indifferent, or you try
to ignore the issue. Maybe it will just go away if you close your eyes
to it.

Apathy—that's the word for the state people get themselves into
when they believe there's no way to change things. Apathy itself then
becomes the problem because it makes any attack upon the real problem impossible.

The opposite of apathy is action. Action—the will to do something
about what troubles you. Action takes commitment, the commitment
of dedicated, optimistic individuals. Whenever you hear of a success
story—of a social problem solved, of an injustice corrected, of oppression ended, the force behind that happy outcome is always the commitment of dedicated people.

Who are these dedicated people? The names of some of them are
ready on our tongues. George Washington leading the American Revo-

lution. Abraham Lincoln piloting the Union to the abolition of slavery. Franklin Roosevelt inspiring an embittered, defeated nation with hope, and devising federal programs to overcome the worst effects of the Great Depression. Martin Luther King rallying the movement that tore down the walls of discrimination and segregation. Great leaders, all of them, but helpless without the countless men and women who are the blood and bone, the heart and nerve of every such struggle to better human existence.

Take Martin Luther King—an obscure young preacher in Alabama until the Montgomery bus boycott challenged his ability to find the form of struggle that would overcome centuries of racist oppression. And how did that crucial movement of blacks to end segregation get started? When Rosa Parks, a seamstress, had enough of apathy and hopelessness and refused one day to sit in the Jim Crow section of the bus. Rosa Parks—until then known only to her family and friends, now in every history book as a pioneer in the battle to end Jim Crow laws.

The Rev. Martin Luther King himself paid public tribute to another man whose words helped him to see the moral necessity of acting against evil. Back in 1846—over 100 years before Rosa Parks had herself arrested for refusing to sit in the Jim Crow seats—a young man of Massachusetts defied the law and had himself put in jail. He was Henry David Thoreau, carpenter, pencil-maker, housepainter, surveyor—the odd-jobs man of Concord. Why did they put him in jail? For refusing to pay his poll tax.

Out of Thoreau's brief prison hours came a great speech and essay called "Civil Disobedience." It was ignored for a long time, until years after Thoreau's death. But it finally proved its universal appeal. What it says goes beyond its immediate subject, the Mexican War and the slavery struggle. Thoreau argued that "it is not desirable to cultivate a respect for the law, so much as for the right" (quoted in Krutch, 1989, p. 86). If unjust laws exist, civil disobedience is an effective way to oppose and change them.

It was Thoreau's expression of that idea that eventually moved people around the world to practice civil disobedience against local and national tyrannies. Gandhi in South Africa and India, the resistance movement of Nazi-occupied Europe, the freedom riders and sit-downers from New York to Mississippi, the antinuclear war pickets here and everywhere, responded to the words of a young "nobody" who decided what was right—and acted upon his belief.

The American past is full of examples of people who tried to shape their own lives, of people who sometimes understood that they could not manage their own life without seeking to change society, without trying to reshape the world they lived in.

Who has heard of Yick Wo? He was an immigrant from China who took up the laundry trade in San Francisco 100 years ago because whites barred the way to most other kinds of work. He grew sick of the ridicule, the abuse, the violence Chinese immigrants suffered in an America where racial prejudice denied them jobs and justice. Despite repeated blows, he didn't cower or crawl. He fought back. He challenged a city ordinance that required laundries to get fire-safety licenses. San Francisco never demanded the license of the white laundries, only the Chinese. He carried his case to the U. S. Supreme Court (*Yick Wo* v. *Hopkins*, 1886). It ruled such discrimination was unjust. So Yick Wo won an important victory for equal protection under the law. The resistance of an unknown immigrant to injustice strengthened the Constitution for all Americans. Later, his case became a precedent for court decisions granting blacks equality in law.

Let's jump now to the year 1912. It's a wintry January. The place is Lawrence, Massachusetts. That Friday morning, one of the giant woolen mills handed out the weekly pay envelopes to the workers, many of them recent immigrants from Eastern and Southern Europe. When they opened their envelopes, they found their pay had been cut without notice. The cut was equivalent to about 2 hours of work, the price of three or four loaves of bread. Count it in nickels and dimes— but it was no minor matter to workers who made only $6 a week! The discipline of years suddenly broke down. Enraged by the cut, a worker named Tony pulled back from his loom and started to walk out. "Tony, if you don't get back to your place, you'll lose your job," yelled his foreman.

"To hell with the job," responded Tony. "I'll pitch it." (quoted in Meltzer, 1991a, p. 121). And walk he did, sweeping out of the mill with hundreds of workers and marching to other mills where they called out thousands more.

That wage cut and the response of Tony and his fellow workers started a strike that lasted for 10 hard and long weeks. It made national headlines and ended in a modest increase in wages. But what was more important was what it signified: the individual awakening of thousands of working men and women, people the upper crust dismissed scornfully as "foreign garbage," "illiterates," and "scum." They had developed their own idea of what a decent society should be like. And they knew it must realize the dignity and rights of all who were part of it. Those anonymous workers of Lawrence wanted bread—and roses too.

These are but a few examples of personal action taken to change the world. History is full of them. Yet we tend to forget that. We think history is what happened *to* us. But history is also what we make happen. Each of us, all of us. Us—a Rosa Parks, a Martin Luther King, a Yick Wo, a Henry David Thoreau, a Tony whose last name we don't even know. These men and women too belong in the history books. History isn't only the kings and presidents and generals and superstars. If we search the records deep and wide enough we can find ample evidence of what the anonymous ones have done and continue to do to shape history. They struggle to survive, they take their lives into their own hands, they organize and agitate to make America realize its promise.

If literature's function is to extend the range of the reader's experience and to heighten sensitivity, then surely this testimony has its place in the classrooms of teachers of English as well as of history. Perhaps few can write with the practiced art of a Thoreau, but their words too come from the heart, and they can move us in a way that no ghostwritten speech can. The searching beam they cast upon the experience of the vast mass of the anonymous and obscure opens up a side of life rarely glimpsed.

In one of my books, *The Black Americans: A History in Their Own Words* (1984), I've used interviews with ex-slaves. These were gathered by people from the WPA Writers Project back in the 1930s (Botkin, 1945). Since these black people were 80 years of age or older, the slave experience they talked about was mainly that of childhood. Here a former slave, from South Carolina, recalls what happened when freedom came in 1865. It is rendered in dialect by the interviewer in an attempt to capture the sound of the words.

When the war was over, Massa come home and says, "You son of a gun, you's supposed to be free, but you ain't, 'cause I ain't gwine give you freedom." So I goes on working for him till I gits the chance to steal a hoss from him. The woman I wanted to marry, Govie, she 'cides to come to Texas with me. Me and Govie we rides that hoss 'most a hundred miles, then we turned him a-loose and give him a scare back to his house, and come on foot the rest of the way to Texas.

All we had to eat was what we could beg, and sometimes we went three days without a bite to eat. Sometimes we'd pick a few berries. When we got cold we'd crawl in a brushpile and hug up close together to keep warm. Once in a while we'd come to a farmhouse, and the man let us sleep on cottonseed in his barn, but they was far and few between 'cause they wasn't many houses in the country them days like now. . . .

I don't know as I 'spected nothing from freedom, but they turned us out like a bunch of stray dogs, no homes, no clothing, no nothing. Not 'nough food to last us one meal. After we settles on that place, I never seed man or woman 'cept Govie for six years, 'cause it was a long ways to anywhere. All we had to farm with was sharp sticks. We'd stick holes and plant corn, and when it come up we'd punch up the dirt round it. We didn't plant cotton, 'cause we couldn't eat that. I made bows and arrows to kill wild game with, and we never went to a store for nothing. We made our clothes out of animal skins. (quoted in Meltzer, 1984, pp. 87–88)

Growing up poor in America—how does it feel? In my book *Poverty in America* (1986) I wrote about the 35 to 50 million Americans living in poverty today. I tried to examine the toll poverty takes both on the poor and on society at large. Often I use the words of the poor themselves to demonstrate that poverty is not some abstraction about income levels, but is a grinding condition of daily life. Here is how a poor, underemployed mother says her children feel.

Now, they'll come back to me, oh, do they, with first one question and then another, until I don't know what to say. . . . They'll be asking why, why, why, and I don't have the answer, and I'm tired out, and I figure sooner or later they'll have to stop asking and just be glad they're alive.

Once I told my girl that, and then she said we wasn't alive, and we was dead, and I thought she was trying to be funny, but she wasn't, and she started crying. Then I told her she was being foolish, and of course we're alive, and she said all we do is move and move, and most of the time she's not sure where we're going to be and if there'll be enough to eat. That's true, but you're still alive, and so am I. (p. 41)

Sometimes I call upon fiction for its documentary as well as artistic value. In my book *The Chinese Americans* (1980), I use the following passage from L. C. Tsung's novel *The Marginal Man* (1963) to tell us something of the lonely life of a Chinese laundryman in America. The "Charles" mentioned here is a well-off Chinese American who has tried to assimilate.

The neon sign of a Chinese hand laundry reminded Charles of the several shirts he had not yet picked up. The sign said Wen Lee, but Charles had never been able to ascertain whether the proprietor's family name was Wen or Lee. He entered the shop and saw the old man still hard at work behind the counter, ironing under a naked electric bulb, although it was already ten o'clock at night. . . .

"How many years have you been in the States?" Charles asked out of curiosity as he paid the man.

"Forty years," the old man answered in Cantonese, and raised four fingers. . . . No expression showed on his face.

"Do you have a family?"

"Big family. A woman, many sons and grandsons. All back home in Tangshan."

"Have you ever gone back since you came out here?"

"No, I only send money," replied the old man. From underneath the counter he brought out a photograph and showed it to Charles. In the center sat a white-haired old woman, surrounded by some fifteen or twenty men, women, and children of various ages. . . . The whole clan, with contented expressions on their faces, were the offspring of this emaciated old man, who supported not only himself but all of them by his two shaking, bony hands. They seemed to represent the flow of a great river of life, originating from a tiny stream. The stream may dry up some day, but the river flows on. The old man put on his glasses . . . and identified each person in the picture to Charles Lin. A toothless smile came to his expressionless face.

Charles Lin realized that this picture was the old man's only comfort and relaxation. He had toiled like a beast of burden for forty years to support a large family which was his aim of existence, the sole meaning of his life. The picture to him was like a diploma, a summa cum laude to an honor student. Behind the facade of sadness and resignation there was the inner satisfaction which made this old man's life bearable and meaningful. (quoted in Meltzer, 1980, pp. 91–93)

In another book, *Never to Forget: The Jews of the Holocaust* (1976a), I tried to turn back into people the brutal statistics of 6 million Jews murdered, letting the men, women, and children who lived the Nazi terror tell it their own way. In this passage from Gerhard Schoenberner's *The Yellow Star* (1973), a man penned in the Warsaw ghetto recalls the children he observed there.

The streets are so overpopulated, it is difficult to push one's way through. Everyone is ragged, in tatters. Often they no longer even possess a shirt. Everywhere there is noise and uproar. The thin piteous voices of children crying their wares—"Pretzels, cigarettes, sweets!"—are heard above the din.

No one will ever be able to forget those children's voices. . . . There are always countless children inside the ghetto. People on the "Aryan" side gape curiously at the piteous spectacle presented by these tattered gangs. In fact, these gangs of children are the ghetto breadwinners. If the German looks away for one second, they run nimbly over to the "Aryan" side. The bread, potatoes and other things that they buy are hidden under their rags, and then they have to slip back the way they came.

Not all the German sentries are murderers and executioners but unfortunately, many of them do not hesitate to take up their guns and fire at the children. Every day—it's almost unbelievable—children are taken to the hospital with gunshot wounds.

The thousands of ragged beggars are reminiscent of a famine in India. Horrifying sights are to be seen every day. Here a half-starved mother is trying to suckle her baby at a breast that has no milk. Beside her may lie another, older child, dead. One sees people dying, lying with arms and legs outstretched, in the middle of the road. Their legs are bloated, often frostbitten, and their faces, distorted with pain. I hear that every day the beggar children's frostbitten fingers and toes, hands and feet are amputated.

I once asked a little girl: "What would you like to be?" "A dog," she answered, "because the sentries like dogs."

Yes, they treated dogs better than children. (quoted in Meltzer, 1976a, pp. 101–102)

In *Never to Forget* I said almost nothing about the people some call the Righteous Gentiles—the non-Jews in every country of Nazi-occupied Europe who helped save the lives of thousands of Hitler's victims. As the years passed I came to realize the great importance of recording not just the evidence of evil but also the evidence of human nobility. Love, not hatred, is what the world needs. So, many years later I wrote a book called *Rescue: The Story of How Gentiles Saved Jews in the Holocaust* (1988b). In its pages are the personal accounts of people who saved Jews—not as Jews, but simply as people struggling to stay alive. To them it wasn't a Jew who asked for help, but a desperate, persecuted human being. And if he or she was a stranger, it made no difference. Aron Blum, a Polish Jew, alone with no documents, no money, no hope, knocked at the door of a Polish Catholic, Frank Dworski. Blum tells what happened.

When I came to his house he did not know me at all. In fact, I did not even know the man who directed me to him. As a welcome he said, "Bread in this house you will not miss." He was as poor as I was, but he shared all. He simply looked upon this help as the most natural thing. He had so much heart and courage. He made papers for me, found me a job, and gave me shelter. After a while, and upon my request, he travelled to Lvov to bring a friend of mine, also a Jew. To make this possible for my friend he arranged false papers. On the way the train was searched by the Nazis. It was customary in such situations to throw away all incriminating evidence. Not he. He hid the papers. Dworski was not afraid, even though he knew he could die for it. But he also knew that, without these papers, he could not bring my friend back, and this in turn would cost my friend his life. Dworski had courage and luck. All went well. He brought my friend, whom he kept in his house as he did everyone else who turned to him. All this he did without ever receiving, or expecting to receive, anything in return. (quoted in Meltzer, 1988b, pp. 37–38)

The kinds of books historians write are varied, and always will be. They look into the past for different reasons, and that shapes the history they produce. Writers like myself, who have come from a submerged class, an immigrant family of workers, find it natural to study the people who make up the bottom rather that the top layers of society.

And for that same reason, I try to write not for the academic, but for the general reader, of whatever age. And I hope, by my stress on what people say about their lives in their own words, to make it more accessible to the reader. The job of the historian is to seek to understand how people behaved in the past and why they behaved that way. I think young readers especially find this approach useful in understanding where we Americans have come from and who we are.

CHAPTER 8

On Ethnic Stereotyping

Ethnicity is more than food and festivals. It is values and beliefs. It is family and community. We need to champion multiethnic programs in the schools, to teach our children to appreciate and respect their own and other people's identities.

In 1976 I published a book entitled *Never to Forget: The Jews of the Holocaust* to help readers recall the ultimate answer to the question of the effects of ethnic stereotyping on children. History, in the person of Adolf Hitler, has told us: death. And the dead included both the stereotyped and those who did the stereotyping. One million of them were children—tortured, starved, beaten, shot, gassed, or burned to death—and the other 5 million had once been children. The victims of stereotyping were of course far more than even that appalling number.

The Holocaust was a measure of the power of evil residing in the stereotype. In Hitler's view the Jews were an inferior race. Again and again he and his legion of propagandists spoke of the Jews as "lice," "vermin," "bacteria." That language made the Jews even less than inferior human beings: It made them nonhuman. And it therefore worked to cut off human response to the plight of the Jews. It helped make it possible for all the Eichmanns to see themselves as only tiny cogs in the machine destroying inhuman objects called Jews. Many of the stereotyped, of course, not only stereotype other groups, but even stereotype themselves. It is a complicated problem, and one whose costs are so painful and potentially catastrophic that it demands our attention—especially those of us who teach or write.

The stereotype reduces the individual character to a single, almost invariably negative, trait. The writer who uses a stereotype does not depict that character as a human being such as we all are in our incredible variety, with our rich complexity and our fascinating contradictions. Think of the stereotype as a virus so dimming the vision that all persons of a certain group appear not as individuals but as blurred and undifferentiated members of that group—and therefore easily subject to prejudice, discrimination, and persecution.

Now literature, as we know, has much to do with shaping our ideas about people. We can all remember certain books, especially those read in childhood, that awakened us to new possibilities within ourselves. There are other books that have an equally powerful but harmful effect upon us. Beginning in the early nineteenth century an endless stream of anti-Semitic books polluted the German culture. Even so great a humanist as Goethe contributed to it, and it was reflected inevitably in children's literature. A German stereotype of the Jew as puny, cowardly, cunning, villainous was shaped. Entrenched as an article of German faith, it had the power of an atomic arsenal when Hitler triggered it.

Have we learned anything from those monstrous pages of the past? The stereotyping of people still goes on in the literature and the media of many nations, including our own. It persists with a desperate kind of stubbornness. It poisons human relationships in every corner of the globe. In New York City its effects can be seen as the ethnic makeup of almost every neighborhood shifts with dizzying speed. Three-quarters of the city's population is now from Latin America or Asia. What used to be a black–white polarity has been made much more complicated. Or take Los Angeles, where 60 different languages are spoken in one high school. From one coast to the other, people who know little or nothing about one another's culture and history find themselves contending for jobs, for housing, for scholarships, for respect.

The result? A Haitian shopper argues with a Korean grocer whereupon an African American nationalist group boycotts the store. Latino, Afro-Caribbean, and Asian immigrant students at a city college protest the policies of an Irish American administration and the attitudes of a largely Jewish faculty. Yugoslav immigrants beat up blacks, but even the Yugoslavs are split by nationalist enmities imported from Balkan history. Black youngsters attack Vietnamese; Cubans are at the throats of Puerto Ricans; Italian Americans kill blacks.

Why such intense racial hatreds and ethnic bitterness? Ours is a country with people of many origins who suffer from isolation, from lack of power, from fear, insecurity, competition. For this newer immigration is occurring in the context of a shrinking economy. Jobs disappear, housing deteriorates, the cost of living soars. Tensions and violence tend to mount when a society does not provide decently for its citizens. And the less well people understand each other's past history and present needs, the more likely will the outcome be disaster and even death.

As the mosaic of America cracks, we see the same phenomenon

occurring in other parts of the world. In France, Jewish graves are pro-
faned and Arab immigrants are spat upon. In Britain, newcomers from
the West Indies are abused. In Germany, migrants coming from the
east are beaten and even killed. Sadly, one of the consequences of the
breakup of the former Soviet Union has been the surfacing of ancient
hatreds—between Bulgarians and Turks, Romanians and Hungarians,
Russians and Lithuanians, Azerbaijanies and Armenians.

If there's one thing in American history that every one of us shares,
it is the immigrant experience. All Americans, the Indians too, have
come here from other parts of the world. Except for the African Americans, they all came willingly and with hope. They became part of a
growing and ever-changing nation. This is a land of many peoples,
many colors, many cultures, many different religious beliefs. We speak
many languages, we live and behave in different ways. But we all want
one thing—to be treated equally. Yet many of us have never known
equality.

As migrants, we've all shared in a great human experience. Migra-
tions are as old as humankind. All through history people have picked
up from one place and moved to another out of the simple desire for
a better life. Maybe the grass was better for the herds. Or there was
more water, or richer soil, or more jobs, or fewer wars.

That hope of making a better life elsewhere seized millions of
people in Europe in the 1800s. There was a large rise in the population
and a great worsening of living conditions. The number of people
grew faster than the ability to provide food and work for them. And
that left the mass of people worse off than before. They began to think
about leaving home. It was said that in the new country across the
Atlantic—the United States—things were much better. No rule by king
or church or aristocracy. Lots of land open to farming, plenty of jobs.
And the cost of travel by sea was cheap enough to be within reach.

So they left home. The whole continent of Europe was on the move
from the 1800s on. Between 1830 and 1930, 40 million Europeans came
to America. It was the biggest migration of peoples the world had ever
seen. And in recent years we have been experiencing another huge
immigration. In the 1970s nearly 7 million people entered the United
States, more than two-thirds of them legally. Immigrant children, who
number about 2.7 million, make up about 6% of public school enroll-
ment. Recent studies of our schools show that they are doing a poor
job of meeting the needs of these immigrant students. The studies note
that dropout rates for immigrant students are high, that suicide
attempts are all too frequent, and that some young newcomers, placed
under extreme pressure, respond by forming gangs for emotional and

physical protection. In some places there is an "English only" or an "English-first" movement, undercutting public funding for school programs serving students who speak little or no English. The newcomers are made to feel that their languages and cultures are unwelcome and inferior. Too many teachers have the attitude that "these kids are dumb; they can't learn."

Stereotypes are false because they generalize about a group of people who are individuals, with all the differences found in every group. But the stereotype makes them all alike, all the same. Examples: Hispanics are lazy, Jews are greedy, blacks are dope fiends, Poles are stupid, Chinese are sly, the Irish are drinkers, Germans are humorless.

Is stereotyping something new? From a book called *Renaissance Europe* by J. R. Hale (1977), I learned that back in the early 1500s people used a kind of stubborn folklore of phrases to demolish the character of people from other countries. To German writers, for instance, it was axiomatic that Poland was the land of thieves, Bohemia of heretics, Saxony of drunkards, Florence of homosexuals. In this folklore, the French were frivolous, Flemings were gluttonous, the English foulmouthed. All this, mind you, almost 500 years ago! I'd guess it was just as true, sadly, back in the days of the ancient Greeks and Romans.

Not all stereotypes are negative. Some are favorable. But they are just as wrong when they are applied uniformly to everyone in a group. Examples: Blacks have musical ability, Jews are smart, Germans are clean, Asians are polite. These stereotypes are less hurtful but they are still a false substitute for real knowledge.

Where do these stereotypes come from? They are the result of racism. Racism is the false belief that some "races" are superior and other "races" are inferior. One group is supposed to be born superior—everyone in the group is bright, wise, talented, strong. And another group is born inferior—everyone in it is stupid, weak, vicious.

Modern science has junked such ideas. It has demonstrated that no classification of races holds up. No one has ever shown scientifically that "race" explains anything about a group of people. There are simply no innate differences in ability or character between peoples.

But racism goes back a very long time, and the false idea is hard to get rid of. In the baggage the first white explorers carried to the New World was the belief that their white skin made them superior. In their mind, colored people were inferior to white. They identified the red people and the black people with evil, with savagery. It gave the white colonists an excuse for enslaving or killing Native Americans and Africans. Colored people were good only for doing the hard and dirty work the white man did not want to do.

These racist beliefs were woven into custom and law, into religion and education. Each white generation learned from preacher and teacher that colored people were inferior. That there was nothing wrong in enslaving inferiors. That it was "natural" and "necessary" to segregate them, to discriminate against them.

A harsh selfishness has marked the treatment of colored peoples. Native Americans were ruthlessly exploited from the beginning. And later, those who were not exterminated were herded onto reservations. The African Americans were enslaved, and after Emancipation, the gains made during the brief years of Reconstruction were steadily taken away. The Chinese in the West were sweated in the mines and in the building of the railroads and then shut out of America completely by the Chinese Exclusion Act of 1882. The Japanese Americans, citizens and noncitizens alike, were penned up in U. S. concentration camps during World War II. In Europe, during the same war, Hitler and the Nazis murdered 6 million Jews because the Nazis said they were an inferior race who should be exterminated, like rats or germs.

So stereotypes are the result of prejudice. They tend to justify prejudice and they certainly strengthen it. It is worthwhile to try to get rid of stereotypes, but that alone would not tear up the roots of prejudice. Still, once you become aware of stereotypes you can spot them for what they are and see what's behind them.

Stereotypes, as we've seen, are applied not only to people of color. Immigrants to America—white or colored—have always been distrusted and feared. And those feelings are reflected in the stereotyping of the newcomers.

When the Irish began coming in large numbers before the Civil War, it triggered anti-Catholic hysteria in what was then a largely Protestant nation. The Pope was scheming to seize the United States, cried the newspapers. The Irish, who arrived poor, were called vicious brutes. They did the dirtiest and hardest work until a much larger flood of immigrants began in the 1880s.

As these new immigrants began pouring in from eastern and southern Europe, the distrust of newcomers was renewed. This time it was not one but a dozen different ethnic groups arriving. Their strange languages, religions, customs, politics again made the dominant white Anglo-Saxon Protestants fearful and hostile. They said the newcomers were inferior people. They would not fit into American life and, disappointed and angry, would overturn the country by bloody revolution.

In hard times—such as we are suffering once more—people are scared of losing what they have. During depressions, working people resent immigrants who compete for scarce jobs. Any rise in immigration seems to threaten the position of wage earners who came earlier. The workers fear that poor and unskilled immigrants will work for very little and take their jobs or lower their pay. Labor unions therefore objected to unlimited immigration. Their leaders thought it would be almost impossible to organize people speaking different languages. In the past, newcomers were sometimes used to scab, taking the jobs of workers on strike. But the unions shared the blame so long as they did little to recruit the immigrants.

When Hispanic newcomers first meet up with discrimination they find it very confusing. The Cubans, the Puerto Ricans, the Chicanos, and all the others have a broad history of racial intermingling. They are a mixture of Native Americans, Europeans, and Africans. Members of a single Hispanic family often will display as wide a variety of racial characteristics as the group itself. When reporters asked hundreds of Hispanics in New York about their race, three out of four refused to identify themselves as black or white. Their nationality or cultural background was what mattered to them, not their color.

But not to the world of the dominant majority, the Anglo world. There racism still operates. Hispanics come to the States because there are jobs to be filled, because their labor is needed. But employers hold them to lower jobs and lower pay. Racism protects that exploitation. It provides an excuse for it by saying Hispanics are good for nothing else. It makes possible greater profits from the cheap labor of an oppressed people.

See what little sense the stereotype makes. The Chicano is pictured as lazy or thieving. Yet it is his willingness to work hard (for low wages) that makes the Anglo boss seek him out. But when there is no more work he is instantly unwanted. He becomes a "greaser" to be gotten rid of.

The newspapers talk about "the Puerto Rican problem," "the Cuban problem," "the Chicano problem." This is seeing an effect as a cause. Racism and exploitation are the problem, not the Hispanics. Do something about the real problem and then see what happens to slums and unemployment and crime and drugs. When Hispanics are denied the opportunity to advance, it is not right to ask what's wrong with *them*. If millions do not enjoy the much-advertised blessings of the American way of life—good education, good job, good home—ask what's wrong with a life that shuts out so many people.

It is much more than racism practiced by *individuals*. It is *institutionalized* racism. By that I mean the major institutions of American society—corporations, banks, courts, police, schools, church, armed services, and much more—often discriminate on racial grounds.

Sometimes they do it knowingly, sometimes not. But the result of being treated as an inferior is to be sentenced to a life of poverty and pain.

To see how it works for Hispanics not in theory, but in real life, let's look at the Chicanos. In the Southwest the Chicano immigrants were expected to live in their own barrios, or ghettos. They were kept out of recreation places supposedly open to everyone. They could get only the most menial and unskilled jobs. In some places they could go only to segregated schools and sit in segregated movie theaters. The police were quick to use violence against Chicanos and ignored their civil rights. In Texas, where discrimination was the worst, food shops refused to serve Chicanos, kindergarten teachers called children greasers, churches held separate services "for Colored and Mexicans." The Anglo view of Chicanos was expressed in what a Texas farmer once said to a reporter: "You can't mix with a Mexican and hold his respect. It's like the black; as long as you keep him in his place he is all right."

It is no wonder that Hispanics distrust public agencies. When Hispanics need to make use of such an agency—for education, job training, welfare, health, justice, immigration—they approach it with suspicion. Cultural differences account for it in part, and of course language is often a barrier. But operating beneath it all is the bitter, repeated experience of racial discrimination. The Anglos are in charge, and too often they treat the Hispanics like second-class citizens.

Discrimination is the basic reason why many millions among our ethnic minority groups are kept poor and ill-educated in the first place. And it is why pressure is put on them not to act for their own good. Fear and isolation make many feel, What's the use? What difference will it make? If they do decide politics is worthwhile, they find society makes it hard for them. Anglo politicians have used fraud and intimidation at the polls. Voting districts are gerrymandered. That means districts with sizable minority populations are cut up so that their vote can't be effective as a block. Literacy tests are a barrier, and so are laws that require voters to live in a district a long period of time.

These facts explain why no national minority has a *smaller* voice in politics than the Hispanics. They are *not* represented fairly in Congress, the state legislatures, the city halls, the federal or local courts. Few have become governors or mayors even in the big barrio cities. The Puerto Ricans of New York have it a little better in this regard. But they are by no means the power in politics that they should be.

The picture is changing. Ethnic minorities have formed organizations to encourage political action and to educate their people to its importance. The goal of self-determination and self-respect may be won only if minorities mobilize to play their part in American political life. Without a voice in politics, one has no say in one's own future.

Wherever laws are written, judicial decisions made, and executive reforms shaped, pressure must be applied to ensure all minorities' full rights. When alliances can be formed among ethnic or racial groups, the chance of success is so much the better.

Forming such an alliance is not an easy thing to do. While minority organizations have things in common, they also have differences in policy and methods. Organizations have all the weaknesses of the human beings they are made up of. To overcome differences for the sake of the common good is hard to do. But how to achieve justice and equality without unity?

Yes, the political, economic, and social fabric of America is being changed once again by the new immigration. From our very beginning our nation defined itself as a land of refuge. But just how welcoming we should be is now the subject of great debate. Although we want the "downtrodden" (often because we need their labor), we often recoil from the cultural baggage they bring. That ambivalence over newcomers has characterized us since before we won our independence. In the nineteenth century the rising tide of non-English immigrants caused such great resentment that we suffered a surge of nativism. Italians, Slavs, Jews, whatever—all were sneered at by those of prestige and power. But in 1965 we came to see that quotas limiting immigration from those outside northern Europe were undeniably racist. And a new set of laws opened our doors to millions from all over the world.

What can be done to make life better for the newcomers, and therefore for all the rest of us? It's a terribly hard question to answer. The schools, many say, have failed in the task of educating children about their country's ethnic heritage and teaching them constructive ways of confronting prejudice and fear. Because parents are often the source of their children's prejudice, schools need to be all the more active in fighting racism.

Do the schools in the larger cities where so many of the newcomers collect do enough to prepare those students to compete for jobs or responsible positions in society? When educators expect little from such students, and lower their standards, students come to believe that they are inferior and that they cannot compete with others. This contributes to a dehumanizing cycle of pathology; parents can do little to help their children because they have become dehumanized themselves. The outbursts of racial incidents in schools and colleges remind us that racism has never vanished in our country. Schools, parents, the churches have not given our children the historical framework to help them understand the differences and similarities between peoples and cultures.

What does all this have to do with books for young readers? In

my childhood, those books had little to say about the values and problems of a multiethnic America. Not until the 1950s did such themes
begin to appear in both fiction and nonfiction. It was a slow start,
sporadic, capricious, sometimes ill-considered. But it was a start that
we writers made, encouraged by concerned editors and publishers.
Like too many other things in American life, multiethnic literature was
the victim of faddism. Great attention today, neglect tomorrow. Publish
to take advantage of a wave of public concern; let the books go out of
print when the headlines fade.

I began writing books for children and adults in the 1950s. Partly
because I grew up in the depression years, and was radicalized by
what I saw and lived through, when I came to write, my work centered
on social issues. My first book was a pictorial history of black Americans, in collaboration with Langston Hughes. A dozen publishers
turned down our book. They all said no one's interested in black
people; most blacks can't read or don't read; and if some do, they can't
afford books. But one publisher knew they were wrong. And that book
is still in print some 40 years later.

As the son of immigrant workers, I grew up in a neighborhood
full of families that had recently come from Ireland, Poland, Russia,
Lithuania, Italy, Greece, Armenia, and Sweden. My parents never
talked about the Eastern Europe they had come from, nor did I ask
about it. That was probably true among most of our neighbors. Nor
did the schools, and the books available to us, have anything to say
about our ethnic roots. They blandly ignored our distinctive cultures
or assured us our differences would all disappear in the great melting
pot of America.

Who can doubt, looking at headlines or TV news programs that
there is a need, more than ever, for children's books that combat racism
and stereotyping? Again America is flooded by a new wave of immigrants, but this time from other parts of the world—Mexico, Colombia,
Haiti, Jamaica, Cuba, Guatemala, Thailand, China, Vietnam, Korea,
Samoa. These strangers too float around like a sea of weeds severed
from their roots. And like the earlier generations of newcomers, they
struggle to find and maintain their identity, to gain a foothold in the
economy, to build family, to fulfill aspirations.

For a while, in the 1960s, as the civil rights struggle erupted and
federal money for libraries was available, there was a flood of books
on black life, for children as well as adults. In my view, many publishers rushed to market with whatever came their way, regardless of quality or whether it simply repeated what had already been done, and
done well. They wanted to cash in on a good thing. Then, as popular

interest faded, so did publishing interest. It became much harder to get such work published. This to me is symptomatic of the faddism that afflicts American life. Something's hot—everyone goes for it; it cools off—everyone drops it. No matter how valid or necessary the subject may be.

I doubt that textbooks today promote stereotypes, as they once did. But still, they can do harm by what they leave out. Even now many fail to do much more than toss in a photo of ethnics with a caption; this is one reason why there is ample room for the trade books that focus on a single ethnic group or personality. Such books illuminate a minority's cultural background and the life they have shaped for themselves.

CHAPTER 9

Writing About the Jews

It took me a long time to choose to write about my own people, the Jews. It was not until 1973 when an editor at Doubleday suggested that I write a history of the American Jews for children that I began to think about it. Her proposal was exciting to me, and at the same time disturbing. Why hadn't I thought of writing about my own people? And since I never had, how did she, the editor, think of me for this book?

I asked her that. Her answer was at first amusing, and then painful. Her staff had been discussing for a long time the need for a book on that subject, and canvassing the names of writers who might best be able to do it. They knew me for the work on black history I had done for Doubleday, as well as several other publishers. Suddenly someone in a meeting piped up: "Hey! Meltzer is also Jewish!" When she told me that over the phone, we both laughed. It was funny, yes. And a second later, I felt the other kind of "funny."

Whatever being Jewish meant to my mother and father, they took for granted. It was passed on unself-consciously to their children. They could not articulate it. Still, their behavior—the way they moved, walked, laughed, cried, talked—their attitudes, the way our family functioned, imprinted upon us something of the social history they brought with them.

If they did not tell me what a Jew was and why I was one, did the world outside? Only in the negative sense: the cost of being a Jew, the insults voiced, the jobs denied, the housing restricted, the club doors closed, the college quotas. And that history—the very calendar that hung in Jewish homes marking the anniversaries, most of which were catastrophes, followed only sometimes by salvation. Passover, to celebrate the escape from ancient enslavement under the Pharaohs. Purim, the time when Haman's plan to exterminate all the Jews of Persia had been foiled by Esther. Hanukkah, which marks the victory of the guerrilla fighters led by the Maccabees over the ruthless despot Antiochus, who tried to suppress the religion and culture of the Jews. And the

Ninth of Ab, which is the fast day for remembering, and mourning, the destruction of the Temple in Jerusalem, the first time by the Babylonians, the second time by the Romans. But so many were the national disasters that followed, the fast day became a reservoir into which have been poured all the misfortunes of the Jews down through Hitler's Holocaust.

No wonder, then, an alarm bell rang whenever I heard or saw the word Jew in an unexpected setting. It might have been the sound of that word slashing into my ears while I played basketball in the gym. Or the sight of those three letters on the page of a book I was reading. Two novels especially, which I read as a youngster, stick in my mind. One was Sir Walter Scott's *Ivanhoe,* and the other was Charles Dickens's *Oliver Twist*—harmless in appearance, but poisonous in effect, as I now see them. I would guess that most readers, asked to recall whether there was anything about Jews in *Ivanhoe,* would remember Scott's sympathetic portrayal of Rebecca. What they forget are the innumerable references to Jews as usurers, liars, hypocrites; as covetous, contemptible, inhuman. The marvelous story Scott told captivated me; I tried to ignore everything in the novel that nourished anti-Semitism. But how can the young reader, Jew or non-Jew, escape the insidious influence of such a book?

And then there was Charles Dickens. I was drawn at once into the wanderings of Oliver Twist, the lost child, the rejected child, full of fear and hope, daydreaming of discovery in the dark places of London. The child's sense of justice was enraged by Dickens's exposure of the vast cruelty and greed, the indifference to humankind that birthed the slums and the haunts of crime the novel moves through. But over everything in the story fell the shadow of Fagin, that "villainous-looking," "repulsive," "greasy," "old shrivelled Jew," to use Dickens's opening description of the master criminal into whose hands the tender and innocent little Oliver comes. In the dark, monstrous visage and the wicked, staring eyes of Fagin, I saw the devil himself. The power of Dickens to draw characters by an intense poetic simplification made the anti-Semitic caricature all the more horrifying. I remember hurrying my eyes over those pages in which he appeared, anxious to get on to passages less painful to me as a Jewish child.

Of course, I encountered Christians in the novel who were vicious, like the brutal Bill Sikes. But my hero and all the other good people were Christians. They more than overbalanced a Sikes. And the fact that Sikes was a villain had nothing to do with his being a Christian. In the case of Fagin, his villainy was made identical with his Jewishness. To be a Jew, one could only conclude, is to be a villain.

If additional force was needed to confirm that image of oneself, there was Shakespeare's *The Merchant of Venice.* Shakespeare's play was used in my high school English classes. We read it aloud and discussed it. That the characterization of Shylock disturbed me goes without saying. Years later, I found Professor Mark Van Doren (1939) putting his finger on how it was done. Shakespeare, he said, had not made the "least inch" of Shylock "lovely."

> He would seem in fact to have attempted a monster, one whose question whether a Jew hath eyes, hands, organs, dimensions, senses, affections, and passions would reveal its rhetorical form, the answer being no ... Shylock ... is a man thrust into a world bound not to endure him. In such a world he necessarily looks and sounds ugly. (pp. 104–105)

Whoever reads or sees the play, he added, "should have no difficulty in recognizing Shylock as the alien element in a world of love and friendship, of nightingales and moonlight sleeping sweetly on a bank" (p. 104).

My high school teacher reveled in the superb lines; she talked of imagery and rhythm, of dramatic structure, of the position of the play in the body of Shakespeare's work. She said nothing of Shylock as Jew. It was not explained to us how church and state cooperated in the medieval centuries to make the Jews outcasts, shut them off from the land, excluded them from the Christian guilds so they could no longer practice their crafts and trades, and forced them to become merchants and moneylenders. As soon as the economy of each European country advanced, such Jews were restricted to smaller and smaller roles. And when they were no longer considered essential, their Christian rivals called them avaricious and heartless—the image perpetuated by Shakespeare's Shylock—and then took over their functions.

It is not only from the medieval mind that such abuse and contempt spring. We encounter it in many national literatures of later times, at least those I have some knowledge of. Take the Russians, whose novels, short stories, and plays I began reading in my college years. Some of the young Jews of Eastern Europe who took part in the revolutionary ferment of the nineteenth and early twentieth centuries were hostile to everything Jewish. They feared their Jewishness would block them from reaching the Russian people. They often came from families that had assimilated. They thought fighting for a revolutionary overturn of czarist society would mean creating a world in which all religions would disappear. There would then be no Jews, no distinction between themselves and everyone else.

Why did they feel so inferior? Why should they hope that a

change in the social system would eliminate their own people? In part, it is due to the Russian literature they were raised on, rooted as it was in the ancient anti-Semitic tradition of the church. Pushkin, Gogol, Lermontov, Dostoyevski, Turgenev all depicted Jews as vile creatures. Russian fiction, drama, and poetry portrayed the Jew as dirty, dishonest, contemptible; as parasite, opportunist, fiend. Their Jewish characters would do anything for money, betray anyone for their own advantage. The Russian writers who were respected for their sensitivity to the human soul could not see in the Jew anything human.

English literature is not much different, with some honorable exceptions such as George Eliot. To the writers I named earlier one could add many more. The French? The same. And the Germans? In the early nineteenth century Germany became the fountainhead of modern anti-Semitism. An endless stream of anti-Semitic books and pamphlets polluted the culture. Some of the most distinguished philosophers and poets contributed to it, among them Fichte and Goethe. It was reflected, of course, in children's literature. The brothers Grimm, whose collection of folktales has delighted children for generations, are also known for their devotion to the study of the German language. They began the classic *Deutsches Worterbuch* (1854/1960), a vast etymological history of the language, which, under the term *Jew*, lists an appalling variety of offensive definitions culled from German literature.

A Jewish stereotype was shaped in widely read German novels. The Jew was puny and cowardly, his eyes gleamed with the "calculated cunning of his race," his foreignness was evidenced in the jumble of Yiddish and German he was made to speak. He was inherently bad, this villain, and few readers would lament the violently cruel death the author invariably sentenced him to. Down deep into the twentieth century this caricature of the Jew appeared and reappeared in popular culture.

And what of American writers? Not until the past few decades have Jewish characters become major figures in American literature. Earlier there were too few Jews in America to write about. The literary artists of the American Renaissance—Emerson, Thoreau, Hawthorne, Melville, Dickinson, Whitman—made only glancing references, if any, to the contemporary Jew. But most Americans, then as now, were not paying attention to our major writers. They were reading popular novels and seeing popular plays created by hack writers who rang endless changes upon the Shylock theme. These writers, like their betters, had little or no connections with Jews and when they wrote about them, fell back on the stereotype. If Jews were present in this cheap fiction, it was usually as ugly, unscrupulous members of that money-obsessed

tribe of Israel. As soon as I began reading dime novels, I became pain-
fully aware of how common this portrait was.

Later, in high school, I read *The Education of Henry Adams* (Sam-
uels, 1939). In Massachusetts we were expected to venerate the native
Adams clan, which had given so much to American political and intel-
lectual life. Yet here was Henry Adams writing of a "furtive Jacob or
Ysaac still reeking of the Ghetto, snarling a weird Yiddish" (p. 238).
Traveling abroad, Mr. Adams looked out his train window and saw "a
Polish Jew . . . in all his weird horror" (p. 238). The Jew, he wrote,
"makes me creep" (p. 238). I soon discovered that nearly all the Boston
Brahmins displayed the same contempt, although Henry Adams earns
first rank for the intensity of his feeling.

Less possessed and more conventional was the antipathy found
in the novelists I began reading in those years—Edith Wharton, Henry
James, Theodore Dreiser, Scott Fitzgerald, Thomas Wolfe; and the
poets—Ezra Pound, T. S. Eliot, e. e. cummings. Anti-Jewish attitudes
were widespread and even fashionable in that era. Not until Hitler's
Holocaust did they go out of style.

I was 15 years old when I first noticed the strange words "Nazi"
and "Hitler" in the newspaper. I lived in Worcester, a city in the center
of Massachusetts. It was September 1930, and I was just starting my
junior year in high school. I used to read the papers, but not very
thoroughly. Sports, the funnies, stories about local people, rarely any
foreign news.

But on this day something caught my eye in a report datelined
from Germany. A hundred-odd members of Adolf Hitler's Nazi party
had just been elected to the German legislature—the Reichstag they
called it—and they had shown up for the first session wearing brown
uniforms and shouting, "*Deutschland erwache! Jude verrecke!*" The paper
obligingly explained what those foreign words meant: *Germany awake!
Jew perish!*

It was those words that had leaped out at me from the small print.
I wasn't looking for them; I didn't know they would be there. Still, I
saw them as with a special sense, attuned to those three letters, J-E-W.
The same sudden alarm would go off in a busy place—the school gym,
the Y swimming pool, the corner hangout—if the word Jew were spoken by someone in the crowd. Through the confusion of noise the
sound would arrow straight into my brain.

I was Jewish, of course, but a feeble kind of Jew, as I think of it
now. I mean I had no religious training and almost no knowledge of
Jewish life, history, or language. Our neighborhood was very mixed,
and so were the schools I went to. I thought of myself as an American.
If someone said yes, but what kind of American, then I'd say Jewish.

Then why did my skin prickle when I saw those words in the newspaper? Whatever kind of Jew I was, I had somehow absorbed the knowledge that Jews lived under threat. I had heard of the Jews of Egypt, enslaved under Pharaoh, and of how Haman's plan to annihilate the Jews of Persia had been foiled by Queen Esther. I knew vaguely about the persecution of the Jews during the Crusades and that the Inquisition had driven the Jews from Spain. Somewhere I had seen the word *pogrom* in print, knew it meant bloody riots against the Jews, and linked it to the immigrants who, like my mother and father, had fled Eastern Europe. On the street I had heard Jewish boys called "kike" and seen them fling themselves upon their tormentors.

But for politicians to stand up now in public and shout that the Jews must die?

I shuddered. "That could never happen here, could it, Pa?" He looked up, then smiled to reassure me. "Don't worry about it," he said. "Hitler and those Nazis of his—they won't last long."

They didn't. Not in the long perspective of time. They took power in 1933; they lost power in 1945. Twelve years. It's the length of time most of us spend in grade school and high school. That's only about one-sixth of the average life span.

But how do you measure the cost of those dozen years of Nazi rule over Germany and most of Europe? By the time Hitler's power was smashed, 29 million people were dead. They were from many different countries, including Hitler's Germany and our United States.

Among the myriad slaughtered were the Jews. Six million of them. Two out of every three in Europe. One-third of the world's Jews. Statistics. But each was a man, a woman, or a child. Each had a name. Each suffered his or her own death.

Historians now speak of Hitler's extermination of the Jews as the Holocaust.

The Holocaust was one of the innumerable crimes committed by the Nazis. Then why single out the extermination of the Jews? Is it necessary to remember? Is it good? Can it even be understood by those who have come after?

I started thinking about these questions when my wife brought me a pamphlet written by a professor at the college where she works. The professor, himself a survivor of Auschwitz, had made a study of the treatment of the Holocaust in history textbooks. In the high school textbooks, he said, the treatment of Nazism was "brief, bland, superficial, and misleading" (quoted in Meltzer, 1976a, p. 217). Racism, anti-Semitism, and the Holocaust were either ignored or dismissed in a few lines. The history books designed for the colleges and universities were not much better. It was hard to believe that scarcely 30 years after, the vilest crime perpetrated by man against man was almost a forgotten chapter in human history.

I did go ahead and write that book. It meant beginning research into a history whose depth and breadth I knew pathetically little about. For that particular book and the readers it was intended for, it turned out to be an advantage. I was discovering for the first time myself what I hoped the young reader would discover from the book.

I decided to try to write about the Holocaust in a way that would reach the young reader, first of all. And at the same time, in a way that would reach any adult who didn't know, except perhaps in the vaguest way, *what* happened in those years, and who hadn't thought about how it could have happened. Or about what it means for him, for her, for humankind.

I did not want the book to be too long, too difficult, or too much to bear. I wanted to start from scratch, to explain all I could about each important aspect as it came up. I assume in this book that my reader—whether of school age or an adult—is not informed about this part of everyone's past. And I say everyone, meaning Jew or Gentile. For in this story both are inextricably involved. You cannot write about the Holocaust and talk only about Jews. It would be like writing about blacks in American history and never mentioning whites. The course that black life has taken in America is profoundly affected by the course white life has taken. Their experience is inseparable. And so it is with Jew and Gentile in the Holocaust. My book is not a book for Jews alone. It is a book for Christians too. Both need to know and to try to understand.

How to make this book alive and meaningful? By making the story as personal as possible. I used a technique that has worked in several of my other books on historical themes. I tell the story of the Holocaust in the words of the people who lived it. I use original sources throughout—diaries, journals, notebooks, letters, interviews, memoirs, eyewitness accounts, testimony at trials and at public hearings, even songs the people wrote to express what they were going through. This is not an anthology, however. All this firsthand material is woven into a narrative that carries the reader from the beginning to the end, from the origins of the Holocaust to its aftermath. Terrible and complex as the events were, they may be brought within comprehension if the reader is helped to see them from the inside. If the reader can be made to feel and to care, he or she will be much readier to try to understand. So the men, women, and children who lived the experience speak of it to the reader in their own words.

How is the book shaped to carry out its purpose? The first part deals with causes and origins. Who were the Jews as an historical people? What is anti-Semitism and how did it rise in Europe and change its character from a religious base to a racial one? Where did Nazism come from, and why did it seize hold on Germany?

The second part of the book begins with Hitler's actions once he held power and tells of his simultaneous steps toward war and his repressive measures against the Jews. It recounts the conquest of Europe, which made possible the carrying out of what he euphemistically called the Final Solution of the Jewish problem—the extermination of the Jews.

The last part of the book tells about what I learned from my research—that everywhere there was oppression, resistance of some kind emerged. The Jews, counter to widespread belief, did not go like sheep to the slaughter. Almost a third of the book traces, through a variety of dramatic actions, how the Jews of Europe carried out the watchword of their resistance: "Live and die with dignity!" Despite the greatest terror, hunger, and privation, Jews upheld that watchword. They would not vanish silently from the earth.

These chapters, I hope, turn the mood of the book, just as in the act of writing them I found an end to the nightmares that afflicted me in the first period of research. I am old enough to have known the 1930s, when Hitler came to power and plunged the world into war. I thought I knew this history—but in the course of writing it I discovered how inadequate was my perception of the truth, how far I had shrunk back from facing the facts, how little I had done to try to change the role played by my own government, which, like other nations, failed to help the beleaguered victims of Hitler when there was yet time to try.

And this is what I come to at the end of the book. This is what happened, I say, insofar as word can tell it. To forget it would not be human. To remember it is to think of what being human means. The Holocaust was a measure of ourselves. We must remember the power for evil that it demonstrates—remember that human beings can treat others as less than human, as only vermin or bacteria. But we must know too of the power of good—of those people who held out a hand to others. By nature we are neither good nor evil. Humankind has both possibilities. And the freedom to realize the one or the other.

All I can do—all you can do—to make the world remember, we must do. It is the least we can do so that it never happens again, to Jews or to any other people.

I was scarcely halfway into that book when I began getting ideas for others related to it. There were so many themes I wanted to explore in this belated process of self-education. One was the immediate past of my own mother and father. Where did they come from in Eastern Europe? I did not even know the names of their home towns. And what was life like for them in those remote places? What made them choose to come to America? How did they get here? What did they do when they arrived? Where and how did they live? Both my parents were long dead when I started on this path. They could no longer give me answers to the questions I wished I had asked them many, many years earlier. But by a combination of research into personal history and research into social history, I built the answers for myself. And they are to be found in what turned out to be two related books. The first, *World of Our Fathers: The Jews of Eastern Europe* (1974c), deals entirely with Jewish life in that part of the world in the latter part of the nineteenth century.

The second book, *Taking Root: Jewish Immigrants in America* (1976b), carries on that history from the time masses of Jews began to leave their homelands in Eastern Europe, heading for what they thought would be Golden America. The difficulties of that decision, the painful voyage across the Atlantic, the hardship of making a home on the Lower East Side or in the other ghettoes of America, of finding work, of bringing up children in an alien culture are all part of the story.

I also carefully set the Jewish immigrant's life against the background of the general mass migration of that time. The reader can then learn much about what all immigrants experience in common, yet see at the same time in what ways this particular ethnic group, the Jews, have differed from the others.

So I have begun to reclaim my culture for myself, scrambling to recover the life of my parents' generation. It was terribly late. Many of their brothers and sisters, my aunts and uncles who could bear direct witness, had gone to their graves, their rich history untold and unrecorded. I have had to build my mosaic out of the fragmentary accounts of survivors and the historical literature on immigrant life.

I have already found that such a work can help to wipe out the cultural amnesia so many of my friends and our children have suffered from. Like me, many had no cultural memory, no loyalty to tradition. They were rootless. And among some of those who prided themselves on being enlightened, there was more than ignorance or indifference; there was hostility to their own Jewish heritage. Incredible as it seems, when one thinks of the 4 millennia of Jewish history, there was the belief that it didn't matter. They had been taught, as I was, that differences are bad. They did not want to be stereotyped as Jews. They believed that they were unique individuals, not members of a group. If

they belonged to anyone, it was the world at large. They felt themselves to be cosmopolitans. They hoped to see a world in which all
distinctions between peoples would disappear.

But why should one want to eliminate one's own people? Only if
one is ignorant of its rich culture and history, if one is embarrassed by
or ashamed of identification with that people.

Is it narrowing, is it limiting, to be intensely concerned with one's
own ethnic group? I do not find it so. True ethnic consciousness can
be a creative force. It is something larger than the self. It provides a
bridge to the past and between generations. It celebrates the beauty of
the differences among the incredible variety of ethnic groups I think
our country is lucky to embrace. It counters the feeling of alienation.
To gain more insight into our cultural distinctions can only strengthen
our national life. For differences do not mean inferiority. We do not
have to give up our uniqueness to share a common humanity.

CHAPTER 10

On Racism

As a white, I am part of the problem. What is my responsibility as a writer of history for young readers?

When you look at the facts, the problem may strike you as overwhelming. So deep-rooted, so universal is institutional racism, that you may feel helpless before it. What can you, a lone individual, do about it? The feeling is understandable. But none of us is really alone, and each of us has the power to speak up, to protest, to organize for change. We are all part of the lives of others. We can think about our own role in our family, our neighborhood, our church, our school, our clubs, in all the institutions we are connected with. Especially in our work. And begin to examine what we ourselves can do to eliminate racism.

For a white writer concerned about racism, the main job today is to combat racism within the white community. That, of course, is equally true for the white teacher and the white librarian. It should be obvious that we cannot deal with the black experience without talking about the white experience. And vice versa. Each has shaped the course of the other.

The quickest glance at our history illustrates the point. Our constitution and our political parties were molded by issues concerning blacks. The new nation's commerce and industrial growth rested on the South's slave economy. Our territorial expansion South and West were a direct product of slavery. The Civil War and the politics and economics out of which it exploded were linked to slavery. Racism has contributed to our imperialist expansion in the nineteenth and twentieth centuries—down to our war in Vietnam. In a speech in the 1930s, President Roosevelt called the South the nation's number one economic problem. And that problem's roots went back to slavery and the subjugation of the black man afterward. From the 1950s to now the nation has been shaken to its foundations by the failure to make any basic change in the lives of black Americans.

What more proof does one need that the black experience and

white racism are central to American life and that no writer, no teacher, no librarian can afford to think of it as some old curiosity to be taken down off a dusty shelf now and then and examined with a yawn?

Although we see how the black experience and the white experience are inseparable, we know that there have been hundreds of histories of America that have left out the black almost entirely, resulting in a history that is all white and all fake. That, thanks to great upheavals, is now being rectified to some degree.

What about the task of the white teacher and librarian within the institutions they are professionally part of? The fact that one may be working in a classroom or a library that has no black students or black book borrowers does not mean there need be no books or other materials about the black experience and no attempt made to interest whites in them.

Books that give black children strength and pride should be read by *white* children too. Any such book will—directly or by implication—reveal to the reader a lot about *white* life in America. And it is the history and role of white racism that our white children need to know. They—all of us—must become far more conscious of the widespread existence of racism in all its forms. We have got to understand what an immense cost the entire nation pays for it. Racism will not vanish just because it is evil. It has to be studied honestly and openly if we are to make any progress in eliminating it. It is hard for whites to deal with it because a layer of myths and lies has been built up over the generations to justify racist practices.

This is where history and biography can help. For the white child, such books can extend his or her perception of how things are for the victims of racism. And this is no act of philanthropy. For if our children are to live in a society less explosive and more just than what we know now, they must share in rooting out racism. The child whose awareness of blacks is limited to the picture of a slave picking cotton but who then reads the autobiography of Frederick Douglass (1855/1969) will find himself lifted out of an abstraction and plunged deep into the experience of slavery. If he knows black militancy only from the television screen but then reads Malcolm X's autobiography (1965), he will feel to some degree the furnace in which those fires of rebellion were built up. And through such life stories he will learn what American institutions have had to do with shaping black life this way. If he thinks the black demonstrators he reads about in the papers are in too much of a hurry, he will see in the century and a half that lie between Frederick Douglass's birth and Malcolm X's assassination how agonizingly long blacks have waited for justice from white America.

The ex-slave Frederick Douglass was one of the most prominent citizens of Rochester, New York. Here he edited his abolitionist newspaper, *The North Star*, and was stationmaster for the Underground Railroad. In 1852 the city honored him with an invitation to deliver the Fourth of July oration. Annually, from the birth of the new republic, Fourth of July orators thundered tributes to the Founding Fathers and the Declaration of Independence. But Douglass was no mouthpiece for dead history. "We have to do with the past," he said, "only as we can make it useful to the present and the future. You have no right to enjoy a child's share in the labor of your fathers, unless your children also are to be blest by your labors" (quoted in Meltzer, 1984, p. 65). He then went on to fling this challenge from black Americans to white Americans.

> What to the American slave is your Fourth of July? I answer, a day that reveals to him more than all other days of the year, the gross injustice and cruelty to which he is the constant victim. To him your celebration is a sham; your boasted liberty an unholy license; your national greatness, swelling vanity; your sounds of rejoicing are empty and heartless; your denunciation of tyrants, brass-fronted impudence; your shouts of liberty and equality, hollow mockery; your prayers and hymns, your sermons and thanksgivings, with all your religious parade and solemnity, was to him mere bombast, fraud, deception, impiety, and hypocrisy—a thin veil to cover up crimes which would disgrace a nation of savages. There is not a nation of the earth guilty of practices more shocking and bloody than are the people of these United States at this very hour.
>
> Go where you may, search where you will, roam through all the monarchies and despotisms of the Old World, travel through South America, search out every abuse and when you have found the last, lay your facts by the side of the everyday practices of this nation, and you will say with me that, for revolting barbarity and shameless hypocrisy, America reigns without a rival. (quoted in Meltzer, 1984, pp. 65–66)

I used this passage in my documentary book, *The Black Americans: A History in Their Own Words* (1984), to help break down people's obsession with themselves. If we don't have the capacity to think ourselves into another's skin, then we are in deep trouble in this polyglot nation. Frederick Douglass tears off the façade to show white Americans what the reality of America is for African Americans.

To ask that a youngster read such books is not to milk tears of sympathy. As many a black has told us, who needs white pity? Reading such books will show the white child a picture of American society as seen by its victims. There are plenty of textbooks written from the standpoint of the executioner. The youngster needs to see our history from below. That is what I tried to do with my documentary history. I had come to realize how unavailable to young readers at that time was the testimony of black people on their own lives. Using material in their own words, I tried to help the reader understand what black Americans have felt, thought, done, and suffered, and how they protested and rebelled and tried to change this world.

In the same vein, history can recover for the young reader those times in our past that have shown the possibility of a better way of life, a more humane, a more decent existence. I've tried to do this with two books about the Reconstruction era. *Freedom Comes to Mississippi: The Story of Reconstruction* (1991c) tells the story of Reconstruction by focusing on that state. Talk about the South today, and Mississippi is on everyone's mind. It is one of the poorest states in the Union. By almost any standard of life's decencies, it ranks near the bottom. Yet freedom *did* come to Mississippi. It was 100 years ago and it didn't stay, but out of the blood and wreckage of the Civil War a new life was born to the South. Slavery was ended and the freedmen in that state tasted democracy for the first time. They voted at last, they built the South's first public school system, they fought to farm their own land, they were elected to local, county, and state offices, and to Congress. Mississippi, today at the bottom of the heap, saw the finest flowering of Reconstruction. True, it lasted less than 10 years, but it *did* happen once. Knowing that it did, young people can learn from it that something else, something better, is possible in this world, that we *can* change things.

The other book, called *To Change the World: A Picture History of Reconstruction* (1971b), is a simple and brief picture history of Reconstruction throughout the South. By using a great many prints and photos of the era, it tries to dramatize for very young readers the same hope embodied in the other books (e.g., *Freedom Comes to Mississippi* and *The Black Americans*).

Is it enough to provide books that make us aware of what is wrong? Certainly that is a beginning. But more is needed. For nearly 400 years the white majority in America has systematically subordinated Indians, blacks, and other racial minorities. Consciously or not, white America has acted as though it believes there is a superiority in its whiteness that justifies actions that harm people of color. Why has racism lasted this long? Largely because we whites profit by it. Millions of us gain economic, political, and psychological benefits from racism. Some of us profit by conscious, individual acts of racism. Others—and far more of us—profit from institutional racism. By that I mean the actions of institutions we are part of—school boards, businesses, churches, trade unions, newspapers, city councils, hospitals, welfare agencies, courts—the institutions of our society that always have and still do place whites first.

Well-meaning though we may be, unknowingly and unthinkingly we whites operate in and through institutions that oppress the life of the racial minorities. The question of intention isn't as important as the effects these institutions have. Their policies, procedures, and decisions do in fact subordinate blacks, Indians, Chinese, Hispanics, and permit whites to maintain control over them. It took a very long time for any attention to be paid to those institutional practices that give advantage to the white and penalize all the others. Few of these institutions are openly racist any longer. Civil rights measures have deprived much institutional racism of any status in law. But institutional practices remain covertly racist nevertheless. Built into them are attitudes, traditions, habits, assumptions that have great power to reward and penalize. History can also illuminate the role of governments and institutions in keeping things as they are. Sometimes this is done by force, sometimes by deception, sometimes by both. To take the race question again: after the Civil War there were three Constitutional amendments—the thirteenth, fourteenth, and fifteenth—giving slaves their freedom, and guaranteeing blacks their citizenship and the right to vote. Armed forces were assigned to the South to protect the new Reconstruction regimes in which blacks played a role. And Congress passed several civil rights laws. But court decisions gutted the fourteenth amendment, and the freedmen never got the promised land to have and hold. It was taken away from them and given back to the white planters, and the Freedmen's Bureau was cleverly used by President Johnson to put the black labor force again in the hands of the white planters and businessmen. With the aid of government blacks again became victims of discrimination, of social ostracism, and of economic subordination.

At the same time, white children—and the children of minority peoples too—need to know that there have been white people who have challenged racism, such as John Brown, William Lloyd Garrison, Wendell Phillips, Prudence Crandall, Theodore Weld, Lucretia Mott, to name only a few. I thought it useful to study the lives of three such whites—Lydia Maria Child, Samuel Gridley Howe, and Thaddeus Stevens—and to write their biographies for young readers. Telling the stories of such brave men and women who fought for equality is important. We are not just showing young people what is wrong with American life when we do this. We are introducing men and women who found that out for themselves, who struggled to overcome white racism in themselves, and who joined in the social and political fight against it. The young reader sees that history isn't made up only of the great and the powerful who oppressed others, or of those who didn't care. We have had heroes and heroines who were frontline fighters against racial injustice. And we will always need them.

No reading of history will guarantee that something better is bound to come. Nothing like that is inevitable. But it can show us that something better is at least conceivable. Black and white did unite to operate the underground railroad and to achieve the goal of abolition. Labor did at last win the right to organize in the 1930s. The Algerians did drive out the French. Ralph Nader has shown that one man can take on giant corporations and institutions and force concessions from them. And the people of Southeast Asia stood up to American aggression with a courage and durability almost beyond belief. Seymour Hersch, a young newspaperman no one had ever heard of, somehow found the way to expose the horror of Mylai to the whole world and make us Americans face up to what we had done.

What we learn from such experience is that citizens—then and now—must act for themselves. They cannot rely on government alone to satisfy their needs or give them justice and equality.

But knowing what is wrong does not necessarily move us to action. We have to believe that something else is possible, that what we do can make a difference. Otherwise, we may decide to live only for ourselves, to retreat into drugs and despair, or cynically to ride with things as they are and to get a little piece of the action for ourselves.

CHAPTER 11

On Wars and Peace

Struggle is action, and it is in action that we begin to find out who we are, what we can do, what we may become.

If you care for life, you can't help thinking about death and all the ways we may encounter it. Our commitment to life calls on us to act for peace, for equality, for social justice. But act how? In what way? You try to think as clearly as you can about such questions. And the best way to do that is to struggle with thought on paper. A theme emerges from the life around you—from what you see, hear, read. Disturbed by, or challenged by, such experience, you seek some element in it you can investigate and then write about. Sometimes it is with an adult audience in mind; more often with young readers. Why the young? Because that is the best age to explore ideas.

I was born during World War I—the war to end all wars, the war to make the world safe for democracy. A sign of how my parents felt—they were immigrants from Austro-Hungary—is a yellowed photograph I still have. It shows my older brother and me, runts trying to stand tall in army uniforms, with campaigner's hats on, and each of us clutching not a gun but a small American flag. I must have been 3 years old then, and my brother 7. We are smiling into the camera.

I was too young to absorb any discussion of the war by my elders. But soon, in my teens, I was reading the novels of disillusionment with the war—Remarque's *All Quiet on the Western Front*, Hemingway's *A Farewell to Arms*, cummings's *The Enormous Room*, Dos Passos's *Three Soldiers*, Barbusse's *Under Fire*. And nonfiction too—the tracts of the British pacifists, the exposés of the powerful war propaganda machine, and the attacks upon the munitions-makers, called the "merchants of death."

It was the time of the Great Depression, and many of us, born poor, struggling to get into college and remain there, but almost hopeless about ever finding a job once we graduated, were ripe for cynicism about the world the older generation was running for their benefit, not ours. We were convinced they had made a terrible mess of both politics and economics, bringing down upon us innocents both war and depression.

Still, when the newborn Spanish Republic was attacked by General Franco and his fascist allies, Hitler and Mussolini, those of us radicalized by the times swung passionately toward support of the battle to save democracy in Spain. Some pocketed their pacifism and volunteered for the International Brigades fighting to make Madrid the tomb of fascism. Others, often members of the traditional peace churches, abided by their deep beliefs while they did all they could to resist fascism at home and abroad by nonviolent means.

Franco won, and World War II began a few months later. My observation was that most Americans disliked Hitler and Mussolini for what little they knew of them, but few were eager to shoulder arms against them. When Hitler's armies overran Western Europe and then in 1941 invaded Russia, it made folks at home nervous, but still not hot to shed blood. The Japanese attack upon Pearl Harbor changed that feeling overnight. I went into the Air Force, 27 years old now and called an old man by my barracks mates, most of them 18 or 19. I spent 42 months in the control tower, helping to train fighter and bomber pilots. Then a few years of relative peace, interrupted by the Korean War. And not long after that the longest war ever for us—in Vietnam. Four major American wars in my lifetime—so far.

Which makes me think that for a country with a rather short history, ours has done quite a bit of fighting. We have taken part in seven officially declared wars. And without the approval of Congress, we have sent our armed forces beyond our borders over 165 times. That comes close to one military intervention per year since the United States was founded.

I mentioned some of the antiwar novels I read as a teenager. But did any of the books assigned to us in school speak out against war? I can't recall any. They had plenty to say about war, but always to justify or even glorify it. Military heroes studded the histories and biographies but what book held up a peace-seeker as an example to follow?

My school years are ancient history. But are the books on the school library shelves any different today? What nonfiction titles there may be on antiwar themes are far outweighed by the others. I've tried to do something to begin correcting that imbalance. My book *Ain't Gonna Study War No More: The Story of America's Peace-seekers* (1985) is the story of the peace-seekers in America, from colonial times to today. It goes into the various kinds of antiwar movements we've known, both religious and secular, and the remarkable men and women who have risked their jobs, their property, their personal safety and freedom, and even their lives to resist war.

I don't take up all this in abstraction. No—the book looks at all the real wars we've fought: the French and Indian, the Revolution, the War of 1812, the Mexican War, the Civil War, the Spanish American War, the two World Wars, Korea, Vietnam, Central America. How did these wars happen? What people resisted them and why?

The peace-seekers are of many kinds. They have taken different paths to carry out their commitment. But there is a common core to their beliefs and acts. They denounce war because it destroys life, corrupts society, and violates morality. And from that conviction they work to develop other means of resolving human conflicts and building social harmony so that peace might flower and endure. In other words, they do not simply oppose war: They try to make peace.

Most of the immigrants who came to America with pacifist principles belonged in their homeland to Christian sects that opposed war on religious grounds. In the Sermon on the Mount, Jesus develops the ethic of nonviolence and love of enemies. "Blessed are the peacemakers: for they shall be called the children of God." And, he told Peter, "All they that take the sword shall perish with the sword" (Matthew 26:52). These last words are taken to mean that violence is futile in the long run. To meet violence with violence is only to perpetuate a cycle of violence that imprisons us.

Scholars believe the early Christians were probably the first individuals to renounce participation in war unconditionally. From the time of the Apostles to about 170 A.D. there is no evidence of Christians in military service. Their refusal to take part in war was one expression of their refusal to take part in the life of the world or the affairs of the state. Public life was a heathen life, and Christians withdrew from it. Military service required an oath to heathen gods, and pagan ceremonial marked many military operations. Devout Christians refused any part in idolatry.

Early Christian refusal to serve in Rome's imperial armies can be traced back to Jewish refusal to bow down before idols. The Jews were the only subject people to win from Rome exemption from military service because it entailed worship of the Emperor and would offend their faith in Yahweh, the one God. The Christian Church began as a Jewish sect, and for a time the Romans granted Christians the privileges already allowed the Jews.

The pagan Celsus sharply criticized the Christians for enjoying the benefits of the empire while doing nothing to ensure its preservation. He condemned them for what would today be called conscientious objection to participation in war. "If all did as the Christians," he wrote (c. 178), "there would be nothing to prevent things from getting into the hands of the barbarians" (quoted in Meltzer, 1985, p. 14). That argument still confronts pacifists.

Replying to Celsus, the Christian scholar Origen (A.D. 185–254) said:

> Christians have been taught not to defend themselves against their enemies; and because they have kept the laws that command gentleness and love of man, they have received from God that which they would not have achieved if they were permitted to make war, though they might have been quite able to do so. . . . The more devout the individual, the more effective he is in helping the Emperor, more so than the soldiers who go into the lines and kill all the enemy troops they can. . . . The greatest warfare, in other words, is not with human enemies but with those spiritual forces which make men into enemies. (quoted in Meltzer, 1985, p. 15)

Like Origen, many early Christian writers condemned war in general and branded killing in war as murder. War was an evil, a madness; and as for the soldier, "How can he be just, who injures, hates, despoils, kills?" (quoted in Meltzer, 1985, p. 15). Peace was more to these writers than the mere absence of war. The followers of Christ must give up the old law of retaliation to walk in the ways of peace. "We who were filled with war and mutual slaughter and every wickedness," wrote Justin Martyr, "have each of us in all the world changed our weapons of war . . . swords into plows and spears into pruning hooks" (quoted in Meltzer, 1985, p. 15).

Many soldiers left the Roman army after being converted to Christianity. They felt that their newfound religion would not permit them to shed blood. The first recorded conscientious objector was the future St. Maximilianus from Numidia in North Africa. At the age of 21, in the year 295, he was called up for military duty because as the son of a Roman soldier he too was bound to serve. When he was brought before the Roman proconsul, Dion, he said he would not serve.

"I will not be a soldier of this world, for I am a soldier of Christ."

"But there are Christians serving in the army," Dion replied.

"That is their business," said Maximilianus. "I cannot fight. I cannot do evil. I am a Christian."

Led away for execution as required by law, the young man proclaimed, "God lives!" (quoted in Meltzer, 1985, p. 16)

Not long after, in 336, the soldier Martin of Tours asked his commanding officer to discharge him. It was the eve of battle. "I am a soldier of Christ," Martin said. "To fight is not permissible to me" (quoted in Meltzer, 1985, p. 16). When he was accused of cowardice, Martin offered to face the enemy alone and unarmed. Do it, the officer replied. But inexplicably the enemy asked for peace. Martin was given his discharge and in time became a bishop and a saint.

Under the Emperor Constantine, Christianity became the official religion of Rome (in 313 A.D.), and the relationship between the Church and the secular power changed radically. The state accepted the Church and the Church accepted the state. Now Christians placed themselves at the service of the emperor. Going into battle in Constantine's army, they inscribed the sign of the cross on their shields and banners. Official Christianity sanctioned military service, and those who disagreed and remained nonviolent were eventually silenced. Pacifism went underground in the Church.

It was late in the fourth century that the classic Christian idea of the "just war" was developed. It began with St. Augustine (354–430 A.D.). He held the traditional view that the individual Christian was barred from violence on his own behalf. But, he argued, defense of one's own community was a different matter. Even in this case the command to love one's enemies even in battle was a solemn obligation of Christian faith. An attempt was made to set up standards for deciding which wars were right and which wrong. Over the centuries the theory was developed and refined.

As many theologians now hold, there are seven standards for a just war.

1. War must be the last resort and used only after all other means have failed.
2. War must be declared to redress rights actually violated or for defense against unjust demands backed by the threat of force. It must not be fought simply to satisfy national pride or to further economic or territorial gain.
3. The war must be openly and legally declared by a legal government.
4. There must be a reasonable chance of winning.
5. The means used must be in proportion to the ends sought.
6. Soldiers must distinguish between armies and civilians and not kill civilians on purpose.
7. The winner must not require the utter humiliation of the loser.

It can be debated whether any war has ever satisfied all these reasonable conditions.

Although the just war theory meant the acceptance of military service under certain conditions, Christianity and violence have not been happily joined. There has never been a period in Christian history without its nonviolent witness. Even when the Church has plunged into extreme violence and cruelty, as during the centuries of the Crusades, there were always Christians who rejected violence. And not only for themselves; they required their followers to do the same. St. Francis of Assisi (1182–1226) is only the most notable example. He founded religious orders—for men, for women, and for laypeople. The rule he voiced was: "They are not to take up deadly weapons or bear them against anyone" (quoted in Meltzer, 1985, p. 20).

In the Middle Ages it was the Holy Roman Empire that dominated Europe. The Emperor was a Christian Emperor and the Pope an imperial Bishop. Two powers equally ordained of God, as they believed, controlling the Christian world. Together they fought wars against enemies without and persecuted enemies within. Religion and politics were inseparable. Opposition or criticism seemed impossible and if it showed itself was quickly driven underground.

How hard it must have been for the voice of Christian pacifism to be heard! But there were some who all through these centuries had the courage to criticize the theory and practice of their time. They were like the early Christians in denouncing war. Only now, they were not rebelling against a heathen empire but against the worldly Church. In their opposition they formed sects, separate from the official Church. Their pacifist convictions found their source in a return to the Bible. That, in an age when it was forbidden and dangerous to possess a Bible. Only the priests could teach and interpret it. These awakened Christians went back to the fundamental ideas of Christianity, to the New Testament, and took the Sermon on the Mount as their ideal.

The Waldenses, the Lollards, and the Moravians were the main heretical groups who repudiated war in the Middle Ages. "The force of arms is altogether inadmissible in matters of religion," wrote one of their leaders. "War under any circumstances is an accursed practice" (quoted in Meltzer, 1985, p. 22).

From these peace-seekers of the Middle Ages we move to the dissenters of the Protestant Reformation. Martin Luther founded the new faith in the early 1500s. Great changes took place in religious, economic, political, and cultural life. The reformers believed that the state was an institution ordained by God as necessary to man's well-being on earth. But some among them denied that government had any right to exercise control in religious matters. Rather than act against their conscience, Christians must refuse obedience and suffer the consequences. Nor could true Christians accept public office, for it would require them to do things contrary to the teachings and example of Christ. The essence of the state, they believed, was to wage war, to exact harsh punishment, and to impose oaths. Since all of these were expressly forbidden by Christ, how could a Christian participate in the state? Be a magistrate? A policeman? A soldier?

Such nonconformists called themselves "defenseless Christians" who lived by a philosophy of nonresistance. They formed the radical wing of the Protestant Reformation. In England they created the Quaker Society of Friends; in Germany, the Dunkards and the Moravian Church. Religious sects of this kind spread across Europe to advance the new truth they found in Jesus Christ. Determined to follow His original way, they committed themselves to the pursuit of peace.

They carried this dedication with them when they migrated to the New World. Shortly before the American Revolution there were 60,000 of them rooted in the colonies, living by their dissenting peace tradition. Up to the twentieth century their vision would be the foundation of organized peace action in America (Meltzer, 1985, p. 23).

Throughout my book I focus on the dissenters from America's wars, the reasons they refused to fight, the punishments dealt out to them, the attempts after the blood stopped flowing to estimate whether the wars cost more in human life and treasure then the results claimed for them. Here different scales of values come into play, and these I discuss too, usually by letting the advocates of the varying views speak for themselves.

Until 1815 it was the peace churches that gave witness against war. It was in 1815 that scattered bands of Americans invented a new form of resistance to war. It was the seed of what became known as "The Movement" during the Vietnam War, nearly 150 years later. Typical of the peace advocates of that earlier era was David Dodge. Dodge was a self-taught and self-made man who rose from Connecticut farm boy to prosperous New York merchant. For many years he never questioned the Christian acceptance of war. He trained dutifully with the militia and carried a pistol on his business trips as protection against highway robbery. But one night at an inn he nearly shot the landlord, mistaking him for a thief. Horrified at the death he almost caused, he was led to question how a Christian could carry weapons. For some years he pondered the spirit and meaning of the Gospel in connection with war, and became firmly convinced that wars of all kinds—offensive and defensive—were wrong, as was the use of physical force in self-defense. In pamphlets, he published his opposition to the violent method of resisting evil. He would rely only on God's protection from harm. (Not until many years later would the early pacifists explore any alternative way to resist evil.)

Dodge brought together about 40 influential merchants and clergymen to form the New York Peace Society. It was the world's first nonsectarian organization aimed at spreading the principles of peace. Within weeks other peace groups formed in various states, and within months the idea leaped the Atlantic and took root in London and Paris. In 1828 scores of local and state groups were pulled together to form the new American Peace Society, the first national organization out to end war.

It is a story full of remarkable men and women whose courage and conviction enabled them to stand up for their beliefs and resist persecution. Persecution was often incredibly brutal and murderous. It was during World War I that the "liberal" President Wilson, a scholarly historian and Ivy League college president, led a savage attempt to repress dissent and punish the peace-seekers.

Now to say a bit more about Catholics and peace. I've already indicated the Church's pacifist stance in the first few centuries of Christianity, and then its changed views under the Holy Roman Empire. I could find no references to Catholic conscientious objectors to any American wars until World War I, when one was recorded. It was in the 1930s that condemnation of war increased among Catholics. The Catholic Worker movement, launched in New York by Peter Maurin and Dorothy Day in 1933, combined religious and radical concerns. Its newspaper, the *Catholic Worker,* carried many articles on the immorality of war and conscription. It rejected the idea of a "just war" as a contradiction in terms and asserted the Catholic's right to take a conscientious objector's position. The movement became the leading voice in American Catholic circles for militant pacifism.

We ought not to forget that during the 1930s a native variety of Hitlerism took hold here. There was Henry Ford's campaign against the Jews; the Protestant Gerald Winrod's preaching that Nazism and fascism stood for life, happiness, and prosperity; and Father Coughlin's weekly radio speeches rousing millions of listeners with praise of Hitler, Mussolini, and Franco as "patriots" rising to the challenge of communism.

But the *Catholic Worker* stood firm against all that. If we are commanded by Christ to feed the hungry, give drink to the thirsty, clothe the naked, shelter the homeless, visit the sick and imprisoned, and if doing these works of mercy is a matter of salvation itself, then, the

Catholic Worker went on to argue, surely we are forbidden to do the very opposite. And war requires the opposite—to cause hunger and thirst, to destroy homes and create refugees, to leave many sick and dying, to burn not only clothes but the flesh as well from others' bodies, and even to imprison those who refuse to do such deadly work.

Many Catholics listened to that voice. They went to prison or into work camps for conscientious objectors rather than submit to military service, from World War II through the Vietnam War. Thomas Merton was but one of those who, while still a layman, refused military service in World War II. Conscientious objection, I recall him writing, seemed to be what Christ himself would have done, and what He would have wanted me to do.

Even in Hitler's Europe there is the remarkable story of the Catholic Franz Jaegerstaetter, an Austrian farmer, sacristan of his village church and a family man, who was beheaded by the Nazis for his refusal of military service even as a noncombatant.

The Second Vatican Council gave clear and formal support to conscientious objectors. And in *Pacem in Terris* (1963) Pope John XXIII said, "Since the right to command is required by the moral order and has its source in God, it follows that if civil authorities legislate for or allow anything that is contrary to the will of God, neither the law made or the authorization granted can be binding on the conscience of the citizens since God has more right to be obeyed than men."

As for those who think a modern war is possible that meets the criteria of the just war theory, there is this simple and often quoted declaration by Pope John XXIII in *Pacem in Terris*: "In this age of ours which prides itself on its atomic power, it is irrational to believe that war is still an apt means of vindicating violated rights."

In the decades since those words were said the world has changed profoundly with the downfall of the communist party in Eastern Europe. We have moved away from, yet there still lingers, the fear of a nuclear disaster, because nuclear weapons remain in the hands of so many countries.

With that unbearable prospect in mind, does it matter much if you or I or anyone else decides to become a conscientious objector? Not in the sense that our personal refusal to fight will prevent the killing of others. For before armies could be ordered into action the signal could be given for nuclear missiles to wipe out hundreds of millions of human beings. But that truth about modern war only underscores the need for nonviolent resisters to muster all their strength, intelligence, and imagination to find practical ways to end the possibility of nuclear extinction.

In the late 1970s there were over 1,300 peace organizations—national, regional, and local—at work. Physicians, the clergy, scientists, lawyers, students, educators, women, business, labor, artists, young people, neighbors formed their own groups to work for a stable and enduring peace. They published leaflets and pamphlets and newspapers. They produced films and recordings. They sent out speakers, they urged antinuke positions on political candidates, they registered voters, they did mailings, they raised funds, they marched, they picketed, they telephoned, they wore buttons and slapped on car stickers, they demonstrated, they petitioned, they protested, they did anything and everything the imagination can devise to help reverse the arms race here and around the world. How many such organizations existed after the cold war ended I do not know.

Yet weapons scientists still work in laboratories and factories of death. We have arms control agreements today and new ones being developed, but they are not enough. They must go along with parallel efforts to reduce political tensions wherever they exist in our world.

For is there any alternative to negotiation? There is no way to peace but to get rivals or enemies down to the hard work of talking. The parties at odds with one another must try to work from their common interest in survival.

Surely the American people have that concern in mind—survival. And happily for the pursuit of peace, a sizable part of the American public no longer stays silent when it sees its government make mistakes in foreign policy. They react to the danger of repeating past errors. They know American leaders can be guilty of intrigue, deception, secretiveness, lawlessness. They learned that dissent has its positive side and should never be crushed. It was only when dissent over Vietnam rolled high enough to reach into Congress and change many minds there that the policy of presidents was obligated to change. We rediscovered the old belief that the truth will make us free. We must continue to say how we see things and speak out for what we believe.

CHAPTER 12

On Terrorism

Late one night in October 1981 when I was watching the news on TV, the lead-off item was a sensational robbery and triple murder in a nearby town. A gang of men and women had ambushed a Brink's armored car outside a bank, stolen nearly 2 million dollars, and in a failed getaway shot and killed a Brink's guard and two policemen. It turned out the suspects were former Black Panthers and members of the Weather Underground.

Like almost everyone else the day the story broke, I was horrified by the robbery and murders. What had brought supposedly intelligent people to do these things? Could political activists believe theft and killing were all part of the game? What kind of revolution stood for this? What did these people want out of life? What did they hope for? What kind of world, I wondered, would they make if they ever got power?

I realized what had happened in the Brink's case was not new. Political extremists—of both the right and the left—had financed their plans by armed robbery, and not hesitated to kill, before this time. But how common is political terrorism? How far back does it go? Is it a worldwide phenomenon?

I learned that it is as old as humankind. It began thousands of years before, and it goes on up to the minute. Almost any day in the newspapers you can find terrorist stories. In a single day in the *New York Times* I clipped six such items, datelined Northern Ireland, Lebanon, Argentina, Greece, Turkey, and West Germany. In the decade 1968–1978 scholars calculated some 10 thousand people were murdered by terrorist actions. Taking my readers back through history, I was able to show in my book *The Terrorists* (1983) that champions of many causes chose to use political terror.

Early on I explain what the adjective *political* means. By it we mean the ways in which the people of any society try to determine or control public policy. People means us, ourselves. We are all involved in politics in one way or another. We take this or that course of action to advance or protect our interests. We act as individual citizens or through parties or pressure groups to influence the election or appointment of those who manage the affairs of state—legislators, mayors, governors, presidents, judges, sheriffs, and many others. If we're passive, if we don't move, our interests are affected by the actions of others. The question really is not *whether* to take part in politics, but rather *how?* And for what goals?

I try to show the reader there can be a variety of political ways to act to achieve a goal. Which way one chooses often depends on the climate of the times and on one's own motives and personality.

The basic means of political struggle haven't changed much over the centuries. Only the technology. At one end the means include voting and attempts to influence opinion by spreading information and ideas. This can be done by word of mouth, by printed material, by speeches, demonstrations, marches, rallies, lobbying, radio, TV, films. And the style can vary from offering the simple facts to rabble-rousing, lies, and slander. At the other end, methods chosen can include conspiracies, assassinations, uprisings, guerrilla warfare, revolution.

It's as old as the unending conflict between the "in's" and the "out's." Those in power strive to maintain their place; those out of power try to take their place. The struggle can be conducted peacefully or violently. Acts of violence kill or injure persons or do significant damage to property. In time of war, of course, states use violence against one another. And in peacetime they use authorized violence to execute convicted criminals.

But violence in the discussion of terrorism might be defined as the illegitimate use of coercion, resulting, or intended to result, in the death, injury, restraint, or intimidation of persons or the destruction or seizure of property. Illegal violence can be used by groups or by individuals, and by the state itself when it ignores its own constitution or laws. The stress is on *unauthorized* and *illegal* acts.

The *American Heritage* dictionary (1976) defines *terror* as "intense, overpowering fear." It is a state of extreme fear caused by the systematic use of violent means by a party or group. It can be used, I explain, to get into power or to maintain power. The party or group inspires the state of fear through acts of terrorism—bombings, kidnappings, hijackings, assassination. It is a policy of intimidation. And it often results from frustration, from failure to reach goals by normal, legal, peaceful means.

It may seem that there is no difference between terrorists and an armed insurrection. But there is. The armed uprising of part of a people seeks to confront the armed forces of the government. The terrorists do not want that; they know they are too few and too weak to survive such open combat. Their aim is to use terror to weaken the will of the community or government and to undermine morale. It is a form of secret and undeclared warfare, psychological warfare, in part.

A key point is that the violence of terrorists is often used *indiscriminately*. All men, women, and children, as I show again and again throughout *The Terrorists* (1983), regardless of their place or function in society, usually are looked upon as potential victims. And the victims are unable to do anything to avoid their injury or destruction because the terrorists have their own code of values by which they judge whom to hurt. The conventions of war have no standing in the eyes of the terrorist. Anyone is fair game.

Even casual reading of the press reveals that terrorism is not the monopoly of any one ideology or cause. Terror has become the weapon of many different ideologies—from extreme right to extreme left—and of religious, ethnic, and nationalist groups.

After this explanation of terms, I go on to trace the evolution of terrorism in history. The story begins with political murder in the ancient world, when kings and tyrants were despatched by poison, the dagger, the spear, strangling. It moves to the eleventh century when the famous Muslim sect, the Assassins, appeared in Persia and Syria. They were the first organized group to use murder systematically for a cause they believed to be righteous. They were part of the Islamic sect, the Shia, which warred against the other major Islamic sect, the Sunni. The Assassins believed they had a religious duty to kill the unrighteous. Each act of murder was a sacred obligation.

How the Assassins operated has set the model for terrorist groups ever since. Their organization was highly disciplined. They lived by a strict code of secrecy. They stressed popular propaganda, spreading their beliefs to the people. They used terror to force local political authorities into compromise or cooperation. They failed to destroy the Sunni orthodoxy, but their tactics survived to be imitated by other terrorists all over the world.

It was during the French Revolution that terrorism was made into the modern political weapon we know today. It was the Jacobin party that introduced the idea of a *policy* of terror to smash the opposition. During the Reign of Terror (1793–94) great numbers of suspects were butchered without trial. They were guillotined, blown up en masse by cannon, buried in mass graves of quicklime, drowned by the hundreds in rivers.

What was new about the French terrorism was its use as a method of *preventive* repression. Not simply individuals came under suspicion, but whole classes, groups, parties were labeled *potential* enemies of the

Revolution. Another innovation was terrorization of *thought*. The people in power tried to control ideas, art, literature, the press by censorship, by intimidation, by terror.

Such revolutionary "justice" was exercised upon the mere whim or will of the terrorists. They murdered anyone they chose in the name of the collective good of the people. The politics of the revolutionaries in power decided who would live and who would die. They took unto themselves the right to determine what the people wanted and to carry that out.

In the name of a "sacred mission" thousands were ruined, tortured, murdered. In the end, one after another, the revolutionary leaders themselves fell before the guillotine. A right-wing terror took over, which continued the killing, only this time of the left-wing terrorists. What had begun as a movement of liberation turned into butchery by rival terrorists. The final outcome was a coup that made Napoleon military dictator of France.

The ideas of the French terrorists swept through Europe and took root in many countries. One of the tribunes of terror was Karl Heinzen, a German who blamed the failures of the revolutions of 1848 on the reluctance of radicals to be ruthless. "Murder is the principal agent of historical progress," he said in a widely reprinted article (Heinzen, 1853/1881) called "Murder and Liberty." Yes, he knew the killing of another human being was considered to be a crime against humanity. But, he went on:

> Against our enemies with their executions and soldiers . . . we are able to achieve precious little with our humanity and our ideas of justice. . . . Let us take the moral horror out of the great historical tool. . . . Once one has overcome the objection that murder per se is a crime, all that remains is to believe one is in the right against one's enemy and to possess the power to obliterate him. . . . It is no great step from this necessity . . . to condemning hundreds of thousands to the scaffold in the interests of humanity. . . .
>
> Once killing has been accepted, the moral stance is seen to have no foundation, the legal is seen to be ineffectual, and the political alone is of any significance. . . . To have a conscience with regard to the destruction of reactionaries is to be totally unprincipled. They wreak destruction, in any way they can, thereby obliging us to respond in kind as defenders of justice and humanity. . . . Even if we have to blow up half a continent or spill a sea of blood, in order to finish off the barbarian party, we should have no scruples about doing it. (quoted in Meltzer, 1983, pp. 15–16)

In the latter half of the nineteenth century, terrorism of several kinds appeared throughout Europe and America. In one sense, it sprang from the same source—the rise of democracy and nationalism.

Conditions that made people unhappy had existed for centuries. But few had felt there was much chance to do anything about them. As ideas about democracy and freedom and national liberation spread, old grievances became less and less tolerable. Protest movements arose to make demands of the ruling classes and the governing powers. When progress was slow, some of the rebels turned to terrorism.

The Terrorists (1983) takes up various branches of the revolutionary movement, especially Marxism and anarchism, tries to explain them, and traces their impact upon the use of terrorism. There are portraits of elitist and cynical revolutionaries, and in contrast to them, of humane and nonviolent radicals. By showing in dramatic detail how their opposing methods worked out, I hope to induce the young reader to think about the inescapable world of politics and political ideas.

To give but one example of my approach: I compare two famous Russian revolutionaries of the nineteenth century, Michael Bakunin (1814–1876) and Alexander Herzen (1812–1870). Both came from aristocratic families, and were friends for a long time, and both devoted their lives to rebellion against every form of oppression. Both men placed the idea of individual liberty at the center of their thought and action. Herzen more than anyone else created the tradition of systematic revolutionary agitation. But unlike Bakunin he would not sacrifice the freedom of individuals to the abstract idea of revolution. He attacked Bakunin and the terrorists for their readiness to slaughter people today for the sake of future happiness. He saw how indifferent his friend Bakunin was to the fate of individual human beings. Bakunin was ready to play with human lives for the sake of social experiment. While such revolutionaries professed horror at Tsarism's arbitrary violence and its victimization of innocent persons, they themselves showed a lust for revolution for revolution's sake. They protested against poverty and oppression in the abstract, but the fate of real people, people's rights and liberties, did not greatly concern them.

Cynical elitists insisted that the uneducated and ignorant masses must be saved by any available means against their own foolish wishes, even if it meant using deceit, fraud, or violence. The majority of radicals in that time did not agree. They were horrified by such tactics. Even the noblest ends would be destroyed by the use of monstrous means.

The Russian revolutionaries wished to train their followers to destroy the Tsarist system and cut down all obstacles to equality and democracy. With themselves in power, they would explain to the masses what they had done and why. Then the masses, ignorant though they might be now, would understand at least enough to let themselves be organized into the new free socialist society.

But Herzen asked, again and again: Suppose the masses, after the revolution, fail to see things the same way you do? What then? The terrorist wing of the radicals had no doubts. Terrorism and more terrorism would achieve complete anarchist liberty. That ideal condition would be imposed at first by the power of the new state, after which it would swiftly dissolve itself.

To which Herzen replied: If the aim of the revolution is to liberate, how can it use the weapons of despots? Wouldn't you only enslave those you hope to make free? You would be applying a remedy more destructive than the disease! We are trying to break the chains of Tsarism, and you would put in their place the no less binding chains of the revolutionary minority. No, Herzen insisted, the only hope for a just and free society requires a long and difficult process. There is no magical, overnight solution. We have to work hard and patiently, day by day, peacefully to convert the people, by rational argument, to the truths of social and economic justice. Only then will democratic freedom come (Meltzer, 1983, p. 27).

It was Bakunin's ideas that took hold, especially in backward peasant societies, like Italy and Spain. When progress was hard to achieve, the belief in terrorism took deeper root. Seeing no mass support for revolutionary change, the radicals in such places took up the idea of "propaganda by the deed." Only violent action, they said, would open the world's eyes to the desperation of the oppressed and the ruthless determination of those who wanted to end it.

But terrorist groups sprang up in advanced countries too, where trade unions were strong and democratic governments held power. To show the range of their ideas and actions, and the variety of societies in which they operate, the book devotes several chapters to selected terrorist organizations. The time periods move from the mid-nineteenth century to today. The most detailed chapter is the story of the young Russian revolutionaries who moved from peaceful education of the workers and peasants to the decision to murder Tsarist officials, which climaxed in the assassination of Alexander II in 1881. This story is powerful because the central figures, teenage boys and girls when they took to revolution, are moved at first by the highest ideals and gradually turn to brutal violence, to acts of terror that serve only to put even worse tyrants in power and thus make even harsher the lives of the people they wanted to emancipate.

Italy, Ireland, France, the Middle East, Latin America, our own country in various times, West Germany are all represented in the story. Toward the end there is a chapter on the systematic terrorism inflicted by governments on their own people. Such authoritarian or totalitarian regimes have enormously greater power to do violence to their citizens than small bands of terrorists. In such modern regimes terror has become the job of specialized agencies of the state. Every one of them—whether Hitler's Germany, Stalin's Russia, Mao's China, or the Latin American juntas—seems unable to do without a secret police force it trains in the methods of murder, torture, and forced confessions. Their job is to hunt down dissenters, political or cultural. To imprison or kill those labeled enemies of the state or the revolution. To spin a web of informers into every corner of the land. To censor thought, to compel conformity.

Our own government's responsibility for such terrorism is also in the record. Young readers ought to know that American sponsorship of authoritarian regimes has aided in the spread of terrorism not only in Central and South America but in other parts of the world as well. The governments of Thailand, Indonesia, the Philippines, Zaire—all in our sphere of influence—have used terror to maintain power and to protect the profits and privileges of the elite. Abroad, official agencies of the United States government have attempted assassination of foreign leaders and have financed bloody covert wars and deadly terrorist programs against internal dissenters.

What about the morality of terrorism?

This is what I hope *The Terrorists* (1983) will get readers to think hardest about. Whenever I take up a specific terrorist group, I let them voice their own beliefs while I show their deeds and the outcome of those deeds. Often I was able to quote the words of terrorists who changed their minds, and explained why they came to see politics in a different light.

In the closing chapter I tackle the issue of morality and take up the arguments terrorists offer in their defense: that limited forms of terror can be justified; that terror that discriminates between the "innocent" and the "guilty" is all right; that terrorists who seek national liberation are really fighting a war; that since the oppressed people whom the terrorists claim to act for suffer harm, it is allowable for terrorists to cause harm to others; and that if a government stands in the way of peaceful change, then violence is the only recourse.

What matters most, it seems to me, is the central question: Does the end justify the means?

Early in their lives Emma Goldman and Alexander Berkman believed the answer was yes. That thinking led them to tinker with a time bomb in a crowded tenement, putting the lives of innocent people in danger. It led them to believe that by taking the life of one man, Henry Frick, the manager of the Carnegie steel mills at Homestead, they would help the working class gain freedom. As Emma's biographer, Richard Drinnon (1961), put it: "The fullness of life was to be achieved by destroying life" (p. 82).

Emma soon outgrew her belief in the end justifying the means. While her study of history convinced her that great changes will always be violent, she could still say, "I feel violence in whatever form never has and probably never will bring constructive results" (Drinnon, 1961, p. 82).

That dilemma of means and ends torments revolutionaries. Terrorists often settle the issue for themselves by deciding that private scruples must be forgotten when the good of the cause is at stake. They see themselves as the instruments of justice. They kill, there is blood on their hands, but it is honored by the rightness of their cause. They lie, they cheat, they steal, they murder, but they see these sins as trivial, when measured by the great end in view. Such immoral means are sacrifices they must make upon the altar of necessity.

The ideal goals of justice and equality and freedom become political rationalizations for the acts of terror. Such left-wing terrorists place the interests of humankind in the *future* above the interests of people in the *present*. A glorious end justifies the most inglorious means.

Most people try to live by a code of ethics that respects the individual, treats a person as end in him- or herself, and seeks to love the individual. The code of the terrorists treats the individual as a cog in the machine, as raw material to be manipulated for society's good. *They*—the terrorists and their revolutionary party—decide what that good is and the path we must take to achieve it. The radical goal they have in mind is the end that justifies the use of any means.

In reality, ends and means cannot be separated. The revolutionary whose goal is some kind of dictatorship leaves no room for individual dissent. His party, and his party alone, knows what the new society must be; it will decide everything for the good of all in the one-party state of the future. And in the struggle to make that revolution, the same kind of thinking operates. The revolutionary will decide what means to use, and woe to those who differ.

Part III

INTRIGUING PEOPLE

Part III is designed for readers, writers, and teachers of biography. Each essay rehearses aspects of a biographical figure Meltzer has written about elsewhere. In addition, these pieces function as meta-biographies, essays about what it meant to write about the figure in question.

In "The Designing Narrator," the lead essay in this section, Meltzer offers a description of both the process he uses and the decisions he makes when writing a biography. For me, the beauty of this essay lies in its concreteness—not only does it provide a step-by-step analysis of Meltzer's approach to his award-winning account of Langston Hughes's life, but it also models the kind of essay students might write as they go about the work of collecting information from documents and informants. It sets out the standards Meltzer uses to judge his own work, and in that sense informs all of the other biographical essays included here. Whereas the other essays in Part III evidence a "problem orientation," this piece presents "the basics," what one needs to know before beginning to research and write.

The second essay focuses on a figure familiar to all American schoolchildren, Ben Franklin. The problem for Meltzer, or for anyone writing about so complex and wide-ranging a life, is where to begin. Meltzer talks in this piece as both storyteller and guardian of the historical record. To make the story work, he has to find a central thread. To be true to Franklin's life, he must make a coat of many colors. The problem raised here will help students look not only at Meltzer's Benjamin Franklin, but at other versions of the statesman's life told for both children and adults.

The next piece, on Lydia Maria Child, sets out another sort of problem. Lydia Maria Child is to Meltzer an important unsung hero of America's past, and yet her name is unrecognized by even college graduates. As a reader, Meltzer helps me fall in love with Maria, as he has. Perhaps this piece will lead others to delve into Meltzer's *Tongue of Flame: The Life of Lydia Maria Child* (1965) as well as *Lydia*

Maria Child: Selected Letters, 1817–1880 (Meltzer & Holland, 1982). My hope is that teachers as well as students will begin biographical work on figures about whom they know little. Teachers and their students might begin by collecting letters from a figure of local prominence or letters about their community. "Lydia Maria Child" provides a direct biographical connection to the essays in Part II and helps us all to write stories about those whom we admire and love.

"Dorothea Lange" might have been another love story, but in his research Meltzer found out that the biographical subject he so much admired as a photographer and social commentator was abusive to her own children. Whereas many historians for young people would gloss over such faults, Meltzer writes here about his own struggle to avoid one-dimensional, flat distortions of truth. Young people who find themselves wary of self-serving history, and those who seek a rosy-bright retelling of the past, can meet together over this piece. An even more difficult example for those in the rosy-bright camp is found in the next piece, on Columbus. Both essays would add immeasurably to a discussion on revisionism. These, and others from this part, could well be read next to textbook accounts of the same characters.

The final essay in this part, subtitled "Four Who Locked Horns with the Censors," is a tribute to writers Langston Hughes, Mark Twain, Lydia Maria Child, and Margaret Sanger—writers whose personal integrity overrode their desire for wealth and prestige. Meltzer's thumbnail sketches tie together these figures around a conceptual stance, making both the argument and the biographical figures more interesting. Good nonfiction can embody subthemes as well as main ideas. This piece led me to ask how each author's passion for truth made them better writers; it finds an appropriate seat next to the Epilogue, which takes a hard look at the difficulties of being a writer today.

As young people begin composing their own lives it is important for them to have the opportunity to see how others' lives stretch across the page.

CHAPTER 13

The Designing Narrator

The biographer's image is not reality itself. The reality is the ceaseless flux of that life, with its billions of moments of experience. That reality is the raw material from which the biographer works. In that reality countless events succeeded each other in the order of time. But the subject's own consciousness of those events is not the biographer's. The subject could not know, as the biographer knows, what lay in the future. Here is where imagination comes into play. The mind of the biographer must be free to seek some arrangement or pattern in the life he or she has studied. The biographer makes connections, holds back some facts, foreshadows others, decides on juxtapositions, attempts to balance this element against that. Using documentary evidence in imaginative ways without ever departing from its truth, the biographer tries to give a form to flux, to impose a design upon chronology.

How does the biographer go about discovering the design for the work? I will use my biography of Langston Hughes as an example. Early in the 1950s Hughes and I had collaborated on a book about black history. Strangers at the beginning, we became friends during the course of the work. Years later, we collaborated on a second book about blacks in the performing arts. As this was entering proof, a publisher asked me to write some short sketches of various people for a project designed to appeal to young readers in black communities. One of the sketches I did was of Langston Hughes's life. When he saw it, he called to say how much he liked it. Then it occurred to me, why not try to do a biography of Hughes for young adults? "What would you think of it," I asked him hesitantly, because of course he could easily do it himself. (He had already published a two volume autobiography for adults.) "Go right ahead," he said, "I'll try to help you however I can." So with a contract from Crowell I set to work.

Since this was to be a book about a writer, the most important source of information was his own work. I knew that my audience was young people, that they were primarily interested in Hughes for his poems, stories, and plays, and that the role of his blackness in his work was of paramount importance. So I began research with very detailed analysis of the two books that make up Hughes's autobiography—*The Big Sea* (1963) and *I Wonder As I Wander* (1964). These volumes carried his life story only up to the age of 40, and now he was 65. In a book for young readers I was constrained to keep the text down to some 40,000 words, not necessarily a handicap. One has to leave out a lot in writing about so richly varied a life. That necessity can be a blessing.

Some biographies are enormous compendia of facts, full of the clutter of daily life, with the subject's every ticket stub and laundry bill thrown in. It is important, however, to remember that the biographer does not imagine the facts. He selects them. His imaginative powers come into play when he creates the form into which the facts will go.

As I made notes on Hughes's writing, I built a list of things to do to clarify, corroborate, or extend what his work suggested to me. Hughes also gave me certain materials from his own files, and he answered the many questions I asked him. In addition, I got help from more than 50 people who had known him, some from as far back as his early school days, some from college years, and some way on up through decades of his long professional career as the first black American to seek to make a living entirely from his writing. Other writers, editors, publishers, agents, actors, directors, singers, dancers, and composers who had played some part in his multifaceted work gave me interviews or answered queries by letter and phone. Some lent me letters, papers, photographs, or clippings. Much material on Hughes is held at Yale University, the Schomburg Center for Research in Black Culture in New York, and Lincoln University in Pennsylvania. Among the liveliest sources were newspapers and periodicals. They carried news stories about him and articles by him, as well as editorial comments on him. And then there were the fat files of his own newspaper columns, which appeared weekly for over 20 years, first in the *Chicago Defender* and then also in the *New York Post*.

Beyond his autobiography were Hughes's other writings, of course. It is an incredibly long bibliography. I read every one of these publications, for they voiced what he taught and felt and dreamed and feared and hoped. The biographer must be constantly sensitive to what he finds that characterizes his subject. Not any fact, but this particular fact or phrase or word is what is wanted. Anything that is vivid and human will help the biographer to discover the configurations of a life.

So I began writing, shuttling from one document to another, trying to form in my mind an image of my subject. Since I was writing about someone I knew, an image was already there, although it may have been modified by what my research had unearthed. My personal relationship with my subject was only one of many such relationships in his life. I saw him from my perspective. Now that perspective was altered by what I had learned from the views of many others. To the testimony of my own eyes I added the testimony of others, which may or may not have been corroborative.

One of the biographer's biggest problems is identification with his subject. It can lead to triumphs or disasters. The biographer seeks to understand a life by coming as close as he or she can to that person. Yet biographers must be careful not to reshape the subject in their own image. When writing about Hughes, of course, the inward and spiritual life was reflected in his work—his poems, songs, plays, stories, novels, autobiography, and columns. It is easier, when your subject is a writer, to take part in his inner life.

But to convey that inner life, while always difficult, is only part of the task. The biographer is interested in every aspect of the subject's history—the physical as well as the psychic, the public as well as the private. The economic and social circumstances that helped shape him are part of the story. The world of his lifespan, as he experienced it, must be considered. In the case of Hughes, I started out with the fact that he was an American and black. And for the black American, life in the land where "white is right" has always been difficult. It is this that Hughes's poetry and his life illuminate. Before he was 25 he had made himself the poet laureate of his people. Their life was his life. So it was that complex life that I had to try to clarify.

When biographers try to do more than compile the facts, they are taking all the risks of the narrative art without the full freedom novelists enjoy. Novelists can summon up all the resources of their imagination; they have the liberty to invent anything they choose to carry out their purpose. Biographers, however, must work within that mass of gathered facts. They must use to the full their freedom to select, to arrange, to depict. Like novelists, biographers seek to capture character in action, personality in performance. Unlike novelists, they owe the reader historical truth. If they succeed, it is because they have found the right design.

There are times, however, when the biographer's designing involves quite a different process, when the historical situation demands that the subjects speak for themselves. I have let them speak like this in several books. One of them, *The Black Americans: A History in Their Own Words* (1984), tries to help the reader understand what black Americans felt, thought, did, suffered, and enjoyed from 1619 to the 1980s. What blacks have had done to them, how they have lived through it, and how they have fought back, is the living stuff of their history. In this book they tell the story themselves—through letters, journals, speeches, autobiographies, proclamations, newspapers, pamphlets. These records reveal what happened to living men, women, and children of the past because they speak with their own voices, recording their experiences from the time the first slave ship landed in Virginia to the present.

Another kind of book, again drawing on living history as reflected in people's own words, is *Brother, Can You Spare a Dime?* (1969/1991b). My narrative weaves together a collective memory. For many those grim years of the Great Depression constitute a past unknown, dim, forgotten. In my history of that tragic time, the unemployed, the poor, the homeless tell about their own lives, in their own words. What they say is not a substitute for history. It is only a part of it, but one sorely neglected. Their voices speak of personal experience, so that we come to feel what it was like to be alive in their time and place. Their voices enrich the group memory and help us recover from the past what still lives.

Both of these books—and many of my others—make use of documentary history, but not in the usual sense of collections of official papers: constitutions, laws, treaties, judicial decisions. Important as those are, they are rarely readable and never personal. Here we have another kind of document: the intimate voices of people who in their own writing, never intended for a public audience, reveal their joys, fears, expectations, griefs, protests, achievements. In the process, the designing narrator crafts the ordering of the narratives, so that readers are caught up in the violence of a mob, the hunger of a child, or the struggle for a job as told in the words of those who lived the experiences.

In both these processes—whether the writer speaks or the subject speaks—the truth comes through the ordering. The biographer's image, the historian's image, although they are not reality itself, take on their own reality, which the reader perceives through the design. Structure and design are meaning. The writer, then, does more than impose an arbitrary order on a single life or the collective life. Whether the writer is the narrator (as in *Langston Hughes*) or the subjects are narrators (as in *The Black Americans* or *Brother, Can You Spare a Dime?*), the writer has collaborated with his subjects and discovered a design that the subjects, bound by their own time, might not have recognized.

CHAPTER 14

Benjamin Franklin

For young readers trying to find out something about our American Revolution, reading about the lives of its great leaders can be both highly entertaining and enormously illuminating. Nothing will bring the past to life more vividly and immediately than the richly colored personal story. Everyone is interested in what other people are like. (That is why we all love gossip, whether we confess it or not.) In the story of Benjamin Franklin (1706–90), born nearly 300 years ago, the young reader can find delightful and startling resemblances to the human nature he or she has begun to observe in contemporary society. But readers can also see in Franklin potentialities for personal growth and development that may lift them out of the rut of their perhaps still narrowly confined world.

One reason I chose Franklin for young readers is that, like most of us, he started life with few advantages. Yet, although born into a family of tradesmen, he became the most celebrated man of his time. No other man of his generation was more multitalented and accomplished. He was the self-made man, the first American to set that pattern which innumerable others have tried to follow. Many of them achieved wealth or political power. But Franklin did more. He proved an astonishing success at whatever he turned his hand and mind to. Printer, publisher, businessman, author, general, inventor, scientist, politician, diplomat, social reformer, philosopher. Yet in whatever he did, wherever he was, he always remained himself.

What are some of the problems of writing a biography? Writing a biography is not a matter of flinging all the facts onto a sheet of paper. My book on Franklin is designed to convey the rich flavor of Franklin and the range of his extraordinary accomplishments. But how could I tell this story and do justice to my subject's power and magic? And do the task within the limits of some 200 manuscript pages? And write it for a group of readers with scanty knowledge of eighteenth-century America and Europe, and no familiarity with the realms of thought and action mastered by Franklin? I should add another limitation—

my own lack of expertise in the many realms Franklin entered and mastered.

What I will try to do is to suggest some of the problems faced by the biographer directing his work to young readers. Wherever possible, I'll use my experience with Franklin to show what I mean.

First, confronting the life of Franklin was very different from approaching the lives of other people I've written about. Most of them, however great their achievement, led lives confined to one field of action. Langston Hughes, Mark Twain, Henry David Thoreau, and Lydia Maria Child were writers; Dorothea Lange, a photographer; Mary McLeod Bethune, an educator; Thaddeus Stevens, a politician; Samuel Gridley Howe, Margaret Sanger, and Betty Friedan, social reformers. George Washington was both a military and a political leader, and of course a revolutionary too.

But Ben Franklin? He was almost everything. With subjects whose lives are pretty much concentrated on one kind of endeavor, learning enough about that field to feel comfortable in it is daunting. Benjamin Franklin forces you to march into so much new territory that you fear you will stumble into a deep pit and be unable to climb out. I always read whatever my subject has written or said. In Franklin's case there is his autobiography (1868/1964), published after his death, which takes him only up to the age of 59; he lived to be 84. And like all such memoirs, it is subject to the natural defects of memory and the use of highly selective recall. He wrote, probably, from the point of view of his own legend, and thus he would show his readers how he became what he knew he had in their minds become. Franklin's other writings—his letters, journals, speeches, articles, almanacs, satires—fill fat volumes, and I mined them diligently for quotations as well as for biographical insights.

My method in research, where the subject's chronology is pretty well established, is to work from a rough outline of the key periods in the person's life. I take notes on 3 × 5 cards as I read the sources and think about what I'm learning, and file them by the tentative outline. Later, the notes will be reshuffled as the outline is modified by what I am finding out. And when I begin to write the story, the notes are clustered by chapter and arranged in the direction I think the chapter might move.

Franklin's time was so distant, that of course I couldn't do interviews with people who knew him. But there were scores of contemporaries who knew the man in one connection or another and had recorded their impressions. That has to substitute for one's own taking of oral testimony by contemporaries, which I've grappled with in some of my other biographies.

Franklin's was a special case for me in that he did so much in so many different fields. Many specialists have done studies of the man as printer, publisher, scientist, inventor, diplomat, author, and so on. I examined most of these too, and then, because I felt my readers would need a broader social context, read broader studies that helped me set Franklin in perspective: printing and publishing, for instance, in eighteenth-century America; apprenticeship in that time; the level of science in the Europe and America Franklin moved in; the state of education in the colonies, and especially his Boston. Where the writer of a life for adults might take some knowledge for granted, I felt I could assume nothing.

I confess to being startled at times by finding connections I had not made before. For example, how close in time Franklin's boyhood was to the witchcraft trials of Salem. They occurred only 14 years before he was born. And the atmosphere of that dreadful demonic time contrasts so sharply with the rationalism Franklin came to stand for. Cotton Mather, who loomed so large in the story of the Salem hysteria, figures in Franklin's boyhood too, for the Puritan minister was still very much alive. The story of Mather's championship of inoculation against smallpox when the plague was wiping out so many Bostonians, and doing this despite the thundering "No"of the medical profession, and while being viciously attacked for it by Franklin's brother in his newspaper, is a startling reversal of what you'd expect to find.

When it came to telling of the education of young Ben, I tried to do more than writers of children's books usually risk. Ben went to school for only 2 years, when he was 8 and 9 years old. Then his father took him out to start his working life as an apprentice in his father's soap and candle making business, and then as a printer in his brother's shop.

But Ben never ended his education. By studying on his own, he would become one of the most learned men of his century. All life long he devoured books. But what books? His insatiable hunger is all the more remarkable when we think how limited was the range of reading offered a boy in his time. There were almost no children's books, no novels, no stories written for boys. But Boston was a bookish town: The written word counted for much in the Puritan mind. Private citizens built up their own libraries. They were often rich in the classics as well as in science, medicine, and natural history. Even Ben's father Josiah, the hard-working tradesman, had a home library, small but varied enough for Ben to feast in.

What I did in this part of the biography was to take up the specific books we know young Ben read, and to discuss them in some detail. They include Bunyan's *The Pilgrim's Progress,* Plutarch's *Parallel Lives,* and Defoe's *An Essay Upon Projects*. (Defoe had not yet written his popular novels, *Robinson Crusoe* and *Moll Flanders*.) It is scarcely likely that any of my young readers will have touched these books. Yet I felt it important to try to show the connection between what a book says and how a reader responds to it. I guess I was propagandizing a bit. I'd like young people to know books matter; they matter terribly.

Bunyan and Plutarch stamped on Franklin's young mind an ideal of progress, and Defoe brought it down to earth for him by showing how the kingdom of God on earth is best advanced by men and women behaving decently, and fairly, with one another. It was Defoe who sent Ben upon the path to social reform.

On another, related aspect of his development, I tried to indicate what helped make Ben such a superbly skilled writer. It was a talent that proved of great use all his life. How he mastered writing while so young is a remarkable story, and I do not pass over it lightly in the book. I felt it might help readers to understand how much thought and effort go into the development of good writing.

One of Ben's Boston friends was another "bookish" boy, John Collins. The two friends enjoyed arguments. For the fun of it, they would take opposite sides of an issue, such as a woman's right to an education, and debate it to develop their skills. Ben thought John, who won more by virtue of his fluency than the strength of his reasoning, a more eloquent speaker. One day Ben sat down to write out his argument, and John replied on paper. They had exchanged a few such letters when Josiah, Ben's father, happened to find them and read them. Without commenting on the merits of the debate, Josiah told Ben that he could spell and punctuate decently, but that his use of language fell short of what it should be (Meltzer, 1988a, p. 40).

Instead of being crushed by his father's criticism, Ben determined to improve his style. A London paper, the *Spectator*, was very popular in America at the time. It was written by two men, Joseph Addison and Richard Steele, who were highly praised masters of English. Ben got hold of a volume of the *Spectator* and read the witty and satirical essays over and over. He was delighted with them. He set about making a few notes on one of the essays, then put them away for a few days before trying to write on the theme in his own words and manner, as best he could. When finished, he would compare his version with the original, discover his faults, and strive to correct them. He would also turn some *Spectator* essays into verse, then back again into prose, enlarging his vocabulary and polishing his style. He got up early in the morning and stayed up late at night to practice writing. His drive for excellence was unlimited.

Ashamed of his ignorance of arithmetic, he found a book on the subject and mastered it. From a book on navigation he took the fundamentals of geometry. Then he read John Locke's *An Essay Concerning Human Understanding*. First published in 1689, it was a monumental work that powerfully influenced eighteenth-century thought. Locke was by nature a moderate man, a man who sought to conciliate differences. In a spirit of tolerance he tried to compromise clashing views without giving up principle. If political authority was legitimate and just, he opposed revolution. But where a government was tyrannical, he advocated effective protest.

Ben was captivated by the book's brilliance. It shaped his own ideas and strengthened the values he would live by. Locke was open to the new, to change, in an ever-changing world. To dismiss something just because it was new, was foolish. I quote him:

> Truth scarce ever yet carried it by vote anywhere at its first appearance: new opinions are always suspected, and usually opposed, without any reason but because they are not already common. But truth, like gold, is not the less so for being newly brought out of the mine. (quoted in Meltzer, 1988a, pp. 41–42)

Locke did not pretend to possess divine authority, the way the Puritan preachers of Boston did. His style of talking with his readers, rather than lecturing them, made it easy to follow his argument. The result was to enlarge Ben's understanding of everything Locke discussed— science, religion, politics, education, ethics, philosophy. Perhaps there were limits to what the human mind could know, but Locke said, "Our business here is not to know all things, but those which concern our conduct" (quoted in Meltzer, 1988a, p. 42).

To be doubtful, to be skeptical, was not a bad thing. The mind, man's power of reasoning, "must be our last judge and guide in everything." Young Ben, still groping for a place to stand, found firmer footing as he read and reread Locke. These were ideas in which he could believe and by which he could live.

Earlier, Ben had found humanitarian principles in one of Cotton Mather's works, *Bonifacius: An Essay Upon the Good* (1710). Many of Mather's flood of publications were dull, boring, impenetrable. But not this book. The Puritan minister, whose family had dominated Boston for generations, thought that good things done in this life prepared the way for the next. Ben had never been concerned with the hereafter. But Mather's lively interest in the world around him was evidence of a generous devotion to the welfare of the people of Boston.

Ben had the same sense of community, and would demonstrate it a thousand times over in the years ahead. He liked to be with others, men and women, to share work and pleasures and ideas with them. The welfare and progress of whatever community he lived in was of great importance to him. Cotton Mather was at the top of Boston's social ladder, and Ben the apprentice was at the bottom. Still, when Mather wrote these words, Ben knew they were meant for him.

> My friend, thou are one that makes but a little figure in the world, and a brother of low degree; behold, a vast encouragement! A little man may do a great deal of hurt. And then, why may not a little man do a great deal of good! It is possible the wisdom of a poor man may start a proposal that may save a city, serve a nation! A single hair applied unto a flyer [a flywheel] that has other wheels depending on it, may pull up an oak, or pull down a house. (quoted in Meltzer, 1988a, p. 43)

One day Ben came across a book that contained excerpts from some 50 dialogues of Socrates, the philosopher of ancient Greece. Because Ben had not gotten very far in his debates with his friend Collins, he was eager to learn about the Socratic method. He was "charmed" by what he read, by the calm temper of Socrates, by his lack of aggressiveness, by the moderate way he talked. He saw that head-on collisions with people who differed from him were not useful. They might think him obnoxious and stop listening. Much better to be modest and tactful in expressing an opinion. The Socratic method of asking leading questions, rather than making self-serving assertions, was effective way back then, and always would be. It was far more likely to lead to the truth.

Let's jump to a later time, when Ben reached middle age and retired from his printing business. At 42, he plunged headlong into his life as a scientist. He had revealed his inventiveness much earlier, in many ways, but here I will mention only one charming bit of evidence. Once, he found that an open pot of molasses in his wife's pantry was crawling with ants. He removed all of the ants but one, then tied the pot to a string suspended from the ceiling, led the string across the ceiling and down the wall, and sat by to observe. The one ant gorged itself in the pot, then clambered along the string and down the wall, and disappeared. About 30 minutes later, the pot was once again thick with ants that had crossed over to it on the string. How, Ben asked himself, has the first ant communicated to the others the feast awaiting them in the pot? (Meltzer, 1988a, p. 111).

Again and again Ben saw in everyday aspects of nature questions that demanded answers. Where others before him had noticed nothing interesting or significant, his mind saw something wonderful. He was born to be a natural philosopher, the term used then for scientists.

To help my readers understand what Ben's scientific achievement amounted to, I had to go back to the time of Sir Francis Bacon, 100 years before, when Bacon began the turn toward modern science.

And here, again, a surprise for me. I didn't realize that that supreme genius, Sir Isaac Newton, lived into Ben's time. And Ben, when he came to London at the age of 18 to work in a printshop, had such confidence in himself that he tried to wangle an appointment to talk things over with Sir Isaac. He failed in that, but he did manage to confer with Sir Hans Sloane, another major scientist and the Queen's physician. Can you imagine yourself, at the age of 18, a nobody, seeking to sit down and chat with Albert Einstein?

I describe how vastly different scientific research was back then, compared with what it is now. You can understand Ben's greatness only if you see it in that context. His voracious appetite for learning made him ask the why and how of everything he came across. In his mind there was nothing that could not be improved. Not only in the material world, but in the social world. From a better stove to a peaceful community of nations.

Franklin's work on electricity is the best-known example of his scientific research; most people think of the spectacular kite experiment. But more important was his experimental approach. It was his genius here that made all his contributions possible, and I was able to handle some of this decently. But when it came to his fundamental electrical experiments, I felt out of my depth. So I relied on quoting the lucid explanation of a twentieth-century physicist, who takes over for me for a few pages.

It's worth noting, in our day of boundless greed and selfish ambition, that Franklin would not patent any of his many inventions to draw profit from them. He delighted in conceiving them but he placed them freely in the public hand. I use the lightning rod as an example of how hard it was for people of Ben's time to set aside the myths and fears they had lived by for centuries and to accept a modern invention. Even 20 years after his lightning rod appeared, many hesitated to erect them for fear they would bring down upon themselves the wrath of the Lord; lightning was viewed as a divine punishment for the sins of mankind. But the practical success of the invention eventually overcame all resistance. Nothing enlarged Ben's reputation so much as the lightning rod. Because it is more than 200 years in the past, it is hard for us to realize the impact it had on people of that time. Ben's contemporary, John Adams, can tell us how his world viewed it.

Nothing, perhaps, that ever occurred upon the earth was so well calculated to give any man an extensive and universal a celebrity as . . . the
invention of lightning rods. The idea was one of the most sublime that
ever entered a human imagination, that a mortal should disarm the
clouds of heaven. . . . His (lightning rods) erected their head in all parts
of the world, on temples and palaces no less than on cottages of peasants
and habitations of ordinary citizens. These visible objects reminded all
men of the name and character of their inventor; and in the course of time
have not only tranquillized the mind and dissipated the fears of the
tender sex and their timorous children, but have almost annihilated that
panic, terror and superstitious horror which was once almost universal
in violent storms of thunder and lightning. (quoted in Meltzer, 1988a,
pp. 130–131)

When others disagreed with Franklin or criticized his research, he
would make no reply. He refused to defend his scientific views, prefer-
ring to let them take their chance in the world. If they were right, he
felt, truth and experience would support them; if wrong, they would
and ought to be rejected. How wise this is, I think, when you compare
it with the acrimony and jealousy and sniping that characterizes exchanges between some scientists of our time. Although Franklin valued his scientific honors—and there were many of them—he seldom
referred to them and even poked fun at them, once calling "a feather
in the cap not so useful a thing as a pair of good silk garters" (quoted
in Meltzer, 1988a, p. 132).

I cannot go into every facet of this Renaissance man's genius. To
describe in detail his discoveries needs another hour of your time and
mine. But just to list some of them will indicate the range of Franklin's
observations and experiments. To start with, the simpler things—those
he made himself. He is credited with clocks, the stove, the lightning
rod, astronomical instruments, bifocal eyeglasses, the flexible catheter,
a chair that can be converted into a ladder, a clothes-pressing machine,
improvements in the printing press, a pole with a manipulable grasp
at the end to take down books from high shelves, laboratory equipment, the musical instrument called the glass harmonica for which
Mozart and Beethoven wrote music. (He could, by the way, play the
harp, the guitar, and the violin.)

One of Franklin's significant innovations was the investigation of
population changes; it led to the development of the science of demog-
raphy. And this gave me the opportunity to let the young reader see
how complex and contradictory Franklin was. Different from others in
this respect? Not at all. Great as he was, he had weaknesses of character and gaps in his understanding such as afflict all of us, barring full-
fledged saints.

A sorry aspect of Franklin's views on population is the racism that was common in his time, even among the most enlightened individuals, including Thomas Jefferson. Franklin was extremely ethnocentric. He did not welcome nonwhites to America, or even whites who were not English. The German settlers in western Pennsylvania upset him. He didn't like the way they clung to their own language and customs, and feared they would become so numerous as to "Germanize us, instead of our Anglifying them" (quoted in Meltzer, 1988a, p. 137). He worried over the fact that white people were a relatively small part of the population of the earth. Why plant in America the dark, the tawny, the swarthy people, he asked. He discouraged their immigration. Then, perhaps feeling a twinge of guilt or shame over this point of view, he added, "But perhaps I am partial to the complexion of my country, for such kind of partiality is natural to mankind" (quoted in Meltzer, 1988a, pp. 137–138).

When Franklin was operating his printshop in Philadelphia, and publishing his newspaper, he ran advertisements for the buying and selling of slaves. He owned slaves himself, used as house servants, and took two of them to England when he went there to represent the Pennsylvania colony. Much later, he changed his views, and became president of the Pennsylvania abolition society. His final public act was to ask the first Congress to take measures against slavery.

None of this is kept out of the biography. The details are there, and the young reader, I hope, will see that even a brilliant thinker and generous man may have blind spots. Or that few of us manage to rise above the prejudices of our time. It takes great imagination and energy to break free of whatever in our culture binds the mind and cramps the spirit.

What about Franklin and women? The rumored scandals would have delighted the publishers of today's sensational press. I do not think such matters should be omitted or glossed over for young readers; they need only to be handled with tact and fairly. When Ben was a young printer away from home and let loose in London, he had affairs with available young women, which he himself didn't hesitate to tell us about in his famous *Autobiography*. He even tried to make love to the mistress of a friend, when the man was away. (He was rejected that time.) And back in Philadelphia, he fathered an illegitimate son, whom his new wife, Debby, generously took in and raised as their own child. That young man later turned Tory and was estranged from his father for a very long time.

In France, Franklin—now an old man, but a delightful and celebrated international figure—was lionized by the ladies of the aristocratic circles he moved in as ambassador from the fresh young American democracy. His success as a diplomat matched his success in the salons. To the ladies of Paris he was "mon cher Papa." Even while raising arms and funds for his country, he found time to court the ladies. French society permitted the paying of frank compliments, and Franklin's wit found full play in conversation and correspondence. To a Boston stepniece he wrote:

> Somebody, it seems, gave it out that I loved ladies; and then everybody presented me their ladies (or the ladies presented themselves) to be embraced—that is, to have their necks kissed. For as to kissing of lips or cheeks, it is not the mode here, the first is reckoned rude, and the other may rub off the paint. The French ladies, have, however, 1,000 ways of rendering themselves agreeable. (quoted in Meltzer, 1988a, p. 246)

There are stories of half a dozen women with whom he had affectionate relationships during his years in France. One of the youngest was Madame Brillon. Thirty-six when she met him, she was a beautiful and intelligent woman married to a man 20 years her senior. He was a government official who acted as an intermediary for French merchants selling weapons to the Americans. Franklin, of course, was almost 40 years older than Madame Brillon, but she found age no barrier to the enjoyment of his company. An excellent musician, she and her daughters entertained Franklin "with little concerts, a cup of tea and a game of chess," often seeing him twice a week at her home in Passy. He wrote his famous "Bagatelles" for her and other intimate friends, printing them on his private press in his house at Passy; these are short essays, charming and whimsical.

A still more intimate friend was Madame Helvetius, a wealthy widow in her sixties who lived at Auteuil. She had been noted for her beauty in her youth, and was still very attractive. She held a weekly salon that drew people like Franklin and Voltaire. She and Franklin hugged and kissed each other in public, a display that "highly disgusted" Abigail Adams, who said she didn't want to know "ladies of this cast." Franklin asked—we don't know how seriously—to marry Madame Helvetius, a proposal she declined amiably, without losing his friendship.

Franklin's life with his wife Debby will interest young readers, I think, because its twists and turns illustrate how oddly matched, or mismatched, marriages can be. They were married when he was a young and poor printer. Debby was a warm, decent young woman, but she was uneducated, barely literate, and could not begin to match his brilliance, although she had plenty of what we call common sense. I think they loved each other, but she was probably scared of the great world he soon moved into, and she always refused to travel with him on the long journeys he took both in America and abroad on government missions. Their letters are affectionate but it's clear she was no Abigail Adams, whose mind could match her husband John's. Debby died in 1774, while Ben was in Europe; he lived another 16 years.

In one of his last letters, to an English friend, Franklin wrote: "God grant that not only the love of liberty, but a thorough knowledge of the rights of man, may pervade all the nations of the earth, so that a philosopher may set his foot anywhere on its surface, and say, 'This is my country!'" (quoted in Meltzer, 1988a, p. 273).

CHAPTER 15

Lydia Maria Child

I was drawn to the story of Lydia Maria Child because hers was an extraordinary life. She was born nearly 200 years ago, but her time was full of clashes and encounters that look remarkably like the map of today's social terrain. She scouted territory that no one had entered before, and put up signposts that still point the way to us. Hers was no conventional success story. On the contrary, she earned fame and money while still young and gave it up in a bitter struggle for freedom and equality. She lived on the thin edge of poverty for the rest of her long life. She married the man she loved but knew many years of loneliness with and without him. She failed to have the children she hungered for. Her life was hard and often miserable. Yet magnificent, too. And to the end she stayed young in her feelings, as interested as ever in birds, and wildflowers, and people. The biography of such a woman can be, I believe, useful to the imaginative teacher who wants to open a child's eyes to fresh visions of a possible future.

Maria, as she was called, was born in a Massachusetts village in 1802, the youngest child of a baker, Convers Francis. With girls denied the same chance at education as boys, she learned all she could from an older brother preparing for the ministry. He taught her to examine every opinion, every idea for herself and to accept or dismiss it without regard for what other people thought. The American Revolution was only one generation past. Maria's generation thought of themselves as chosen by God to lead the way to universal freedom. Why couldn't they work out a new society based on the gospel of humanity?

Maria read a lot in early American history. She looked up the old veterans of the Revolution and talked to them about their struggles and hopes. She visited the Abnaki Indians who lived a few miles up the river, and listened to their tales of the old days before the white man came. She began to think that our own history would make great material for literature. One day she sat down at a desk and in a few hours wrote the first chapter of a novel about the Indians. Her brother read it and encouraged her to go on. Six weeks later she finished it. She told a very sensational story for her time, for it dealt with an interracial marriage between an Indian and a white girl, an independent girl who dared to defy her bigoted father.

Overnight young Maria became famous. There was a great curiosity about the lives of American Indians and their history. Everyone rushed to buy her book, entitled *Hobomok, A Tale of Early Times* (1824). The literary critics welcomed it as one of the very first novels to deal with the subject. Boston society lionized her. A year later there was another historical novel, this time about Boston just before the Revolution. This book, *The Rebels: Or Boston Before the Revolution* (1825), was also a great success. Publishers knocked at her door to beg for her work. Since very few writers in America at that time could make a living by their pen, she opened a private school. A new idea grew out of her experience in teaching. Children must learn to read, but they should enjoy the learning. Yet there was so little literature written for them. Why not start a children's magazine? She did, and *Juvenile Miscellany*, first issued in 1826, became the pioneer children's magazine in America and an immediate success.

Maria married David Child, a young lawyer. An idealist, he began to edit a political newspaper and raised issues that demanded action. One of the first causes he championed was that of the Cherokee Indians, whom the new president, Andrew Jackson, was trying to force off their land.

David drew Maria into this political battle. She wrote a pamphlet about the Cherokees, trying to make clear that racial prejudice was at the root of the merciless way whites were driving Indians off their homeland. It was a prejudice that went back to the religious bigotry of the old Puritans, she said. Many of the first settlers thought God had ordained them to conquer the "red devils." The Puritans were chosen to do God's work, they claimed, so *any* action they took was in *His* name. This was an easy excuse to rob, beat, exile, and even kill the Indians.

Maria and David did their best, but editorials and pamphlets alone proved weak weapons against greed and racial hatred. The Cherokees took their case to the Supreme Court. It ruled in their favor, which should have been enough to end the injustice. But court rulings mean nothing if presidents don't ensure that they are carried out. And President Jackson refused to enforce the decision. Bribery, fraud, and guns drove 15,000 Cherokees into exile in the west.

A housewife now, as well as a writer and editor, Maria had to learn how to make ends meet. Her husband gave his energy to causes, not to saving money. She had to be creative about getting by on next to nothing. Out of what she learned came a new book, *The American Frugal Housewife* (1855). For years it was one of the most popular and valued books in American households. She wrote more manuals, one for mothers, another for girls, and both were very popular. Whatever Lydia Maria Child wrote, people wanted to read.

She could have gone on as a popular, noncontroversial writer, earning more and more money, making life easier and more comfortable for herself and David. But a young printer named William Lloyd Garrison had come to town to build a bonfire under the Bostonians. He spared no one. Our politics are rotten to the core, he said. Slavery is a national sin, and we are all alike guilty. New England money has bought human flesh. New England ships have carried black cargoes. New England men have helped forge the fetters of those who groan in bondage. It is the duty of men in the free states, who were constitutionally involved in the guilt of slavery, to speak out against its continuance and to assist in its overthrow. Why delay the work? There must be a beginning, he said. *Now* is the time!

This stranger was reaching the hearts of some whites who were sick of the lie they knew their country was living. Here was a new nation, which held it a self-evident truth that all men are created equal, endowed by their Creator with the unalienable rights of life, liberty, and the pursuit of happiness—and here too was the horrible fact of human slavery.

Maria took up Garrison' challenge in her book *An Appeal in Favor of That Class of Americans Called Africans* (1833/1968). "We first debase the nature of man by making him a slave, and then very coolly tell him that he must always remain a slave because he does not know how to use freedom. We first crush people to the earth, and then claim the right of trampling on them forever, because they are prostrate. Truly, human selfishness never invented a rule which worked out so charmingly both ways!" (p. 169).

She took up the common charge that blacks were, after all, fit to be slaves, for when did they ever resist it? She replied: "By thousands and thousands, these poor people have died for freedom. They have stabbed themselves for freedom, jumped into the waves for freedom, starved for freedom, fought like very tigers for freedom! But they have been hung, and burned, and shot—and their tyrants have been their historians!" (p. 170).

What could be done about it? A great deal, she answered. She cited what the Quakers were doing for conscience's sake, and what the newly organized Anti-Slavery Society stood for. Their object was to turn the public against this evil, by plain and unrelenting exposure of the facts.

She was shunned by former friends and neighbors. Never again would she know anything but a bare and meager existence, always borrowing to stay afloat. But she came to know other and infinitely greater satisfactions. Her indictment of slavery and racism proved to be the most influential book of its kind until the arrival twenty years later of *Uncle Tom's Cabin* (Stowe, 1852/1981). There were old friends who stayed loyal and new ones who came to her because their lives were changed by the power of her thought and feeling. The *Appeal* (1833/1968) was widely read and won innumerable converts to the cause. It appealed to reason and to the heart. Its calm, strong tone, its systematic treatment, its careful statements made it the most convincing book of its time.

Soon after Maria's *Appeal*, the antislavery presses began to issue many pamphlets, newspapers, magazines, and books. Maria's own pen was rarely still. She followed up the *Appeal* with more abolitionist writings. Her way of trying to change the world was through moral persuasion, not physical force. She fought the battle with reason. She was one of a tiny band, the pitifully few who dared oppose government, business, law, society. They stood naked and alone in those early years, defenseless against the vast majority. Yet they had such passion for their cause they soon began to touch the conscience of the nation.

But it was never easy or peaceful for abolitionists, and especially for those who were women. The Southern press and politicians demanded that they be silenced in only one way—with terror and death. The Northerners accused them of plotting the government's destruction. By 1835 the air was heavy with anger. Mobs raided their meetings, attacked their speakers, wrecked their presses, burned their literature. In just one week a hundred incidents of mob violence were reported.

The farmers and mechanics who swung the axes and clubs or burned down the meeting halls were not solely to blame. Maria pointed out that behind them were the leaders of the North who did millions of dollars of business with the South. They would not stand idle while their interests were threatened. Maria showed her courage in many a meeting raided by mobs bent on beating the speakers and frightening the abolitionists into silence.

Women had to struggle for equality with men in the abolitionist movement. The men objected to "female orators" and to their appearances before mixed assemblies of men and women. Maria decided that girls had to be encouraged early, helped to see the world with clearer eyes. So she created a series of popular biographies about outstanding women of the past. She wrote about women who went to jail for their heretical opinions, women who fought against tyrants, women who had wit, talent, learning, and love for beauty which they tried to use for good ends. From this series Maria went on to write the groundbreaking *History of the Condition of Women in Various Ages and Nations* (1835/1972). She showed how they had been enslaved through the centuries. Maria took a double step toward progress when she made her next move, taking up the editorship of a new publication in New York, the *National Antislavery Standard*. She proved to be a superb editor and managed to steer pretty clear of the quarrels and factionalism that were always splitting the abolitionist movement.

After 2 years at the helm, Maria resigned, returning to writing for children. Again she pioneered for women in journalism, this time by writing a regular column about New York, which was carried in several newspapers. She produced a book called *Fact and Fiction* (1846), which was a plea for women's rights. It showed the wrongs suffered by women in a society whose laws were written by men in their own favor.

Maria moved for a time to New Rochelle, NY, a village some distance from New York City. She made her home a station on the Underground Railroad, helping runaway slaves move north to freedom.

When the western territories were thrown open to slavery by Congress in the 1850s, Maria turned herself into a propaganda mill, pouring out letters to the press to gain support for the antislavery colonists in Kansas. She reached still more people by writing a novel about the struggle in Kansas, which the *New York Tribune* ran as a serial.

The Dred Scott decision came, with the Supreme Court proclaiming that African Americans were pieces of property with no rights that the white man had to respect anywhere. The whole country split wider and wider apart. The South took aggressive steps to strengthen slavery. Then in the fall of 1859 tremendous news crackled across the country's front pages—John Brown, with a small band of 16 whites and five blacks, had invaded the South. The raid on Harpers Ferry failed, but it gave a new direction to events. The Union's political power had been—and still was—in the slaveholders' hands. But here came John Brown invading their land and striking slavery at its roots. His armed attack showed that there were people in the North no longer content merely to *moralize* against slavery. The South was hysterically fearful. How many others were arming themselves to follow Brown's example?

As soon as she read Brown was wounded and lying in prison among enemies, Maria offered to come and nurse him. She asked Virginia's Governor Wise for permission. She never was allowed to go, but her exchange of letters with Governor Wise and with Mrs. Mason, the wife of the Virginia Senator who authored the Fugitive Slave Law of 1850, intensified public debate over slavery. The letters were printed in the *New York Tribune* and had a powerful impact on public opinion. The abolitionists broadcast the letters in a pamphlet. Over 300,000 copies were sold, an enormous audience for that day, greater than for anything else Maria had written.

Only 10 years before, there were countless thousands in the North who would not listen to the slightest criticism of slavery or the South. Now there was a vast public spirit that approved John Brown's open war on slavery. And one of the forces that created this change of spirit was Lydia Maria Child. Her heart, her intelligence, her will, her pen helped prepare the North for the final conflict that was soon to end slavery.

The heritage of slavery—the racism that corrodes America—is still with us. But surviving too are people like Maria, knowing pain and anger and injustice, committed to their humanity, struggling to be free.

CHAPTER 16

Dorothea Lange

When I began work, there was no biography of Dorothea Lange. For that matter, only a few of the major American photographers have had anything substantial written about their lives. And even in these books the center of attention is more the photographs than the life out of which they came. What little we know about many of the other significant figures is contained in the brief introductions to collections of their photographs.

But just as we find it useful to learn more about the lives of great painters and poets and dramatists and composers, so should we find it worthwhile to probe the life of a photographer. With Lange I have attempted a narrative of her development as an artist and a portrayal of a life burdened with illness and the conflicting demands of family and profession.

No one, I think, can provide the key to the mystery of human personality or to the creation of art. And Dorothea Lange's personality was as complex and contradictory as we should find the lives of most of our friends to be, if only we could learn this much about them. All the biographer can hope to do is to unearth the facts that have not hitherto been widely known and to offer as clear and truthful an account of her personal development as the evidence permits. In this limited way, perhaps he can contribute something of value to the historians of photography and to the critics of that art.

There are three basic divisions in the nearly 50 years of Lange's work as a photographer. The first begins with her apprenticeship in New York. For about 5 years (1912–1917) she served several photographers in turn, from commercial hacks to such great talents as Arnold Genthe and Clarence White. She then went to San Francisco and ran her own studio for nearly 15 years, establishing herself as one of the leading portraitists on the West Coast.

The second period (1935–1945) is the decade of her work as a documentary photographer for several government agencies. It is for these photographs that she is best known to the public. She was one of that extraordinary cluster of photographers, including Ben Shahn, Walker Evans, and Arthur Rothstein, who served under Roy Stryker at the Farm Security Administration.

Her third period (1945–1965) embraces the last 20 years of her life. Throughout this period, she was handicapped by serious illness. In the intervals when she was able to work, she renewed herself through independent photography. She created many personal photographic essays on a rich variety of themes, working close to home first of all, but traveling widely, too, in Ireland, Egypt, Asia, and Latin America.

Lange had never planned to become a great photographer; she simply wished to make her own work as good as it could be. "Good" meant "being useful, filling a need, really pleasing the people for whom I was working" (Lange, 1968, p. 54). She didn't make any portraits for their own sake. Nor, on the other hand, did she seek out celebrities to photograph for the publicity it would bring herself. Beyond San Francisco, her portrait work was unknown. She was not invited to exhibit her work.

Less than a year after her move to San Francisco, Lange married Maynard Dixon. She was young and unknown. Dixon, then 45, was a distinguished painter of the western wilderness, its people, and its landscapes. At the center of San Francisco's art world, he brought Dorothea into it. Dixon's habit was to make many painting expeditions into the more remote regions of the West, sometimes with Dorothea and more often without. It was on an extended trip into the Navajo and Hopi country in 1923 that she began making photographs of a different kind—of the Indian people and the landscape. Unfortunately, few of them seem to have survived. The only one to be exhibited is titled "Hopi Indian, New Mexico." This trip must have been the seed of her documentary photography. There are photographs made a year later of blacks and of the Chinatown of Carson City, its houses, yards, streets. In 1925 she made a significant decision to move from her expensive Sutter studio. She had begun to feel that the secure living from her portrait studio, this small personal business, wasn't really what she wanted. "I had proved to myself I could do it," she said, "and I enjoyed every portrait that I made in an individual way. . . . But I wanted to work on a broader basis" (Lange, 1968, p. 147). She took space in an unfashionable San Francisco neighborhood—not really risking much, for she had the right clientele and they were willing to follow her.

She continued to use her camera beyond her studio walls, chiefly on her occasional trips with Dixon. Almost unconsciously, she was heading in a new direction. Looking back on the last years of the 1920s, she saw in her portrait work a documentary feeling beginning to emerge. "You were able to sense, if not see, a good deal more about the subject than just faces. They were *larger* photographs" (Dixon, D., 1952, p. 72). In the summer of 1929, the whole family—she and Dixon now had two very young sons—took a vacation in the back country of California. She tried for something new, but her landscape photographs of this trip were terrible, she thought, and she was beginning to feel depressed. Until one day, as she recalled it,

> I was given a big boost by a turbulence of nature. That afternoon I had gone to be by myself for a while, when I saw a thunderstorm piling up. When it broke, there I was, sitting on a big rock—and right in the middle of it, with the thunder bursting and the wind whistling, it came to me that what I had to do was to take pictures and concentrate upon people, only people, all kinds of people, people who paid me and people who didn't. (Dixon, D., 1952, p. 72)

This, she told her son Daniel, was one of the great spiritual experiences of her life.

A few weeks later, in October 1929, the stock market crashed. Production slowed down that winter, and unemployment rose to several million. Lange and Dixon, self-employed professionals, were hit like the rest. When the stocks owned by patrons of the arts shot down in value, the rich stopped ordering portraits and buying art. Commissions for murals were canceled, plans for exhibits were dropped, painters could not collect for work sold earlier. "There was a sense of something ominous and unavoidable impending," Dixon said, "of being caught in the slowly closing jaws of a vise, of complete helplessness in the face of fate" (Dixon, M., 1936, p. 25). This feeling became an obsession, and in the need to free himself of it, he tried to externalize it on canvas. When he exhibited his painting, called "Shapes of Fear," its grim foreboding touched a common chord.

In 1931, although they were still making enough to keep the family afloat, they felt the world was too full of trouble and suffering and decided to get away from it by going to live in Taos, New Mexico. They spent 7 months there, Dixon painting and Lange taking care of the family, but doing little photography. In Taos she saw Paul Strand at work and was amazed at his intense discipline. She hadn't known photographers who gave themselves so completely, so passionately, to their work. She did not think of her work as important enough to require the concentration Strand gave to his photography. She was cooking meals, driving the family here and there, taking care of visitors. "I couldn't work then, really," she said later. "Of course, if I had stated my terms with life, I could have. Maybe I kept myself too busy. But what Paul Strand was able to do, I wasn't. Women rarely can, of course, unless they're not living a woman's life" (Lange, 1968, p. 139). She did take some photographs in New Mexico, but no prints survive.

As the Depression deepened, their income shrank. They gave up their home, boarded the children out, and lived in their studios. Separated from the children except on weekends, she was driven to work harder, and differently. Even her studio portraits of the early 1930s show a change—less abstract, more sharply focused, a greater sense of the here and now. She was still making portraits of the diminishing number of people who could afford them. But the habitual pattern of life was broken. From the window of her corner studio one flight up she could watch the flow of street life. It was no longer firm and purposeful. It was erratic, drifting, uncertain.

> One morning, as I was making a proof at the south window, I watched an unemployed young workman coming up the street. He came to the corner, stopped, and stood there a little while. Behind him were the waterfront and the wholesale districts; to his left was the financial district; ahead was Chinatown and the Hall of Justice; to his right were the flophouses and the Barbary Coast. What was he to do? Which way was he to go? (Dixon, D., 1952, pp. 73–75)

She thought again of that time in the mountains when she had realized she had to take pictures of all kinds of people, not only the rich and the comfortable who could pay her. And thinking to herself, "I better make this happen," she felt compelled to leave the studio and go down into the streets to photograph. If her life had not been shaken up by the Depression, if she had not been separated from her children by the pressure of circumstance, she might have said to herself, "I should do this, but I can't because. . ." giving herself all the plausible excuses for not risking something new. "As so many women say to themselves over and over again, which is one reason why men have the advantage" (Lange, 1968, p. 147). She felt driven to act.

This was 1932, the depth of the Depression, when 14 million people were out of work. She said, "The discrepancy between what I was working on in the printing frame and what was going on in the street was more than I could assimilate. I knew that if my interests in people were valid, I would not be doing only what was in those printing frames" (Herz, 1963, p. 9). Many unemployed drifted about the streets with no shelter, no prospect of jobs, helpless because there was no planned relief—certainly not on the huge scale required.

Nearby Dorothea's studio, a rich woman called the "White Angel" had set up a bread line, and Dorothea decided to photograph it, taking along her brother Martin for protection, for she had no knowledge of how the down-and-out would react to a cold-eyed camera. As it turned out, she needed no bodyguard. "Almost at once," as she told her son Daniel later on, she discovered that photography inside and photography outside were even more sharply different than she had thought. Before, she had been able to arrange her subjects, but now she had to train herself to select them; before she had been concerned chiefly with detail; now she was concerned also with situation. All the tidy routines and methods to which she had been accustomed were, in the streets, swept away by shocks, intrusions, and elusiveness. But even so, it was an easy change for her to make—so natural to her, in fact, that on that first day she took what has since become one of her best-known photographs—"White Angel Bread Line."

What were her feelings when she observed that man on the bread line?

> I can only say I knew I was looking at something. You know there are moments such as these when time stands still and all you do is hold your breath and hope it will wait for you. And you just hope you will have time enough to get it organized in a fraction of a second on that tiny piece of sensitive film. Sometimes you have an inner sense that you have encompassed the thing generally. You know then that you are not taking anything away from anyone: their privacy, their dignity, their wholeness. (Herz, 1963, pp. 9–10)

She took the print of "White Angel Bread Line" and put it up on the wall of her studio, to see how people would react to it. Her portrait customers came in, glanced at it, and turned away. The only comments she got were, "What are you going to do with this kind of thing?" Remembering these exchanges, in years to come, she would tell young photographers, "Don't let that question stop you, because ways open that are unpredictable, if you pursue them far enough" (Lange, 1968, p. 145).

She herself couldn't answer that question. She didn't know what to do with a photograph like "White Angel Bread Line," but looking at the photograph on her wall, she knew it was worth doing. Now, some 60 years later, it has become one of the great images of the Depression era, of people in trouble. As George P. Elliott (1966) has pointed out, this was

> her first photograph to become widely known and her first important one to provide the viewer with something of the context of the lives of the people in it. What has made the picture celebrated is in large part the

image of the unshaved, hunched-up little man in the foreground, leaning on a railing with a tin can between his arms, his hands clenched, the line of his mouth bitter, his back turned to those others waiting for a handout. This image does not derive its power from formal elegance so much as from its being inextricably entangled with the comment it is making. It is art for life's sake. (Elliot & Museum of Modern Art, 1966, p. 9)

It was in this season, the fall of 1932, that what came to be known as Group f/64 was formed in the Bay region. It was short-lived, but it represented a powerful influence in the development of photography. It started in Oakland, in an old studio at 683 Brockhurst, which Willard Van Dyke had taken over from the photographer Annie Brigman and turned into a gallery. As a protege of Edward Weston, Van Dyke had been absorbed in the straight approach to photography. The Brockhurst gallery was soon a hangout for Bay photographers who had turned away from academic pictorialism. Although she knew the f/64 people, Lange was not part of the original group of seven, nor did she join it later. She was more interested in doing socially aware work. The others were more concerned with the formal elements of photography, with the whole technical process; she with *subject*. She did exhibit with the group and learned from them much about technique. "Her conscious aim," as Beaumont Newhall put it, "was less esthetic than informational: the greater the detail, the more her photographs carried that conviction so essential to her needs" (Lange, 1967, p. 6).

After that first day in the streets and "White Angel Bread Line," Dorothea got out of the studio every chance she got. It wasn't easy; she was just gathering her forces. "I wasn't accustomed to jostling about with a camera in groups of tormented, depressed and angry men." But she quickly forgot her fears. Soon, she said, "I'd begun to get a much firmer grasp of the things I really wanted to do in my work" (Dixon, D., 1952, p. 75).

In March 1933, Roosevelt took office and moved to alleviate human suffering by taking swift measures to provide relief and jobs. Still, his administration couldn't solve the crushing problems of the Depression. (It never did, not in peacetime. Only the coming of World War II ended mass unemployment.) Demonstrations by the unemployed continued. On May Day 1933, Dorothea gave herself the task of photographing the demonstration at the Civic Center. She said, "I will set myself a big problem. I will go down there, I will photograph this thing, I will come back, and develop it. I will print it and I will mount it and I will put it on the wall, all in 24 hours. I will do this to see if I can grab a hunk of lightning" (Doud, 1964).

This was the day she made another of her famous photographs, the one of the big policeman with his back to the demonstrators, called "Street Demonstration, San Francisco, 1933." She was still doing portraits, mostly to finance the photographs she wasn't getting paid for, and to contribute her share to the support of her sons. She didn't know what would happen to her documentary photography. She thought often in the early 1930s of how good it would be if she could get paid to do that kind of photography and be spared the strain of trying to maintain it on her portrait business. Early in 1934 the Dixons took a house together again, on Gough Street, reuniting the family. To economize on rent, Dorothea gave up her studio and converted some space at home into her workrooms.

Maynard Dixon, too, had discovered new themes in the Depression. Like many artists of his generation, he had dodged the responsibility of facing social conditions. The Depression, he said, "woke me up to the fact that as an artist I had a part in all this. . . . Painting, as I see it, must be human rather than arty—it is a means to an end. It is my way of saying what I want you to comprehend. It is my testimony in regard to life" (Wallace, 1937, p. 82).

San Francisco was now in the first stages of the turbulent maritime strike of 1934. The port's seamen and longshoremen were among the worst exploited of all workers. Led by Harry Bridges, the unions were demanding changes in wages and working conditions that would permit them to live at last as human beings. Both Dixon and Lange were drawn to the waterfront struggle. Angered by the brutality of the employers and the police, they tried with paintbrush and camera to capture the sense of crisis. Dixon found that although his paintings evoked a sympathetic response, no one wanted to buy pictures of strikers nursing broken heads or homeless men trudging the highways. Even the art critics who were usually attentive to his new work managed to ignore these paintings. He stopped painting social themes. Other artists, like Ansel Adams, shied away from what they dismissed as "soapbox art." Adams wrote Stieglitz that spring that he was

> dreadfully tired of being used as a tool for radical interests—artists in the main are asked to do "proletarian" work, photographers are asked to photograph May Day celebrations, old human derelicts in a dingy doorway, evictions, underpaid workers, etc. I grant that the times are portentous, but I'll be damned if I see the real *rightness* of being expected to mix political economy and emotion for a purpose. . . . I do not like being expected to produce propaganda. Half my friends have gone frantic Red. (Newhall, 1964, p. 98)

That summer Willard Van Dyke gave Dorothea an exhibit at his gallery in Oakland. It was the first public showing of her documentary photography, and the occasion that led to her meeting Paul Taylor, a man her own age and then associate professor of economics at Berkeley. One of the rare academics with a driving concern for the oppressed, he had already done detailed studies of migratory labor. And most important for Lange's future, he had begun to use his amateur's camera as an aid to revealing what he was seeing and learning. Paul Taylor was interested in photog raphy not as a medium for its own sake, but as a tool of social research. An article on migrant labor he wrote in 1931 for *Survey Graphic,* the national magazine, was illustrated by a dozen photographs taken by Ansel Adams, a commission Adams got from the magazine's editor, Paul Kellogg (Meltzer, 1978, p. 82). (*Survey Graphic's* role as a pioneering force in documentary photography has been overlooked. Kellogg was one of the earliest editors to provide serious analyses of contemporary social problems and to make strong use of photographs to complement the text.)

Paul Taylor was not, of course, the first to see this application of the camera. As far back as 1850, only 11 years after photography's invention, the Harvard scientist Louis Agassiz had commissioned a South Carolina photographer to daguerreotype slaves for purposes of documentary identification of race. When he began to use a Rolleiflex, Taylor was confirmed in his opinion that no amount or quality of words alone could convey the problems of the migrant labor he was studying. The camera gave him another language.

Hearing that a man named Van Dyke had a gallery where he sometimes had exhibits that reflected his social concerns, Professor Taylor went to 683 Brockhurst. On the wall he saw a striking array of photographs by a Dorothea Lange, someone he had never heard of. One of the most powerful images, made during the maritime strike, was of a labor leader addressing a crowd through a microphone. Taylor needed just such a shot to go with an article on the strike he had written for *Survey Graphic.* Reached by phone, Dorothea agreed to let him use it, getting $15 from Kellogg as her fee.

That summer of 1934 Dorothea decided her independent photography was the path she wanted to take. There was no name for such photography then. Soon they would be calling it "documentary," a word she never liked. The waterfront photograph, her first documentary picture to be published, appeared in *Survey Graphic* in September 1934. A month later the magazine *Camera Craft* carried the first criticism of her documentary photographs. Written by Willard Van Dyke (1934) it is a marvelously perceptive piece. She had scarcely started along this path and yet he saw in her all the qualities that would swiftly make her one of the finest artists in the field.

It was Van Dyke's initiative that led to Lange's first meeting with Paul Taylor. Some of Van Dyke's friends wanted to photograph the human impact of the Depression, but were uneasy about going into the field and pointing their cameras at people in trouble. Appealed to for help, Professor Taylor arranged for a small group to accompany him to Oroville for a weekend of photography of the self-help coopera-tive that had sprung up there as one way of meeting the problems of the unemployed. Besides Van Dyke, the group included Imogen Cunningham and Dorothea. (Maynard and Dorothea were separated at this time; the divorce was finalized a while later.) That was when Lange and Taylor met for the first time. It was of great significance for both of them. They would marry about a year later, a marriage that would last 30 years and would end with her death, in 1965. For Doro-thea professionally, Taylor would be a great influence. At Oroville she watched him talk to the co-op people in their cabins after their day's chores were finished. She had never seen a social scientist conduct an interview. She was absorbed in the way he drew facts and feelings from people without their being aware of how much they were telling him. Even though he wrote in his notebook while they talked, they didn't seem to be made self-conscious by it. She saw how eager most people were to talk even to strangers, especially if they were talking about themselves, their own experience, their own involvement. He used his notebook unobtrusively and didn't make them stop talking while he wrote. They liked the fact that he was taking down at least part of what they said; it implied he thought they had important things to say.

Professor Taylor arranged for 80 of the photographs made at Oro-ville to be exhibited on the Berkeley campus. He asked the photogra-phers to sign their prints. All signed some, but refused to sign others because, however useful the prints might be, not all the work came up to their professional standards. This notion of a double standard interested him. In their minds there was one standard for "art" photog-raphy and another for "documentary" photography. And only some of their work met both standards. A generation before, the work of Jacob Riis and Lewis Hine in documenting the slums and child labor held no interest for art critics and little for art photographers. But this group Taylor had taken to Oroville at least "recognized the importance of documentation. They weren't concentrated or fixed exclusively on exhibition photographs" (Taylor, 1975, pp. 123–125). Group f/64's ideas on straight photography surely influenced them toward superior doc-umentary work.

That December there was a second show of Lange's work, this time at a public library branch. Viewing it, Ansel Adams saw in her photographs something different from the soapbox art he had recently decried. He wrote:

> She is both a humanitarian and an artist. Her pictures of people show an uncanny perception, which is transmitted with immense impact on the spectator. To my mind, she represents the almost perfect balance between artist and human being. I am frankly critical of her technique in reference to the standards of purist photography, but I have nothing but admiration for the more important things—perception and intention. Her pictures are both records of actuality and exquisitely sensitive emotional documents. Her pictures tell you of many things: they tell you these things with conviction, directness, completeness. There is never propaganda. . . . If any documents of this turbulent age are justified to endure, the photographs of Dorothea Lange shall, most certainly. (Newhall, 1964, p. 82)

It was Paul Taylor's discovery of Lange's work in Van Dyke's gallery, and his realization that she was the photographer he needed for his visual approach to socioeconomic research, that gave her the patron (government) and the means (a regular paycheck) she could not do without.

In the winter of 1934–35, Taylor was asked by California officials to prepare a study of the staggeringly large and complex migration of penniless farm families from the Dust Bowl into California. He asked the state to furnish him the usual staff of researchers and technicians, and then insisted too upon hiring a photographer. Astonished at such an unprecedented request from a social scientist, they resisted. But Taylor insisted that the people in Washington, who would read and evaluate his reports, and make the crucial decisions, must be able to *see* what the conditions of the new migrants were like. His words alone would not be enough to convey the truth with the force and detail required to produce *action*.

In the early 1930s, photographs of a social problem made by either professional or amateur photographers were extremely rare. There were Jacob Riis's pictures, to be sure, and Lewis Hine's, but most people in California had never heard of either man. As for the social scientists themselves, only the anthropologists had begun to use photographs. The other social scientists feared photography was too emotionally loaded to be scientific. It would be distracting. And, said Taylor, "there was then—even more than now—a resistance to facing people as human beings. You free yourself from some responsibilities if you can reduce people to numbers. You don't have to bother with

people. They are just numbers you can manipulate any way you want"
(Taylor, 1975, p. 129).

It took a lot of talk before the agency got used to the idea of using
a photographer for social research. Still, there was no authority to hire
one, no slot for a photographer in the table of organization, and no
funds. It seemed an impasse, until "in a sort of defiant euphoria," as
he put it, the office manager broke the rules and hired Dorothea Lange
at $1,560 a year, listing her as a clerk-stenographer. To get around the
problem of expenses in the field, he increased Paul Taylor's per diem
allowance for travel and entered the cost of her film under "clerical
supplies." Since the agency had no darkroom, and no supplies or staff
for it, she was to develop and print her own work. The division direc-
tor, when told that Dorothea was on the payroll, lectured the office
manager sternly on proper procedure and warned, "We'll try it for a
month, then we'll see" (quoted in Meltzer, 1978, p. 94).

When Dorothea learned her job was safe only for a month, it was
a strain on her. What did she have to do to prove she was worth keeping? Her test came quickly, when disaster threatened the pea pickers
in Nipomo. Several hundred migrant families had flocked into the
small valley in San Luis Obispo County, on the south-central coast,
seeking work in the early pea crop. But bad weather had set in, spoil-
ing the crop, and an endless cold rain fell on desperate families hud-
dled in their old jalopies or under makeshift tents of blankets and
tarpaulins. Like the crop, they lay rotten in the empty, sodden fields,
without shelter, sanitation, food, or the gas to move on. Taylor realized
at once the drama of the pea pickers' plight. In Nipomo he could find
the documentation necessary to attract national attention and force
action to help the migrants. He chose a team of four to go into the
field—three men and Dorothea. Two of the men—Edward Rowell and
Tom Vasey—were graduate students in economics at Berkeley. Taylor
told Rowell this would be the first time they'd have a photographer in
the field. He didn't know how she would be received. He instructed
Rowell to stick with her, to help carry her cameras, and to see that
nothing bad happened. He told Dorothea not to worry on her first day
out. No one knew how the people at Nipomo would feel about someone shooting pictures. "If you don't make a single photograph the first
day," he said, "that's all right with me" (Taylor, 1975, p. 30).

When they got to Nipomo, she went straight to the migrants and
started taking pictures. Right from the beginning, Taylor said, she
showed she could use not only her eye but her ear. Their first times
out she would take pictures and talk with people, listening intently to
what they said, then sidle over to Taylor and repeat what she'd heard

as he scribbled it into his notebook. Later she herself jotted down the phrases people used, the often vivid words in which they distilled their experience. There is, to cite but one example, her photograph of a pea picker leaning against his flivver, and under it what the man said: "This life is simplicity, boiled down."

How she worked the first few times in the field was recalled by Tom Vasey when I interviewed him in 1976: "She was a small person with a slight limp. The characteristic pose was with the Rollei on her left shoulder, held by the left hand. From here it always seemed least distracting to the subject as she brought it down for use after a bit of talk. She was particularly adept in getting closeup cooperation with the women and children." In break periods and at mealtime Vasey found her conversation "always stimulating. Dorothea shared easily but did not dominate" (quoted in Meltzer, 1978, p. 95).

It was on one of those first trips that the reality of the mass migration hit home. Returning from a day's shooting in the field, she stopped to get gas and watched the car full of people ahead of her as she waited her turn at the pump.

> They looked very woebegone to me. They were American whites. I looked at the license plate on the car and it was Oklahoma. I got out and asked which way were they going, were they looking for work? And they said, "We've been blown out." I questioned what they meant, and then they told me about the dust storm. They were the first arrivals that I saw. These were the people who got up that day quick and left. They saw they had no crop back there. They had to get out. All of that day, driving the next miles, I saw these people; and I couldn't wait—I photographed them. (Doud, 1964)

But she quickly proved she could do it all by herself. When she was shooting alone, her method was often to walk up to the migrants, look around quietly, wait until they appeared to be used to her and wouldn't mind, and then take pictures. Sometimes she did it while talking with them, sometimes not. She said she wore her "cloak of invisibility"—the same protective look she had adopted while walking the Bowery as a child. It was almost like playing a game—"they can't see me"—but what made her successful was her natural skill in relations with people, an ability to put them at ease, to make them feel she cared.

She would never intrude her camera upon anyone's privacy. If a person refused to be photographed she would not find some sneaky way to shoot the picture. If nothing was said but she felt unwelcome, she would fool around with her equipment or just go sit down in a corner and let them look her over. She was aware that some people withdrew because they felt she did not belong with them. Tactfully, then, she would speak to them about who she was and what her family was like, where she came from, what she represented, so that she told them much about herself, and truthfully. Then, if she asked questions, it was a fair exchange. It took more time to work that way, but she thought it a human way of meeting her fellows on the same level.

When they spoke to her, she wanted to get down their exact words. Knowing the limit she could hold in her head, she would find some pause in which to scribble down the words in her own short-hand, relying on the rhythm of the speech, and knowing that if she lost just one word it often meant that rhythm would collapse. She believed strongly in the use of those words. To her they were not a repetition of or an intrusion upon the images, but their extension: "What the right words can do for some photographs is enormous" (quoted in Meltzer, 1978, p. 97).

Later, she commented on the difference between what she was doing in the field and what she had done in the streets of San Francisco.

> I had begun to talk to the people I photographed. For some reason, I don't know why, the people in the city were silent people, and we never spoke to each other. But in the migrant camps, there were always talkers. This was very helpful to me, and I think it was helpful to them. It gave us a chance to meet on common ground—something a photographer like myself must find if he's going to do good work. (Meltzer, 1978, p. 97)

But in another respect, the migrants—homeless, cut off from the stable rural communities they had once known—were hard to photograph. "Their roots were all torn out," she said. "The only background they had was a background of utter poverty. It's very hard to photograph a proud man against a background like that, because it doesn't show what he's proud about. I had to get my camera to register the things about those people that were more important than how poor they were—their pride, their strength, their spirit" (Meltzer, 1978, p. 97).

Professor Taylor's reports, illustrated by many Lange photographs, had a powerful effect in Washington. They won support for emergency relief funds to build migrant labor camps. (Incidentally, that housing for migrants turned out to be the first federal public housing in the United States.) But more important, the illustrated reports made Washington realize the migrant problem in the far west was different from elsewhere. It was not simply poverty or tenancy, it was deep dislocation. And Lange's documentary portraits forced the agricultural scientists to stop thinking in narrow terms of land, production, and machinery. This was a question of *people*, too.

In April 1935 a new federal agency for rural rehabilitation was created, called the Resettlement Administration (RA)—later to be renamed the Farm Security Administration. Dorothea was transferred to its Information Division. Now she was officially recognized for her true role and given the job listing of Field Investigator: Photographer. Her assignment would be regional—California and four neighboring states.

Soon after, a Columbia teacher, Roy Stryker—he was not a photographer, but an economist—was hired to start an Historical Section within RA's Information Division. His job was to find ways to bring the agency's programs before the public. Like Paul Taylor, he had long been intensely interested in using photographs for social purposes. He was just feeling his way in his new job, not knowing exactly what to do or how to do it, when the Taylor–Lange reports landed on his desk. They made a powerful impression on him, as did her photographs of migrant labor appearing in current issues of *Survey Graphic*. He wanted her on his payroll, and on September 1, 1935, she transferred to his unit. Now her title was reversed—Photographer: Investigator. Photographer came *first*.

So at the age of 40—she was the oldest photographer on Stryker's staff—she was at last doing what by hindsight we are bound to think she was destined to do. She had found her special gift as a photographer.

CHAPTER 17

Christopher Columbus

If my book departs from the familiar legend of Columbus as heroic explorer, it is not with the goal of muckraking. Rather, it is in the hope that a creative interpretation of the basic truths to be learned from his story will help readers to reject stereotypes and myths that do harm to us all.

Let's look at the man, one of the dominant characters in history. How accurate is the image of Columbus most of us hold in our minds? I began work in 1990 on his biography, called *Columbus and the World Around Him* (1990a), because I was well aware that 1992 would mark the five hundredth anniversary of Columbus's first voyage to the western hemisphere. I had done enough research on European and American history over many years to know that what I had learned about Columbus in my schooldays was remote from the harsh truth. Yet the myth built up about the man had taken powerful hold on the imagination of Americans. And in book after book, even recently written, about the events of Columbus's life, that myth still goes unchallenged.

The conventional story would have us believe that Columbus was one of the best and bravest men of his time. Because he loved adventure, he got the king and queen of Spain to provide him with three ships so he could sail across the ocean to open up a new route to Asia—and to prove the world was round. Landing on some islands in the Caribbean, he "discovered" America and took possession of the land for Spain. He called the red-skinned people who greeted him "Indians." He gave them some trinkets and returned to Spain with a few of the Indians to show them to Ferdinand and Isabella.

This version of the events of Columbus's life for the most part hasn't much to do with the historical record. And it is just as harmful for what it leaves out. Not to make the facts available to young readers is to miseducate them in how international affairs are shaped. It starts with the motives given for the Columbus enterprise. Bland acceptance of such myth makes it easier for the people who wield political power to get away with the platitudes and pieties they feed the public so they can carry out their policies at home and abroad. If we do not learn how to ask probing questions about the past, how will we meet the challenges of the present?

I am not suggesting that children do not need to have heroes and heroines. But must we have only plaster saints? Without sin, without weakness, without fear? Can't leaders be portrayed with at least some of the complexity all human nature has? Men and women can achieve great things, can do wonders in our world, and still be flawed in ways most of us can recognize. Haven't scholars found that to be true of Martin Luther King? And isn't it true too of Thomas Jefferson, whose contradictory impulses and actions I have explored in my biography of the man?

In contrast with the standard version of the life of Columbus, my book takes passages from primary sources to illuminate a different Columbus, the man we need to reconceptualize if the significance of his exploits is to be truly grasped.

To illustrate the point, I will focus on a single issue. Most of the books children read—textbooks as well as trade books—concentrate on the voyages, on the so-called discovery of America. They pretty much ignore the people and the land Columbus found in the New World. But in the encounter between the white Europeans and the Native Americans, what happened? What did the Spaniards do to the indigenous people and to their land?

For evidence we go not to guesswork, not to hypothesis, not to assumption, but to the documents left by Columbus and his men. Here, from the journal of the first voyage kept by Columbus, is an entry made when he landed on the Caribbean shore and saw some people he called Indians. It was Friday, October 12, 1492.

> I, in order that they might develop a very friendly disposition towards us, because I knew that they were a people who could better be freed and converted to our Holy Faith by love than by force, gave to some of them red caps and to others glass beads, which they hung on their necks, and many other things of slight value, in which they took much pleasure. They remained so much our [friends] that it was a marvel . . . (Morison, 1963, pp. 64–65)

That first day in the West Indies, Columbus noted in his journal what struck him most about these strange people.

> They all go quite naked as their mothers bore them; and also the women, ... And some paint their faces, others the body, some the eyes only, oth- ers only the nose. They bear no arms, nor know thereof; for I showed them

swords and they grasped them by the blade and cut themselves through ignorance. . . . These people are very unskilled in arms, as Your Highnesses will see from the seven that I caused to be taken to carry them off to learn our language and return; unless Your Highnesses should order them all to be taken to Castile or held captive in the same island, for with 50 men they could all be subjected and made to do all that one wished. (Morison, 1963, pp. 65–68)

Their generous ways puzzled him.

. . . They are so artless and so free with all they possess, that no one would believe it without having seen it. Of anything they have, if you ask them for it, they never say no; rather they invite the person to share it, and show as much love as if they were giving their hearts. . . . (Morison, 1963, p. 183)

Columbus and the Indians looked curiously, and warily, upon one another. The whites did not know what to make of the Indians, nor were the Indians sure of who and what the whites were. The tendency of the whites was to treat the Indians like animals, while for their part the Indians wondered if the whites might be gods.

For the most part the Indians of the West Indies were peaceful people. Now they collided with Spaniards bent on conquest of the Americas. Trained as a warrior class during the civil wars in Spain between Christians and Moslems, the Spaniards came to the New World fired with religious zeal and a great lust for wealth. The Spaniards believed there was only one God in heaven, and their Catholic Majesties were here on earth to rule it. The natives they would meet must become subjects of the crown and serve it.

The idea that the Indians might have a right to determine their own way of life and to govern themselves never occurred to Columbus. His mission was to bring them under the authority of God and Spain, peacefully if he could, by the sword if necessary. Although he believed he was in the realm of some Asian ruler, he did not hesitate to proclaim that he was taking possession of these lands for the king and queen of Spain.

Thus Your Highnesses ought to resolve to make them Christians, for I believe that if you began, in a short time you would achieve the conversion to our holy faith of a multitude of folk, and would acquire great lordships and riches and all their inhabitants for Spain. . . . (Morison, 1963, p. 92)

Here Columbus was opening the door to the conversion of untold numbers of people to Christianity. He put himself forward as a soldier of the faith, a redeemer of souls. And with this image of himself he justified all the consequences of his Great Enterprise. One of those consequences he brought up himself almost immediately: enslavement. These innocent and trusting Indians could easily be made not only good Christians but "fine servants," by which he meant slaves.

Later, in a letter to his royal patrons, Ferdinand and Isabella of Spain, Columbus remarked how easy it would be to exploit these gentle people.

> . . . You may believe that this island and all the others are as much yours as Castile, that here is wanting nothing save a settlement, and to command them to do what you will. I, with the people on board, who are not many, could overrun all these islands without opposition; for already I have seen that when only three of the mariners went ashore, where there was a multitude of these Indians, all fled, without seeking to do them ill. They bear no arms, and are completely defenseless and of no skill in arms, and very cowardly, so that a thousand would not face three; and so they are fit to be ordered about and made to work, to sow and do all else that may be needed; and you may build towns and teach them to go clothed, and to [adopt] our customs. (Morison, 1963, pp. 122–123)

Columbus could conceive no other connection between Spaniards and Indians than that between master and slave. He had already seen how the Portuguese enslaved the natives of the Canary Islands and the blacks in Africa, and noted how the Church condoned it. Not every Spaniard saw the Indians in this light. Bartolomé de Las Casas (1875–76/1971), the first priest to be ordained in the Americas, knew Columbus well. In one of his books he had this to say about the Admiral's attitude.

> Note here, that the natural, simple, and kind gentleness and humble condition of the Indians, and want of arms or protection, gave the Spaniards the insolence to hold them of little account and to impose on them the harshest tasks that they could, and to become glutted with oppression and destruction. And sure it is that here the Admiral enlarged himself in speech more than he should, and that what he here conceived and set forth from his lips, was the beginning of the ill usage he afterwards inflicted upon them. (quoted in Meltzer, 1990a, p. 101)

On his way home from the first voyage, Columbus wrote a letter to a Crown official, a letter meant for Their Majesties' eyes. After telling how peaceful and generous the Indians were, he says:

I gave them a thousand good, pleasing things which I had brought, in order that they might be fond of us, and furthermore might become Christians and be inclined to the love and service of Their Highnesses and of the whole Castilian nation, and try to help us and to give us of the things which they have in abundance and which are necessary to us. (Morison, 1963, p. 184)

Coming to his landing at Hispaniola he describes the tiny cluster of huts as "a large town" and Guacanagari as "King of the land" with whom he "established a warm friendship. But should he change his attitude the men I have left [at Navidad] would be enough to destroy the entire country" (quoted in Meltzer, 1990a, p. 110).

Holding out the promise of much more, he notes that this was only "a very hasty voyage." If Their Majesties would give him a little more help, "I will give them as much gold as they need . . . spices . . . cotton . . . resin . . . aloes . . . and as many slaves as they ask" (quoted in Meltzer, 1990a, p. 110).

Some of the recent children's books stress Columbus's deep faith in God and his desire to convert "heathens" to Christianity as one of the main motives for his voyages. But what he was really after can be glimpsed in this passage from a journal of the second voyage kept by Cuneo, an adventurer in the fleet.

After we had rested for several days in our settlement it seemed to the Lord Admiral that it was time to put into execution his desire to search for gold, which was the main reason he had started on so great a voyage full of so many dangers. (quoted in Sale, 1990, p. 143)

To give some examples of how the Spanish colonists treated the Indians, we go to Las Casas (1875–76/1971) again. He had come to the Spanish colony on Hispaniola in 1502 and left a vivid description of the almost unbelievable abuses committed by his fellow colonists. Again and again, he says, "I saw all the above things. All these did my own eyes witness." He reports that the Spaniards "made bets as to who would slit a man in two, or cut off his head at one blow; or they opened up his bowels. They tore the babies from their mother's breast by their feet, and dashed their heads against the rocks . . . they spitted the bodies of other babes, together with their mothers and all who were before them, on their swords" (quoted in Sale, 1990, p. 157). When they desired more formal punishment of the Indians, Las Casas reports, they hung them from a gallows, "just high enough for their feet to nearly touch ground, and by thirteens, in honor and reverence for our Redeemer and the twelve Apostles, they put wood underneath and, with fire, they burned the Indians alive" (quoted in Sale, 1990, p. 157).

Once, as he was walking with a file of Spanish soldiers, Las Casas (1875–76/1971) saw them come upon a group of Indians sitting around the plaza of their village. Earlier that day the soldiers had sharpened their swords on whetstones in a river bed. Now they were eager to test out the edges of their swords, and this was their chance. He reports:

> A Spaniard, in whom the devil is thought to have clothed himself, suddenly drew his sword. Then the whole hundred drew theirs and began to rip open the bellies, to cut and kill those lambs—men, women, children and old folk, all of whom were seated, off guard and frightened, watching the mares and the Spaniards. And within two credos, not a man of all of them there remains alive. The Spaniards enter the large house nearby, for this was happening at its door, and in the same way, with cuts and stabs, begin to kill as many as they found there, so that a stream of blood was running, as if a great number of cows had perished. . . . To see the wounds which covered the bodies of the dead and dying was spectacle of horror and dread. (quoted in Sale, 1990, p. 157)

In his book about the Indies, Las Casas offered this summary of what happened in those first years of the Spanish occupation.

> In this time, the greatest outrages and slaughterings of people were perpetrated, whole villages being de-populated. . . . The Indians saw that without any offence on their part they were despoiled of their kingdoms, their lands and liberties and of their lives, their wives, and homes.
>
> As they saw themselves each day perishing by the cruel and inhuman treatment of the Spaniards, crushed to the earth by the horses, cut in pieces by swords, eaten and torn by dogs, many buried alive and suffering all kinds of exquisite tortures, some of the Princes, particularly those in Vega Real . . . decided to abandon themselves to their unhappy fate with no further struggles, placing themselves in the hands of their enemies that they might do with them as they liked. There were still those people who fled to the mountains. (quoted in Sale, 1990, p. 159)

Las Casas lived many years after his experiences in the West Indies. At the end, in his will, he sat down and wrote this agonized prophecy:

> I believe that because of these impious, criminal and ignominious acts, perpetrated unjustly, tyrannously, and barbarously upon them, God will visit His wrath and His ire upon Spain for her share, great or small, in the blood-stained riches, obtained by theft and usurpation, accompanied by such slaughter and annihilation of these people—unless she does much penance. (quoted in Sale, 1990, p. 158)

Bearing in mind all the above, we read these justifications by Spaniards, some 50 years after Columbus, of what they did—and would continue to do—to the indigenous peoples of the New World. First is a Dominican monk, Tomas Ortiz, who drew this sketch of the Indians as wild beasts, a sketch that reminds us of the dehumanizing propaganda against the Jews that Hitler spread before the German people.

> They are more given to sodomy than any other nation. There is no justice among them. They go naked. They have no respect either for love or for virginity. They are stupid and silly. They have no respect for truth, save when it is to their advantage. They are unstable. They have no knowledge of what foresight means. They are ungrateful and changeable. . . . They are brutal. . . . The older they get the worse they become. About the age of ten or twelve years, they seem to have some civilization, but later they become like real brute beasts. I may therefore affirm that God has never created a race more full of vice and composed without the least mixture of kindness or culture. (Todorov, 1984, pp. 150–151)

Next is the Spanish nationalist, Juan Gines de Sepúlveda. He writes:

> Compare then those blessings enjoyed by Spaniards of prudence, genius, magnanimity, temperance, humanity, and religion with those of little men [the Indians] in whom you will scarcely find even vestiges of humanity, who not only possess no science but who also lack letters and preserve no monument of their history except certain vague and obscure reminiscences of some things on certain paintings. Neither do they have written laws, but barbaric institutions and customs. They do not even have private property. . . . How can we doubt that these people—so uncivilized, so barbaric, contaminated with so many impieties and obscenities have been justly conquered? (Hanke, 1949, pp. 122–123)

There is such primary evidence as this in my book, but I take up other issues too. My book tries to illuminate the European culture Columbus grew up in, an age moving from medievalism to the intellectual challenge of the early Renaissance. Readers will see, I hope, how these large social forces shaped the thinking of Columbus, and his burning desire to acquire riches, power, and fame. I don't pretend that Columbus was a unique villain, markedly different from the conquistadors of Spain and other countries. Like many of his day he saw the people of the Americas as inferior beings ripe for enslavement, and their lands as prizes to be seized and exploited by the superior Europeans. The book seeks to explain why.

It isn't only scholars of our own time who have questioned the myths about Columbus and other adventurers of the period of colonial expansion. Back in 1759 Samuel Johnson, the English author, weighed the fruits of the explorations encouraged by King Henry the Navigator of Portugal. He said:

> Much knowledge has been acquired, and much cruelty been committed; the belief of religion has been very little propagated, and its laws have been outrageously and enormously violated. The Europeans have scarcely visited any coast but to gratify avarice, and extend corruption; to arrogate dominion without right, and practice cruelty without incentive. Happy had it then been for the oppressed if the designs of Henry had slept in his bosom, and surely more happy for the oppressors. (quoted in Sale, 1990)

Johnson added that no part of the world has yet had any reason to rejoice that Columbus found support at the Spanish court for his voyages.

Here in the United States, Columbus is honored with his name placed almost everywhere you look—on cities, counties, towns; on rivers, streets, and parks; on colleges and universities and libraries. No one but George Washington has more monuments and statues erected to him. Surely it is time for young people, as well as ourselves, to see the man in all his dimensions.

CHAPTER 18

Hughes, Twain, Child, and Sanger: Four Who Locked Horns with the Censors

I am not a constitutional authority on the First Amendment and freedom of speech or the press. I am neither an investigator of nor a reporter on acts of censorship. I am aware of such events as the attempt to label some publications in the St. Charles County library system "subversive" and the attempt to remove certain periodicals and books from local libraries in California on the ground that they are obscene. The antismut campaign seems to be growing into a serious threat to the freedom to read. The Supreme Court decision that permits the regulation of the reading and viewing of minors has given heart to the censorship forces. I hear that a good many localities and state legislatures have introduced or adopted so-called Ginsberg laws to establish motion picture and literature review boards. Their goal is to shut young people off from obscenity. The difficulty, of course, is to define what obscenity is.

I would like to say something here about censorship and writers. As I think back on the men and women I have written about, I realize that a good number of them had to do battle with censors. Perhaps there is something to learn from their experiences.

Two of the lives I have written about began in Missouri—one in the town of Joplin, the other in the village of Florida. Both men grew up to become writers. Both suffered from censorship. Both had the courage to resist it.

LANGSTON HUGHES

The man from Joplin was Langston Hughes. He was black, born in a country where "white is right." From the beginning he voiced the condition of the black American. He listened, and heard; he saw, and understood; he touched, and felt; he knew, and remembered. Within a few years of his first book, he was the poet laureate of his people. Their life was his life, and he wrote about it as it was.

Hughes was not a poet who wrote about abstract emotions. He wrote about love, to be sure, but it was love in a very particular place. Harlem usually, where people in love had their problems too. Hughes had personal troubles, but because they were often common to his people, many of his poems could be called social poems. Basically, his own desire to realize the dream of American life—"land where opportunity is real, life is free, and equality in the air we breathe"— was the same as that of millions of Jim-Crowed blacks (quoted in Meltzer, 1968, p. 233).

Because he told the truth, and persisted in it, his poems got him into trouble. During the 1920s he was forbidden to visit Cuba by the Machado dictatorship because he had written some poems about the way the sugar plantation owners exploited the cane workers. But it was not until he had returned from a trip to Soviet Russia that censorship got bad enough many times to keep him from appearing on public programs. It started when he was scheduled to be one of several speakers at a program in the colored YMCA branch in Los Angeles. Some people charged he was a communist and the scared Y secretary said that unless Hughes was dropped, the program couldn't go on. Hughes had never been a communist but he soon learned it didn't make any difference to the people making the charge. Anyone visiting Russia in those days and reporting anything favorable, was liable to have the label slapped on him. The voices who cried "red" the loudest, Hughes noted dryly, were never known to be raised against segregation.

In spite of the Y secretary's ruling, the youth committee refused to give in to pressure. But the police were put at the door to keep Hughes out that Sunday afternoon. The young people then told the assembled audience what was happening, and moved the meeting to another place where the poet was allowed to speak.

A near riot broke out in November 1940, when Hughes was to read a few poems with several other authors at a book-and-author luncheon in a Pasadena hotel. Somebody malicious gave Aimee Semple McPherson, the highly publicized evangelist, a copy of Hughes's youthful poem "Goodbye Christ." It was ironic in tone and meant to be a poem against those he felt were misusing religion for profit. In it he mentioned Miss McPherson. She was furious and claimed the poem was anti-Christian. From her pulpit she preached against Hughes, saying, "There are many devils, but the most dangerous of all is the red devil. And now there comes among us a red devil in a black skin!" (quoted in Meltzer, 1968, p. 236).

Her followers showed up to picket the hotel the afternoon Hughes was to speak. They sent a delegation into the hotel "to interrogate me," he said, "on the state of my immortal soul" (p. 236). As their sound truck blared out "God Bless America" the howling mob blocked all traffic. The frantic hotel manager said Hughes would have to leave or he would cancel the entire luncheon. Rather than inconvenience the several hundred guests already there and the half-dozen speakers, Hughes withdrew, barely getting through the mob as the police cars came in answer to a riot call. The afternoon papers revealed that the whole demonstration had been organized by Aimee McPherson's publicity man, and that when the police arrived he had been arrested for refusing to give up the keys to his sound truck stalled midway in the street to block traffic. Hughes said, "This simply proved the point I had tried to make in the poem—that the church might as well bid Christ goodbye if his gospel were left in the hands of such people" (p. 237).

A few years later Hughes was picketed again, this time in Detroit by the "Mothers of America," a group organized by Gerald L. K. Smith. Smith was the man who fomented a riot in Detroit's Sojourner Truth housing project in the hope of keeping blacks out of the government homes built for them.

To be picketed—and it would continue to happen every now and then—was never pleasant, but at least Hughes felt he must be saying something worthwhile. He wasn't turning his back on his people's problems or his country's. Nothing like this would have happened to him if he had limited the subjects of his poems to roses and moonlight. But almost all the beautiful roses he had seen were in white people's yards, not in his.

Once in Gary, Indiana, black teachers were threatened with the loss of their jobs if Hughes accepted their invitation to speak at a public school. In another city a white high school principal, hounded by a few reactionary parents, sought assurance from the FBI, who seemingly told him the scheduled speaker was not a communist. But the principal of the white school still needed to bolster his respectability. When Hughes showed up for the assembly he found that all the black ministers and other black notables in town had been invited to sit on the stage in a semicircle behind him. Stepping out to read his poems, he felt like Mr. Interlocutor in a modern minstrel show. The students must have been overwhelmed, he thought, by this sudden wave of blackness after all those years when they had never seen any blacks at all on their stage.

Coming back home once after completing 45 speaking dates, he wrote, "It's been a running feud with Klan-minded censors from Florida to California who like neither poetry nor Negroes" (quoted in Meltzer, 1968, p. 238). And so it went into the 1950s. There was no telling when a wave of know-nothing patriotism might seize a community or the whole nation. In 1951 even the venerable W. E. B. DuBois was threatened with jail by the federal government for speaking out against militarism. Hughes came to the defense of his childhood hero in a syndicated newspaper column written in words of fire. At the end he said:

> Somebody in Washington wants to put Dr. DuBois in jail. Somebody in France wanted to put Voltaire in jail. Somebody in Franco's Spain sent Lorca, their greatest poet, to death before a firing squad. Somebody in Germany under Hitler burned the books, drove Thomas Mann into exile, and led their leading Jewish scholars to the gas chamber. Somebody in Greece long ago gave Socrates the hemlock to drink. Somebody at Golgotha erected a cross and somebody drove the nails into the hands of Christ. Somebody spat upon his garments. No one remembers their names. (quoted in Meltzer, 1968, p. 239)

Thousands of men and women were victimized in those years for their dissenting opinions. For a long time, during the years when Senator Joseph McCarthy dominated Washington and the headlines, any writer with an independent mind and the courage to speak was fair game for state or congressional investigating committees.

And Hughes was among them. He was summoned before the McCarthy committee in March 1953, when the Wisconsin senator was trying to embarrass a government agency by accusing it of purchasing radical books for distribution to libraries overseas. The effect upon Hughes, as upon so many others, was serious. His lecturing, an important source of his income, fell off badly for a long time. McCarthy was finally discredited before the nation and censured by his fellow senators. But there is no guarantee that such hysteria will not come again.

MARK TWAIN

The other man from Missouri was Mark Twain. He liked success and he delighted in the comforts wealth provided, but he could not abide the worship of money or the sacrifice of human values to the getting of it. He was a funny man all his life, but in the fame he won for his genius, his serious side is too often overlooked. With the same gusto he gave to his get-rich-quick speculations, he heaved bricks at the Vanderbilts, Rockefellers, and Wanamakers. *The Gilded Age* (1873/ 1967) was his first major satire on politics and society. As more and more work came from his pen in the 1870s and 1880s, his scorn of pretense and his hatred of injustice found ever fuller voice. Beneath the laughter you could hear the rage. Mark Twain too was censored. When *The Adventures of Huckleberry Finn* appeared in the 1880s, the Concord Library in Massachusetts banned the novel on the ground that it was morally injurious to the young. The press, taking sides in the censorship fight, put Huck on the front pages. Twain commented: "They have expelled Huck from their library as 'trash suitable only for the slums.' That will sell 25,000 copies for sure" (quoted in Meltzer, 1960, p. 173). On the other end of the town's moral seesaw, the Concord Free Trade Club promptly elected Twain an honorary member.

The book was off to a great sale. But the critics were indifferent or cold. Not one of the country's major newspapers reviewed it, and only one of the national magazines did. Some of the papers editorialized that Twain's day as a writer was done. *Huck Finn,* Mark Twain's master-piece and one of the world's great novels, was too vulgar, coarse, and inelegant for the censors of that genteel age when such robber barons as the ineffable Jay Gould ruled the land.

The book banning continued. In 1905, both *Huck Finn* and *Tom Sawyer* were removed from the children's room of the Brooklyn Public Library because they were, and I quote, "bad examples for ingenuous youth" (Meltzer, 1960, p. 173).

Huck Finn has been criticized by some blacks as racially offensive. At one time, the Associated Press reported that the book had been dropped from the required reading list at Dade Junior College in Mi-ami because black students had complained that the novel of nine-teenth-century life on the Mississippi River embarrassed them.

Twain, on occasion, censored himself. When he was editor of the *Buffalo Express,* a New York newspaper, he fought against segregation in the schools and conducted an antilynching campaign. He wrote edi-torials against injustice wherever he found it and never hesitated to name the wrongdoers, no matter how prominent. Except where his father-in-law, a wealthy coal dealer, was concerned. The rival paper in Buffalo used to wonder publicly why the editor of the *Express* was so docile and quiet about the great coal monopoly question, when he tore into everything else. Later, as a publisher, Twain refused to print a book by one of the muckrakers attacking the oil tycoon Henry H. Rog-ers, who had stepped in to save Twain from financial disaster.

These few acts of self-censorship seem minor, however, when

viewed in the light of Twain's courageous public indictment of his country for what it had begun to do to the rest of the world by the 1890s. The ambitious and ruthless men who became the rulers of steel and oil and railroad kingdoms, used their power in national government to extend an American empire across the globe. Twain joined his friend William Dean Howells in the Anti-Imperialist League and issued many manifestos designed to awaken the country to the "unhuman methods" the McKinley Administration was using against the Filipinos. When General Funston came home from the Spanish-American War to be hailed as a hero, he advised his critics to be silent or risk being labeled traitors. Twain argued that Funston couldn't be blamed for his brutal conduct "because his conscience leaked out through one of his pores when he was little" (quoted in Meltzer, 1960, p. 254).

Of that war in the Philippines, Twain told the New York *Herald* early in 1900:

> We do not intend to free but to subjugate the people. We have gone there to conquer, not to redeem. It should, it seems to me, be our pleasure and duty to make these people free and let them deal with their own domestic questions in their own way. And so I am an anti-imperialist. I am opposed to having the eagle put its talons on any other land. (quoted in Meltzer, 1960, p. 255)

In 1901 Twain wrote an article attacking the imperialism of all nations. It brought him both furious condemnation and high praise, showing, he said, that "the nation is divided, half-patriots and half-traitors, and no man can tell which is which" (quoted in Meltzer, 1960, p. 255). Twain drew up a savage bill of particulars against the great powers for the way they exercised their "civilizing" missions in South Africa, China, the Philippines, the Congo. He called it, "To a Person Sitting in Darkness." It was a superb sermon from a pen warmed up in hell (Anderson, 1972). And it is still, in a century of incessant wars and antihuman acts, as timely as it was in 1901.

What should be remembered now, is that Mark Twain showed his courage when it was needed most—in the midst of the battle. Our army was fighting against the Filipinos when Twain published his conviction that they, the enemy, were right, and we were wrong.

There was no official censorship of the press at that time. Pressure against the expression of dissent came from the popular passions stirred by the jingoist newspapers. Those who spoke out fearlessly suffered private abuse and public denunciation. Many other writers felt the same way as Twain and Howells. Publications eager to print what notable authors had to say on almost any other subject, found no space for dissenting opinions. William and Henry James, William Vaughn Moody, Hamlin Garland, Thomas Wentworth Higginson, Ambrose Bierce, Finley Peter Dunne, Edgar Lee Masters, Edwin Arlington Robinson—they all vigorously opposed militarism and interference in the affairs of other nations. And many of these writers were called traitors for exercising their freedom of speech and conscience.

There is no way of proving it, but I am convinced that if the government had imposed censorship, Twain and his fellow writers would have taken to an underground press to continue their fight for peace and freedom.

LYDIA MARIA CHILD

In the generation before Mark Twain was born there were writers who had to carry on a kind of literary guerrilla warfare against the forces of censorship. Lydia Maria Child was one of them. At 22, this self-educated Massachusetts woman had written one of the first American novels to deal with the Indians—and from their point of view, not the white invader's.

William Lloyd Garrison, a printer, got hold of the strings of Mrs. Child's conscience and pulled her into the abolitionist movement. The substantial citizens of Boston, not wanting to be disturbed, hated the abolitionists. But Mrs. Child, like Garrison, believed it was necessary to damn and torment the complacent until their consciences awoke. For anyone—lawyer, preacher, professor—to be silent in the face of slavery was to share in the guilt of its existence.

The free blacks in the North lived an existence cramped and confined by all kinds of discriminatory laws and customs. Just as in the slave South, education of the blacks was violently opposed. Almost everywhere schools for blacks were planned or opened, they were dropped or destroyed.

Mrs. Child decided to write about slavery and to make an attack upon race prejudice the core of her book. In 1833 she published *An Appeal in Favor of That Class of Americans Called Africans* (1968). It was the first antislavery volume to be published in the United States and was equally distinguished as one of the earliest arguments against race prejudice.

After a masterful attack upon the slave South, she pointed out that the people of the North could not flatter themselves that they were any better. "The form of slavery doesn't exist among us," she said, "but the very spirit of the hateful thing is here in all its strength" (1833/1968,

p. 195). Our prejudice against the blacks, she warned, is just as deep-seated and chronic. In what schools are blacks treated equally? In what theater can they expect a decent seat? In what church do they share our pews? In what restaurant do we dine together? In what boat or stagecoach or railroad or streetcar are they not segregated? To what business—besides cutting hair, shining shoes, or waiting on tables—are they allowed to aspire?

Yet, Mrs. Child went on, who in this country dares to publish anything on this subject? Our books, our magazines, our newspapers, have all been silent, or exerted their influence on the wrong side. We made slaves, she said, and slavery makes the prejudice. "Let us no longer act upon the narrow-minded idea that we must always continue to do wrong, because we have so long been in the habit of doing it" (1833/1968, p. 134).

She knew the power and wealth of the country were up in arms against the abolitionists. She knew ridicule and abuse would be heaped upon anyone who joined the antislavery cause. But, she said, "the gold was never coined for which I could barter my individual freedom of acting and thinking upon any subject. . . . The only true courage is that which impels us to do right without regard of consequences" (1833/1968, pp. 206–207).

Mrs. Child had need of that kind of courage. Although her indictment of slavery and racism in the *Appeal* proved to be the most influential book of its kind until the arrival of *Uncle Tom's Cabin* (Stowe, 1852/1981), some 20 years later, the consequences to her of publishing the *Appeal* were swift and terrible. She felt as though she had marched into the enemy's camp, alone. Only yesterday the leading literary magazines had all hailed her. She was the most popular woman writer in the country, South as well as North. And suddenly, for lending her pen to the cause of the slave, an overwhelming tide of abuse swept over her. The magazines refused her work. The respectables of Beacon Hill, who had patronized her for 10 years, at once shut their doors against her. The sales of all her other books dropped disastrously. Outraged mothers canceled subscriptions for her magazine, *Juvenile Miscellany*, and within a year the publication was dead.

Commenting on Mrs. Child's case some years later, Wendell Phillips, who was converted to abolitionism by reading her book, said no young author ever made a costlier sacrifice. Fame and social position were in her grasp, every door was opening to her, a life of hardship was changing to one of ease, she was tasting the sweetness of having her talents recognized. "No one had supposed that independence of opinion on a moral question would wreck all this" (quoted in Meltzer,

1965, p. 43). But confronted suddenly with the alternative of leading a gagged life or seeing that life wrecked, she never hesitated.

MARGARET SANGER

Censorship was the enemy in the life of another rebel with a cause, Margaret Sanger. To Mrs. Sanger, birth control was the first freedom for women. "No woman can call herself free," she said, "until she can consciously choose whether she will or will not be a mother" (quoted in Meltzer, 1969, p. x).

The right of a woman to plan her family through birth control is one of the most crucial ideas of this century. Today, the use of birth control by "pill" or many other medically approved methods is supported by the U. S. Supreme Court and all state laws. It is so accepted by society that it is hard to believe Mrs. Sanger went to jail nine times to win this fight.

A trained nurse, this beautiful redheaded daughter of an Irish-American Catholic family began with the goal of changing women's attitudes toward sex, emphasizing that "the procreative act is natural, clean, and healthful." In language that anyone could understand she wrote a series of articles called "What Every Girl Should Know" and published them in the *Socialist Call* in 1912. Until then, no newspaper or magazine had dared to tell women the important facts about their own bodies. The reason for this silence was the wall of prudery and fear that had been piled stone upon stone during the nineteenth century to shut away sex as a dirty secret. Almost anything about sex was unmentionable in those decades. An all-powerful censorship law adopted by Congress in 1873 classified all such information as pornography. The law was named after Anthony Comstock, founder and secretary for life of the Society for the Suppression of Vice. With his fanatical followers, he got some 30 states to follow Congress with their own "little Comstock laws." The Post Office Department gave Comstock himself a special agent's power to open any letters, packages, pamphlets, or books going through the mails. He personally decided what was "lewd," "obscene," "indecent," "immoral." Since no one had drawn up any rules or guidelines as to what these words meant, Comstock was judge and jury of what could be sent through the mails.

I will not go into detail about Mrs. Sanger's fight against Comstockery. It is enough to say here that the government censorship Comstock instituted made enormously difficult the emancipation of American women. At every step Mrs. Sanger tried to take, censorship stood guard. But she and her small band of followers were fearless. Arrested again and again for publishing her opinions on sex, or for opening a clinic for birth control, she was advised by lawyers to compromise, to give in here and there, to take suspended sentences in return for pleading guilty. She refused. "I'm not concerned about going to jail," she would insist. "The question is whether or not I have done something obscene. If I have not, I cannot plead guilty" (quoted in Meltzer, 1969, p. 73).

She dramatized the issue by going into court without a lawyer. She stood alone against the federal government, defying a stupid law as a woman speaking with the voice of all women. Not defense, but attack! That was always her weapon. She lectured; she published; she spoke on street corners and at factory gates, at mine pits and shipyards, in slum tenements and high society parlors; she organized locally and nationally; and slowly, year by year, she changed public opinion.

Today we know what a great difference this one woman's life has made in all our lives. The censorship forces had to give way in the end to this fragile little woman who was determined that her sex, as she put it, should not remain "a brood animal for the masculine civilizations of the world" (quoted in Meltzer, 1969, p. 73).

REMOVING THE BLINKERS

You may ask, what is the relevance of all this history to the young? It has the meaning of all true history, the meaning of what it is to be American. We cannot endure as a people, as a nation, unless we can distinguish between that which is true and that which is false about this country. Ours is not a past of sweetness and light, no matter what the textbooks tell us. Textbooks avoid the conflicts and the disorders that have taken place in our past. No wonder they bore students.

In the recounting of our past we have been the victims of censorship, a censorship more disastrous by far than any brought about by the hunters of the obscene and the pornographic. For when we have not learned the truth about our past, we cannot find the truth in the present. Sometimes the censorship I speak of has been active, conscious, deliberate—the blotting out of some aspects of the truth by Comstocks who crusaded for their blinkered version of life. More often it has been a censorship by omission, a censorship by people so unaware of any vision of life but their own that they cannot see the humanity and the suffering of people different from themselves. Here, of course, the most obvious examples are those of us who look at the world through white eyes. That perspective is deadly narrow. It has created a white American nationalism and self-righteousness that have imprisoned us. It was that perspective which Twain and some of his fellow writers learned to detest for the gross damage it did to the world and to us.

"America—ever onward and upward." "America, God shed his grace on thee, and crown thy good with brotherhood from sea to shining sea." Listen to those words with a black ear. And know then what Langston Hughes meant when he wrote the line, "America, you've never been America to me," in his poem "Let America Be America Again" (Hughes & Bontemps, 1949).

Think of American history from the side of color—the Native Americans, the Hispanics, the African Americans. And not only color—I mean any minority group, any ethnic group that has stood outside the WASP citadel. Look for the story of the Puritans burning the Indians while giving thanks to God. Of Jackson forcing the Cherokees out of their ancestral homeland to take the long Trail of Tears to the West. Of the concentration camps for these, our first families, which we call "reservations." Of the way we crushed the Cuban rebellion in 1898 and then went on to do it to the Filipinos too. Of our domination of the Latin nations to the south of us. And most of all, of the way we enslaved black people, Bible and prayer book in our hand.

This is part of our tradition, this violence to individuals, to races, to classes, to other nations. So too is the violence that has protested the status quo—the Boston Tea Party and the American Revolution, the slave revolts and the Civil War, the great strikes and the uprisings in the black ghettoes.

Are these tensions, these conflicts, inevitable? Do they stem from the kind of society we are? Does this happen in other lands and in other kinds of society, and for what reasons?

None of us has easy answers, but we need to know the facts and to think about their meaning. We can learn these facts only from the study of American history. And as I and many others have pointed out elsewhere, we need stronger reflection of these issues in our textbooks. When blandness, comfortable platitudinizing, and national arrogance characterize our history books, they leave children unprepared for the struggles we are all part of now. We cannot heal ourselves unless we know our wounds.

Epilogue:
On Being a Writer

What is it like to be a writer?

Of course it differs for all of us in this profession, in many ways. But there are also things that we share in common. Now I'm at that stage where I can look back and examine the path that took me to this point. That path has had many twists and turns, wholly unexpected, and with unpredictable consequences. One of the frightening ones occurred several years ago.

As James Thurber (1955) is said to have put it at a comparable stage of his life—that is, entering old age—I had developed inflammation of the sentence structure and a definite hardening of the paragraphs. While traveling downtown on a crowded bus, a man who looked to be even older than I felt, offered me his seat. I refused it, of course, implying politely that I was just as sturdy as he was. Then we started to chat, and he asked me if I knew the medical definition of the moment of death. No, I said—tell me. Well, he said, when you're over 65, and you wake up in the morning, and you start getting out of bed, and nothing hurts—then you know you're dead.

These old bones were not yet in that blissful, painless condition. I was still writing, although not the number of hours daily I had once been able to enjoy. As time passed, I seemed to want a different balance of my days. More time for music, and more time to walk the streets of the city or the fields and paths in the country. At one point I thought I'd have to give up writing altogether. My batteries seemed to have run down. I felt tired, drained, listless. I couldn't focus on the work at hand. I had no ideas for what to write next. Months went by in this horrid dull state, and I concluded that my days as a writer were over. I happened to be entering my sixty-fifth year when this occurred, and I seized on that as the reason for my sorry disintegration. The time for my annual medical checkup came round just then, and I went through the usual battery of tests at my doctor's. A couple of days later he called to tell me that my blood tests revealed I was at the tail end of a siege of viral hepatitis, and that the condition I had complained of was entirely due to that illness. Instantly I felt wonderful! Almost before I put down the phone, ideas began to bubble up in my mind and before the week was up, the writing was flowing as though my pump had been magically primed.

My entry into the world of book authorship had its roots in a crisis of age too. I'd been a professional writer all my adult life, but in the fields of journalism and public relations. I'd started at Columbia, determined to be a teacher, but when one of my professors sent a paper I'd written to a magazine editor, and it was published, it made me think perhaps there was another way I could earn my living.

If only someone had pointed out to me what John Steinbeck reportedly said when accepting the Nobel Prize in 1962: "The profession of book-writing makes horse-racing seem like a solid, stable business." Well, I had no such warning ready at hand. So seeing my name in print was one reason I gave up teaching. The other reason was the Depression. These were the early 1930s, and, despite the New Deal, many millions were still jobless. My father never earned much of a living, but in those hard times it became impossible. Somehow he managed now and then to tuck a five dollar bill into letters from home and with that, daily duty in the college dining hall for my meals, a Saturday job selling ladies shoes downtown, and a scholarship for my tuition, I got by.

But gradually, college began to seem pointless. Few people with college degrees were finding jobs, unless their family had the right connections. My father died in my senior year, and my mother needed help, so I quit school—my mother never forgave me for that—a few months before graduation and tried to find a job, any job. I failed. So I went on relief to keep from starving. Some months later, clutching that copy of my one published piece as proof of my professional standing, I managed to get work on the WPA Federal Theater Project. There I wrote background material on the great variety of plays the project produced, material funneled to teachers who brought their classes to see our performances. Those three-and-a-half years on the Federal Theater were among the richest of my life. Not only for the worth of what we were all trying to do, but for the insight into the real world it gave me. Besides an education in one of the major arts, it was a kind of postgraduate political training layered on top of the student movement I had been part of at Columbia. No, we were not making bombs in basements or stacking guns for some impossible revolution. We were joining demonstrations of the unemployed to demand jobs, we were walking picket lines with working people seeking better wages, we were helping dispossessed tenants pick up their furniture from the sidewalk and put it back in their apartments, we were writing editorials against Fascist or Nazi professors from abroad invited to speak on our campus, and then picketing outside college halls when they gave their messages of hate.

On the Federal Theater Project, we spent endless hours picketing and sitting-in and demonstrating at WPA headquarters in New York and busing down to Washington to confront Congress with our plain need to survive. Those jobs paying us $23.86 a week were all we had to keep ourselves and our families alive, as well as our human dignity. Sometimes our protests staved off drastic budget cuts, more often they failed, but we never gave up.

The budget cuts of the Reagan–Bush years could look back proudly to their Neanderthal ancestors of the 1930s, who wouldn't give a dollar bill to save a single soul. In the end, the coalition of conservative southern democrats and northern republicans killed the Federal Theater, and, soon after, all the other arts projects too. Until very recently, I would look at what was happening and say to my wife, "Let's go, Hildy. Isn't this where we came in?" Thinking about it as an historian, I wonder if anyone reads history, or ever absorbs its lessons.

But to get back to my first book. For some 20 years I had used writing as my tool to make a living. After the WPA job collapsed, I managed to keep going on various editing and writing jobs. Then came World War II. I spent nearly 4 years in the Air Force as an air traffic controller, keeping my hand in by writing stray pieces for camp newspapers and service magazines. After the war I became a researcher and staff writer for a weekly dramatic documentary called *Assignment Home* on the CBS radio network. Later I worked for Henry Wallace while he aimed for the Presidency in the 1948 election—and missed badly. And then I joined the public relations staff of a big corporation, writing all kinds of material on the job—from news releases and speeches to film scripts, and editing technical volumes for the scientific community.

By now I was edging 40—the male climacteric. I worried that my time might be running out. And what had I done with my life? Who would ever want to read anything I had written? What use had it all been?

Somehow, writing a book seemed the way to solid ground. (I never stopped to think it might be a rotten book.) Yesterday's newspaper was stone cold dead. But a book? That, to my naive mind, promised to be read forever. While I was casting about for a subject, it occurred to me that with a wife and two children I couldn't afford to give up the weekly paycheck. My wife was very understanding. "I'll let you out of the dishes," she said, "if you write a book." Later, she turned this around and told everybody the only reason I wrote books was to get out of doing the dishes.

I found my subject—a history of black people in America, to be told with a big and solid text combined with a thousand illustrations (Meltzer & Hughes, 1956). When I began to make notes, I knew only a little about black history, and the enormous magnitude of the research task became clear only as I made some headway. But it was never a chore. It was a stretching of my mind, a deepening of my emotional capacities, a disciplining of my organizing powers. And of course, when I decided to find a collaborator and Langston Hughes agreed to work with me, it meant the beginning of a friendship that lasted until his death in 1967. I owe much to him for his professional example, his encouraging sympathy, his understanding of the world black and white Americans are living in together—if so differently.

That first book launched me on a bifurcated career for the next dozen years. I held full-time jobs while I wrote many books on my own time. Then in 1968 came the moment when I felt confident I could give up a salaried editorship in medical journalism and survive by giving all my energies to writing what I cared most about.

I didn't anticipate, back in 1968, how very soon stagflation and the mergers and conglomerates in the book business would have a terrific impact on many aspects of publishing. The big book or "blockbuster" has meant that works of literary or social merit are often bypassed for more readily marketable "products." It has meant a steep decline in editorial standards in recent years. Not universally—but in too many places. Now the fate of many serious writers who try to make their living solely by books is to struggle simply to stay alive.

Many of us cannot afford to write any more, unless we are lucky enough to have salaried spouses or a job. Or, as in my case, we are lucky enough to reach the age when we can draw retirement benefits from Social Security. And even here, if we earn anything above a certain modest income, we are bound to return one dollar for every two.

But of course many writers do write only for money. Or at least end up that way.

Let's get down to basics: What is a writer?

Simply a man or woman who writes. It is a profession that has no entrance requirements. To be a doctor you need a medical degree, to be an architect you need a license. To be a writer you need only find someone to publish you. And if you have the money, you can even publish yourself.

Writing is the chief activity of the serious writer—although it may not be the activity that takes up most of his time. One of our great poets, William Carlos Williams, spent more of his life as a family physician, delivering babies and tending the sick, than at his desk writing poems. T. S. Eliot, until he was about 60, gave most of his time to being a banker, an editor, and a publisher. Wallace Stevens was a Hartford insurance executive all day long, and one of our leading poets only in his spare time. But to all of them—and to most writers—writing is their central purpose. They write because they have something to say, or think they have something to say. A great many have nothing to say, but nevertheless manage to get published. And, unfortunately, if they and the publisher make some money out of it, they continue to get published. Sadly, some writers do have enough to say to make a novel or two, but go on trying to make other books after the well has gone dry. Others, and not many others, can tap a spring that never fails to run clear and bright.

If a writer has something to say, he can't think about writing without thinking about readers. He wants to communicate, to talk to somebody, to have his words overheard, at least. It may be disputed, but I think that's true of even the most abstract poets. I think no one really writes for himself alone, although writers disappointed in their dreams of publication may console themselves with that notion.

The medium the writer works in is language. The writer works with words, the painter with pigments, the sculptor with stone or wood or metal, the composer with tones, the potter with clay. Each is a craftsman, itching to make something real, some object or artifact that will exist independently, that will have a life of its own, that will have some effect, some meaning in the lives of people the craftsmen will never see.

Most writers, like most craftsmen, believe in the importance of their medium. Language is the special gift of humans (unless we now must add, of porpoises too) and the force that holds a nation and a civilization together. Everyone, literally everyone, adds to language's resources, inventing and improvising, modifying and molding. Writers plunge into that vast pool and comes up with the best they can find, adding to it their own creations, shaping something new and, hopefully, something permanent.

A little later I will say a bit more about the creative aspect of writing; here I thought you might like to know something about the practical, or bread-and-butter side of the writer's life. First, then, is the fact that very, very few writers can earn a living simply by writing books. Perhaps there are now 20,000 people in our country who consider themselves professional authors, and yet one authority estimates that only some 200, or 1%, earn the major part of their incomes, year in and year out, by writing books.

It begins this way. When the writer has an idea, he presents it in some form—usually an outline and perhaps sample chapters—to a publisher for consideration. If the idea is liked, the publisher pays the writer an advance to go on with the work.

A southern writer once equated the writer's situation with that of the tenant farmer who goes to the plantation store to get credit so that he can start next year's crop. That man is a cotton sharecropper, while the writer is a literary sharecropper. The system is set up so that each has minimal economic security. The planter and the publisher keep each man alive so that they can create cotton and books, by the sale of which the planter and publisher earn their living. Each sharecropper gets an advance—the tenant farmer a small sum per month, just enough so that he can eat and clothe himself while he farms, and the writer a lump-sum advance so that he can eat and clothe himself while he writes. For both, the advance is barely enough to keep body and soul together.

The advance the writer draws is of course against the future royalties his book may earn. It should be pointed out that some authors, like many tenant farmers, never get out of debt and never receive a check for earned royalties. One or two of such commercial fiascos—no matter how high the intrinsic value of the book—and the writer is no longer on the publisher's list.

Nowadays, the average advance that writers get is not sufficient to feed and clothe them and their family while they write the book. The high cost of living forces writers to find means of financing themselves. They must either do other kinds of writing that bring direct cash returns or take some kind of job with a regular paycheck. That is, unless they have been clever enough to be born with an inheritance or to marry a rich woman or a rich man. Sometimes a foundation will put some money into the writer's project, so that he or she can devote all his or her time and energy to it, but that is still rare enough not to be broadly significant.

What about when the book is finally published? No jackpots are at the end of that rainbow, except, once more, for a very, very few writers. A major book club choice, serialization in a national magazine, a sale to TV or to Hollywood: These are possible for only a handful of writers.

For most authors, whatever income there will be will come from bookstore sales, and this is a sad picture. Although the price of almost everything else has gone up, authors' royalties have gone down. Sixty years ago royalties were 20% of the retail price for popular novels, but later they dropped to a maximum of 15%, and this was reached at the end of a sliding scale. Ten percent is the royalty on the first several thousand copies sold, and, unfortunately, most writers never get to enjoy the next step up the ladder. If a book is priced at $20 and manages to sell 5,000 copies in a year, the author will collect royalties of $10,000.

If it took the writer a year to do the book—and many books take longer than that—the writer earned the equivalent of $200 a week for that year's work, or about the minimum hourly wage provided by law for the most unskilled labor. He may spend another year or two on his next book—and fail to sell it to any publisher.

If the sale goes up to 20,000 copies, the author will earn about $40,000. But a bookstore sale of 20,000 copies is extremely rare. Sad to say, in our country with a population of 250 million, if a hardcover book goes over 20,000 copies it may make the national bestseller lists. Most novels don't sell over 5,000 copies and are losing ventures for both author and publisher. Nonfiction does somewhat better. As for poets, a sale of 800 or 1,000 copies is about the average. It is said that only two American poets earned their living with their poems—Robert Frost and Ogden Nash.

The writer who does produce a bestseller has everything rigged against him. A tremendous proportion of his earnings will be taken away from him, for the income tax laws are very rough on writers, actors, athletes, and others who have brief periods of prosperity. Writers have, for almost 100 years, been pressing for remedial legislation that would take into account their long dry spells, but nothing has been changed thus far. The depletion allowance that has fattened many a Texas millionaire shows that oil is considered a more vital natural resource than imagination.

How, then, does the writer keep alive? Some very good writing has come from authors who have jobs completely unrelated to writing. They earn their living installing plumbing, selling refrigerators, or teaching, and do their writing in their spare time. But, with the exception of those who teach, this has been true of very few, I think. Usually the job is too exacting or too tiring, and no energy is left for the rigorous task of writing.

If, on the other hand, the writer finds a more congenial job, involving the use of his craft, he is often too tired of writing upon order by the end of the day to sit down at home and work on what he would call his real, his best, writing.

Most professional writers therefore make a living by their trade. Writing for magazines provided a major source of income in the heyday of the big-circulation publications. But that field has shrunk considerably. The general or family-type magazines have failed one after another. Now picture magazines, news magazines, and special interest magazines have replaced them. But these are often completely or largely staff-written, and reach narrower markets, which usually mean lower rates are paid.

Some writers pick up occasional fees from lecturing to forums, to women's clubs, or on the campus. Others do that for love, or to promote a book, or because they have children in the audience.

Writers hired to write on salary have probably increased in number tremendously since World War II. The federal government made considerable use of them for propaganda and information services at that time, and the practice has grown steadily. Now local and state governments, too, hire writers for a great number of functions. Corporations, of course, hire writers by the dozens, to draft speeches or prepare press releases, or write articles for house organs. Film, radio, and television companies need writers; and newspapers, magazines, advertising agencies, and publishing houses have always found them indispensable.

The freelance writer—if he has iron nerve and a family that doesn't worry about missing meals—has an infinite variety of chores open to him, from ghosting the sinful autobiographies of fresh young presidential candidates, from which the sin has been carefully extracted, to collaborating with celebrities whose studies the public is eager to read. Such writing jobs can put bread and meat on the table and sometimes even champagne and lobster. But almost always this work is done not for love, but for money. Even those writers who earnestly want to do their best find, within a few years, that they must choose between quality and quantity. To eat regularly, quantity is usually demanded.

At this point I might say a word about the great prominence of the promoted book, that is, the book that is not the author's own idea, but that he has been persuaded or directed to write by a publisher or an agent because there seems to be a market for it. The promoter with the idea seeks out a freelance writer who will take on the assignment, not out of any sense of inner urgency, but because he wants the money held out to him. Often a quite successful writer will not find the time to write the book he really wants to write because he has signed contracts to write books someone else thinks people will want to buy. E. B. White, I believe, once said a writer should be permitted a special space on his income tax form for the capital loss he sustains—either from writing something he doesn't want to write at all, or from failing to write something he wants terribly to write.

All this is part of the steadily intensifying problem in our country of maintaining writing as a profession with dignity and independence. Some years ago, the distinguished American novelist, the late Glenway Wescott, questioned—only semi-humorously—whether he could really be considered a professional writer in the sense in which professional is applied to other fields of work. In any walk of life, he said, to be a professional must mean not only to devote one's best energies and perhaps a 40- or 50-hour week to it, but to make or try to make one's living by it. Mr. Wescott, who was then in his sixties, said that except for a 10-year period when he was in his twenties, he hadn't produced enough publishable manuscripts to be self-supporting. In over 40 years of writing he had had only two novels that sold well, and those appeared 18 years apart.

Mr. Wescott thought the basic problems for authors and other creative people are chiefly economic—the costs of training and apprenticeship, the development or the shrinking of markets and outlets, the impact of the new mass media on old methods of publishing books.

We have all found out, Wescott said, that in a plutocratic democracy money is a symbol as well as a livelihood and a necessity. When a famous writer ends his life in poverty or living off the benefactions of friends or relatives, he does not suffer any more than any other old person, but the general cultural effect throughout the nation is worse. It serves notice to all and sundry that writing is a second-class way of life.

Let's go back about 150 years to remind ourselves of one American who lived for his writing, but was never able to make a living by it. When Henry David Thoreau was asked to supply a biographical entry for a Harvard record book, he wrote:

> I am a Schoolmaster, a private Tutor, a Surveyor, a Gardener, a Farmer, a Painter, I mean a House Painter, a Carpenter, a Mason, a Day Laborer, a Pencil Maker, a Glass-Paper-maker, a Writer, and sometimes a Poetaster. My steadiest employment is to keep myself at the top of my condition. (quoted in Harding & Bode, 1958, p. 186)

Thoreau had much to say about living, and the problem of earning a living. In his essay *Life Without Principle*, he wrote:

The ways by which you may get money almost without exception lead downwards. To have done anything by which you earned money merely, is to have been truly idle and worse. If the laborer gets no more than the wages which his employer pays him, he is cheated, he cheats himself. If you would get money as a writer or lecturer, you must be popular, which is to go down perpendicularly. Those services which the community will most readily pay for, it is most disagreeable to render. You are paid for being something less than a man. (quoted in Krutch, 1989)

Thoreau goes on to state:

Those slight labors which afford me a livelihood, and by which it is allowed that I am to some extent serviceable to my contemporaries, are as yet commonly a pleasure to me and I am not often reminded that they are a necessity. So far I am successful. But I foresee that if my wants should be much increased, the labor required to supply them would become a drudgery. If I should sell both my forenoons and afternoons to society, as most appear to do, I am sure that for me there would be nothing left worth living for. I trust that I shall never thus sell my birthright for a mess of pottage. I wish to suggest that a man may be very industrious, and yet not spend his time well. There is no more fatal blunderer than he who consumes the greater part of his life getting his living. All great enterprises are self-supporting. The poet, for instance, must sustain his body by his poetry, as a steam planing-mill feeds its boilers with the shavings it makes. You must get your living by loving. (quoted in Krutch, 1989)

Did any writer ever get less, commercially, from his work than Thoreau? He wrote his *A Week on the Concord and Merrimack Rivers* while he was at Walden Pond from 1845 to 1847. The book itself, rejected by several firms, was not published until 1849, and then only when Thoreau guaranteed to underwrite the cost of the book if it did not sell.

It did not sell. The publisher demanded payment of the cost of publication. Thoreau was driven to—for him—the desperate expedient of trying to make business deals. He came near to speculating in cranberries, and then was obligated to manufacture $1,000 worth of pencils and slowly dispose of, and finally sacrifice, them in order to pay the publisher the $100 he owed. It took Thoreau 4 years to raise that $100.

The unsold stock of copies of *A Week* was then shipped to him— 706 copies out of a total printing of 1,000—and Thoreau lugged them on his back up to the attic. "I now have a library of nearly 900 volumes, over 700 of which I wrote myself," he noted wryly in his journal that night (quoted in Meltzer & Harding, 1962, pp. 178–179).

In those same 2 years at the pond, Thoreau wrote a good part of his other book, *Walden* (Krutch, 1989). It seemed so close to publication that an advertisement announcing it was bound into the back of *A Week*. But the failure of *A Week* postponed the publication of *Walden* for another 5 years. No publisher wanted to risk a second failure.

Thoreau, however, did not lose faith in himself or in his writing. He reworded the manuscript of *Walden*, revised it, polished it, cut it, and added to it through eight distinct, complete revisions. Finally, largely through his friend Emerson's intervention, the new firm of Ticknor and Fields was persuaded—reluctantly—to take a chance and issue *Walden*. It appeared on August 9, 1854, and it sold 2,000 copies—in 5 years.

The world, then, ignored Thoreau. Only a handful of his literary neighbors recognized his worth as a man and as an artist. Nobody out there beyond Concord seemed to be listening. He published two books and a scattering of magazine articles in a lifetime of writing, and, for a generation after his death, that seemed to be the end.

But it was not the end. In addition to *A Week* and *Walden*—*Walden* has never been out of print in the more than 130 years since Thoreau died of tuberculosis at the age of 44, and has gone into over 150 editions—there are now the four volumes of his collected pieces and the 14 volumes of his rich and beautiful *Journal* (1981). And surrounding this shelf of 10,000 printed pages there is a steadily growing mountain of hundreds and hundreds of books about Thoreau and his work, to which I happily added two small contributions.

To return finally to what we started with, the writer's situation . . . Thoreau had something to say for those—writers or not—who, faced by hard resistance to their hopes and dreams, take the path of least resistance. He tells us:

> It is remarkable how easily and insensibly we fall into a particular route, and make a beaten track for ourselves. I had not lived there [at Walden] a week before my feet wore a path from my door to the pondside; and though it is some time since I trod it, it is still quite distinct. It is true, I fear, that others may have fallen into it, and so helped to keep it open. The surface of the earth is soft and impressible by the feet of men; and so with the paths which the mind travels. How worn and dusty, then, must be the highways of the world, how deep the ruts of tradition and conformity! I did not wish to take a cabin passage, but rather to go before the mast and on the deck of the world, for there I could best see the moonlight amid the mountains. I do not wish to go below now.

I learned this, at least, by my experiment: that if one advances confidently in the direction of his dreams, and endeavors to live the life which he has imagined, he will meet with a success unexpected in common hours. . . . If you have built castles in the air, your work need not be lost; that is where they should be. Now put the foundations under them. (quoted in Krutch, 1989, p. 343)

Bibliography

The American Heritage dictionary of the English language. (1976). New York: Dell.

Anderson, F. (Ed.). (1972). *A pen warmed-up in hell: Mark Twain in protest.* New York: Harper & Row.

Barbusse, H. (1983). *Under fire.* London: Dent.

Barnes, G. H. (1933). *The antislavery impulse, 1830–1844.* New York: D. Appleton-Century.

Botkin, B. A. (Ed.). (1945). *Lay my burden down: A folk history.* Chicago: University of Chicago Press.

Chernyshevsky, N. G. (1986). *What is to be done?* Ann Arbor, MI: Ardis.

Child, L. M. (1824). *Hobomok, A tale of early times.* Boston: Cumming Hillard Co.

Child, L. M. (1825). *The rebels: Or Boston before the Revolution.* Boston: Cumming Hillard Co.

Child, L. M. (1846). *Fact and fiction.* New York: C. S. Francis & Co.

Child, L. M. (1855). *The American frugal housewife* (33rd ed.). New York: Samuel S. & William Wood.

Child, L. M. (1968). *An appeal in favor of that class of Americans called Africans.* New York: Arno Press. (Original work published 1833)

Child, L. M. (1972). *History of the condition of women in various ages and nations.* Gordon Press. (Original work published 1835)

Coleman, J. W. (1940). *Slavery times in Kentucky.* Chapel Hill: The University of North Carolina Press.

Collier, J. L., & Collier, C. (1974). *My brother Sam is dead.* New York: Four Winds Press.

Collier, J. L., & Collier, C. (1985). *The winter hero.* New York: Scholastic.

Collier, J. L., & Collier, C. (1987). *Who is Carrie?* New York: Dell.

Collier, J. L., & Collier, C. (1992). *War comes to Willy Freeman.* Magnolia, MA: Peter Smith.

Coman, C., & Dater, J. (1988). *Body and soul.* Boston: Hill & Co.

Cullinan, B. (1986, January/February). Books in the classroom. *Horn Book Magazine, LXII*(1), 108–110.

cummings, e. e. (1978). *The enormous room.* New York: Liveright.

Daugherty, J. H. (1939). *Daniel Boone.* New York: Viking Press.

de Trevino, E. B. (1965). *I, Juan de Pareja Elizabeth Borton de Trevino.* New York: Farrar, Straus & Giroux.

Defoe, D. (1697). *An essay upon projects.* London: R R for Thomas Cockerill.

Defoe, D. (1807). *Robinson Crusoe*. New Haven, CT: Sydney's Press of Increase Cooke & Co.

Defoe, D. (1962). *Moll Flanders*. New York: Collier Books.

Dickens, C. (1984). *Oliver Twist*. New York: Dodd, Mead. (Original work published 1838)

Dixon, D. (1952, December). Dorothea Lange. *Modern Photography, 16*(12), 68–77.

Dixon, M. (1936). *Outline of his life* [prepared for WPA Monograph]. Unpublished in Edith Hamlin Collection, San Francisco.

Dos Passos, J. (1964). *Three soldiers*. Boston: Houghton Mifflin.

Doud, R. K. (1964, May 22). [Interview with Dorothea Lange]. Archives of American Art, Detroit.

Douglass, F. (1845). *Narrative of the life of Frederick Douglass, an American slave*. Boston: Anti-Slavery Office.

Douglass, F. (1969). *My bondage and my freedom*. New York: Dover. (Original work published 1855)

Drinnon, R. (1961). *Rebel in paradise: A biography of Emma Goldman*. Boston: Beacon Press.

Egoff, S. (1969). Precepts and pleasures: Changing emphasis in the writing and criticism of children's literature. In S. Egoff, G. T. Stubbs, & L. F. Ashley (Eds.), *Only connect* (pp. 419–446). New York: Oxford University Press.

Elliott, G., & Museum of Modern Art. (1966). *Dorothea Lange*. Garden City, NY: Doubleday.

Fisher, M. (1972). *Matters of fact: Aspects of non-fiction for children*. New York: Crowell.

Fitzgerald, F. (1979). *History of America revised: History schoolbooks in the twentieth century*. Boston: Little, Brown.

Forbes, E. (1944). *Johnny Tremain*. Boston: Houghton Mifflin.

Franklin, B. (1964). *The autobiography of Benjamin Franklin*. New Haven, CT: Yale University Press. (Original work published 1868)

Freedman, R. (1987). *Lincoln: A photobiography*. New York: Clarion Books.

Fritz, J. (1982a). *What's the big idea, Ben Franklin?* New York: Putnam Publishing Group.

Fritz, J. (1982b). *Why don't you get a horse, Sam Adams?* New York: Putnam Publishing Group.

Fritz, J. (1982c). *Will you sign here, John Hancock?* New York: Putnam Publishing Group.

Gara, L. (1961). *The liberty line: The legend of the underground railroad*. Lexington: University of Kentucky Press.

Gay, P. (1976). *Style in history*. New York: McGraw-Hill.

Grimm, J., & Grimm, W. (1960). *Deutsches worterbuch* (1st ed.; 16 vols.). Leipzig: S. Hirzel. (Original work published 1854)

Hale, J. R. (1977). *Renaissance Europe*. Berkeley: University of California Press.

Hanke, L. (1949). *A Spanish struggle for justice in the conquest of America*. Philadelphia: University of Pennsylvania Press.

Harding, W., & Bode, C. (Eds.). (1958). *The correspondence of Henry David Thoreau*. New York: New York University Press.

Hardy, B. (1987). *The collected essays of Barbara Hardy: Narrators and novelists* (Vol. 1). Sussex, Great Britain: The Harveste Press Ltd.

Heinzen, K. P. (1881). "Murder and liberty" [a volume of pamphlets]. Indianapolis: Lieber. (Original work published 1853)

Hemingway, E. (1988). *A farewell to arms*. New York: Macmillan.

Herz, N. (1963, April). Dorothea Lange in perspective. *Infinity, 12*(4), 5–11.

Hirsch, E. D. (1988). *Cultural literacy*. New York: Random House.

Hitler, A. (1962). *Mein kampf*. Boston: Houghton Mifflin. (Original work published 1940)

Hughes, L. (1963). *The big sea*. New York: Hill & Wang.

Hughes, L. (1964). *I wonder as I wander*. New York: Hill & Wang.

Hughes, L., & Bontemps, A. (Eds.). (1949). *The poetry of the Negro, 1746–1949*. New York: Doubleday.

Jan, I. (1973). *On children's literature*. London: Penguin.

Krutch, J. W. (Ed.). (1989). Walden *and other writings by Henry David Thoreau*. New York: Bantam Books.

Lange, D. (1967). *Dorothea Lange looks at the American country woman*. Commentary by B. Newhall. Los Angeles: Amon Carter Museum at Fort Worth and Ward Ritchie Press.

Lange, D. (1968). *Dorothea Lange: The making of a documentary photographer*. A volume of transcribed interviews (conducted 1960–61) by Suzanne Riess, Regional Oral History Office, The Bancroft Library, University of California, Berkeley.

Langton, J. (1972, July 17). Fair or unfair? Confessions of a literary contest judge. *Publishers Weekly*, 88–90.

Las Casas, B. (1971). *History of the Indies*. (A. Collard, Trans.). New York: Harper & Row. (Original work *Historia de las Indias* published in Madrid: Imp. de M. Ginesta in 1875–76)

Latham, J. L. (1955). *Carry on, Mr. Bowditch*. New York: Houghton Mifflin.

Lilienblum, L. (1842). *The sins of youth*. Boston: Massachusetts Sabbath Sunday Society.

Locke, J. (1689). *An essay concerning human understanding: In four books*. London: Printed by Eliz. Holt for Thomas Basset.

Malcom X. (1965). *The autobiography of Malcom X*. New York: Grove Press.

Mather, C. (1710). *Bonifacius: An essay upon the good*. Boston: Printed by B. Green for Samuel Gerrish.

Meigs, C. (1968). *Invincible Louisa: The story of the author of* Little Women. Boston: Little, Brown. (Original work published 1933)

Meltzer, M. (1960). *Mark Twain himself*. New York: Crowell.

Meltzer, M. (1965). *Tongue of flame: The life of Lydia Maria Child*. New York: Crowell.

Meltzer, M. (1967). *Thaddeus Stevens and the fight for Negro rights*. New York: Crowell.

Meltzer, M. (1968). *Langston Hughes: A biography*. New York: Crowell.

Meltzer, M. (1971a). *Slavery: From the rise of Western civilization to the Renaissance*. New York: Cowles Book Company.

Meltzer, M. (1971b). *To change the world: A picture history of reconstruction*. New York: Scholastic.

Meltzer, M. (1974a). *Bound for the Rio Grande: The Mexican struggle*. New York: Knopf.

Meltzer, M. (1974b). *Remember the days: A short history of the Jewish American*. New York: Doubleday.

Meltzer, M. (1974c). *World of our fathers: The Jews of Eastern Europe*. New York: Farrar, Straus & Giroux.

Meltzer, M. (1976a). *Never to forget: The Jews of the Holocaust*. New York: Dell.

Meltzer, M. (1976b). *Taking root: Jewish immigrants in America*. New York: Farrar, Straus & Giroux.

Meltzer, M. (1978). *Dorothea Lange: A photographer's life*. New York: Farrar, Straus & Giroux.

Meltzer, M. (1980). *The Chinese Americans*. New York: Crowell.

Meltzer, M. (1983). *The terrorists*. New York: Harper & Row.

Meltzer, M. (1984). *The black Americans: A history in their own words*. New York: Harper & Row.

Meltzer, M. (1985). *Ain't gonna study war no more: The story of America's peace-seekers*. New York: Harper & Row.

Meltzer, M. (1986). *Poverty in America*. New York: Morrow.

Meltzer, M. (1987a). *The American revolutionaries: A history in their own words, 1750–1800*. New York: Crowell.

Meltzer, M. (1987b). *The landscape of memory*. New York: Viking Penguin.

Meltzer, M. (1988a). *Benjamin Franklin: The new American*. New York: Franklin Watts.

Meltzer, M. (1988b). *Rescue: The story of how gentiles saved Jews in the Holocaust*. New York: Harper & Row.

Meltzer, M. (1988c). *Starting from home: A writer's beginnings*. New York: Viking Penguin.

Meltzer, M. (1990a). *Columbus and the world around him*. New York: Franklin Watts.

Meltzer, M. (1990b). *Crime in America*. New York: Morrow.

Meltzer, M. (1990c). *Underground man*. New York: Harcourt Brace & Jovanovich.

Meltzer, M. (1991a). *Bread—and roses: The struggle of American labor, 1865–1915*. New York: Facts on File. (Original work published 1967)

Meltzer, M. (1991b). *Brother, can you spare a dime? The Great Depression, 1929–1933*. New York: Facts on File. (Original work published 1969)

Meltzer, M. (1991c). *Freedom comes to Mississippi: The story of reconstruction*. New York: Modern Curriculum Paperback.

Meltzer, M., & Harding, W. (1962). *A Thoreau profile*. New York: Crowell.

Meltzer, M., & Holland, P. G. (Eds.). (1982). *Lydia Maria Child: Selected letters, 1817–1880*. Amherst: University of Massachusetts Press.

Meltzer, M., & Hughes, L. (1956). *A pictorial history of negro Americans*. New York: Crown.

Meltzer, M., & Lader, L. (1969). *Margaret Sanger: Pioneer of birth control*. New York: Crowell.

Monjo, F. N. (1968). *Indian summer*. New York: HarperCollins.

Monjo, F. N. (1970a). *The drinking gourd*. New York: Harper & Row.

Monjo, F. N. (1970b). *The one bad thing about father*. New York: Harper & Row.

Monjo, F. N. (1972). *The secret of the sachem's tree*. New York: Coward, McCann & Geoghegan.

Monjo, F. N. (1974). *Grand papa and Ellen Aroon: Being an account of some of the happy times spent together by Thomas Jefferson and his favorite granddaughter*. New York: Holt Rinehart & Winston.

Monjo, F. N. (1976). *Willie Jasper's golden eagle: Being an eyewitness account of the great steamboat race between the Natchez and the Robert E. Lee, as told by a boy on board the Natchez*. Garden City: Doubleday.

Monjo, F. N. (1977). *The house on Stink Alley: A story about the Pilgrims in Holland*. New York: Holt, Rinehart & Winston.

Monjo, F. N. (1980). *Prisoners of the scrambling dragon*. New York: Holt, Rinehart & Winston.

Monjo, F. N. (1991). *Letters to horseface: Young Mozart's travels in Italy*. New York: HarperCollins.

Morison, S. E. (Ed.). (1963). *Journals and other documents on the life and voyages of Christopher Columbus*. New York: Heritage Press.

Newhall, N. (1964). *Ansel Adams: The eloquent light*. San Francisco: Sierra Club.

Northup, S. (1853). *Twelve years a slave: Narrative of Solomon Northup, a citizen of New-York, kidnapped in Washington City in 1841, and rescued in 1853, from a cotton plantation near the Red River, in Louisiana*. Buffalo, NY: Auburn, Derby & Miller.

O'Dell, S. (1980). *Sarah Bishop*. Boston: Houghton Mifflin.

Olmsted, F. L. (1862). *The cotton kingdom: A traveller's observations on cotton and slavery in the American slave states. Based upon three former volumes of journeys and investigations* (2nd ed.). New York: Macmillan. (Original work published 1861)

Plutarch. *Parallel Lives* (Vols. 46–47, 65, 80, 87, 98–103). Loeb Classical Library.

Remarque, E. M. (1984). *All quiet on the western front*. Boston: Little, Brown.

Sale, K. (1990). *The conquest of paradise: Christopher Columbus and the Columbian legacy*. New York: Random House.

Samuels, E. (Ed.). (1939). *The education of Henry Adams*. Boston: Houghton Mifflin.

Schanberg, S. H. (1985). *The death and life of Dith Pran*. New York: Penguin.

Schoenberner, G. (1973). *The yellow star: Persecution of the Jews in Europe, 1933–1945*. New York: Bantam Books.

Scott, W., Sir. (1962). *Ivanhoe*. New York: Collier Books. (Original work published 1830)

Shakespeare, W. (1992). *The merchant of Venice*. New York: Washington Square Press/Pocket Books.

Siebert, W. H. (1898). *The underground railroad from slavery to freedom.* New York: Arno Press.

Still, W. (1872). *The underground rail road.* Philadelphia: Porter & Coates.

Stowe, H. B. (1981). *Uncle Tom's cabin.* New York: Penguin Books. (Original work published 1852)

Taylor, P. S. (1975). *Paul Schuster Taylor: California social scientist.* A volume of transcribed interviews (conducted 1970–72) by Suzanne Riess and Malca Chall, Regional Oral History Office, The Bancroft Library, University of California, Berkeley.

Thomas, B. P. (1950). *Theodore Weld, crusader for freedom.* New Brunswick, NJ: Rutgers University Press.

Thoreau, H. D. (1981). *Journal.* Princeton, NJ: Princeton University Press.

Todorov, T. (1984). *The conquest of America* (R. Howard, Trans.). New York: Harper & Row.

Townsend, J. R. (1968). The present state of English children's literature. In S. Egoff, G. T. Stubbs, & L. F. Ashley (Eds.), *Only connect* (pp. 407–418). New York: Oxford University Press.

Tsung, L. C. (1963). *The marginal man.* New York: Pageant Press.

Twain, M. (1884). *The adventures of Huckleberry Finn (Tom Sawyer's comrade).* London: Chatto & Windus.

Twain, M. (1897). *The adventures of Tom Sawyer.* Hartford, CT: American Publishing Co. (Original work published 1875)

Twain, M. (1967). *The gilded age.* London: Cassell. (Original work published 1873)

Van Doren, M. (1939). *Shakespeare.* Westport, CT: Greenwood Press.

Van Dyke, W. (1934, October). The photographs of Dorothea Lange: A critical analysis. *Camera Craft, 41*(10), pp. 461–467.

Van Loon, H. W. (1985). *The story of mankind: The classic history of all ages for all ages.* New York: Liveright. (Original work published 1921)

Wallace, G. (1937). *Maynard Dixon: Painter and poet of the far west.* California Art Research Project [WPA Project No. 2874], San Francisco.

White, E. B. (1945). *Stuart Little.* New York: Dell.

White, E. B. (1952). *Charlotte's web.* New York: HarperCollins Children's Books.

White, E. B. (1973). *Trumpet of the swan.* New York: HarperCollins Children's Books.

Yates, E. (1967). *Amos Fortune, free man.* New York: Dutton Children's Books. (Original work published 1950)

Yick Wo v. Hopkins. (1886). 118 U.S. 356, 6 S.Ct. 1064, 30L.Ed. 220.

Books by Milton Meltzer

CHEAP RAW MATERIAL: HOW OUR YOUNGEST WORKERS ARE EX-
PLOITED AND ABUSED (1994)

ANDREW JACKSON AND HIS AMERICA (1993)

GOLD: THE TRUE STORY OF WHY PEOPLE SEARCH FOR IT, MINE IT,
TRADE IT, STEAL IT, MINT IT, HOARD IT, SHAPE IT, WEAR IT, FIGHT
AND KILL FOR IT (1993)

LINCOLN IN HIS OWN WORDS (ill. by Stephen Alcorn) (1993)

THE AMAZING POTATO: A STORY IN WHICH THE INCAS, CONQUISTA-
DORS, MARIE ANTOINETTE, THOMAS JEFFERSON, WARS, FAM-
INES, IMMIGRANTS, AND FRENCH FRIES ALL PLAY A PART (1992)

THOMAS JEFFERSON: REVOLUTIONARY ARISTOCRAT (1991)

AFRICAN AMERICAN HISTORY: FOUR CENTURIES OF BLACK LIFE (with
Langston Hughes) (1990)

THE AMERICAN PROMISE: VOICES FROM A CHANGING NATION (1990)

THE BILL OF RIGHTS: HOW WE GOT IT AND WHAT IT MEANS (1990)

COLUMBUS AND THE WORLD AROUND HIM (1990)

CRIME IN AMERICA (1990)

AMERICAN POLITICS: HOW IT REALLY WORKS (1989)

VOICES FROM THE CIVIL WAR (1989)

BENJAMIN FRANKLIN: THE NEW AMERICAN (1988)

RESCUE: THE STORY OF HOW GENTILES SAVED JEWS IN THE HOLO-
CAUST (1988)

STARTING FROM HOME: A WRITER'S BEGINNINGS (1988)

THE AMERICAN REVOLUTIONARIES: A HISTORY IN THEIR OWN
WORDS, 1750–1800 (1987)

THE LANDSCAPE OF MEMORY (1987)

MARY McLEOD BETHUNE: VOICE OF BLACK HOPE (1987)

GEORGE WASHINGTON AND THE BIRTH OF OUR NATION (1986)

POVERTY IN AMERICA (1986)

AIN'T GONNA STUDY WAR NO MORE: THE STORY OF AMERICA'S
PEACE-SEEKERS (1985)

BETTY FRIEDAN: A VOICE FOR WOMEN'S RIGHTS (1985)

DOROTHEA LANGE: LIFE THROUGH THE CAMERA (1985)

THE JEWS IN AMERICA: A PICTURE ALBUM (1985)

MARK TWAIN: A WRITER'S LIFE (1985)

THE BLACK AMERICANS: A HISTORY IN THEIR OWN WORDS (1984)
A BOOK ABOUT NAMES (1984)
THE TERRORISTS (1983)
THE HISPANIC AMERICANS (1982)
THE JEWISH AMERICANS: A HISTORY IN THEIR OWN WORDS: 1650–
     1950 (1982)
LYDIA MARIA CHILD: SELECTED LETTERS, 1817–1880 (Edited with Patricia
     G. Holland) (1982)
THE TRUTH ABOUT THE KU KLUX KLAN (1982)
ALL TIMES, ALL PEOPLES: A WORLD HISTORY OF SLAVERY (Ill. by Leo-
     nard Everett Fisher) (1980)
THE CHINESE AMERICANS (1980)
THE COLLECTED CORRRESPONDENCE OF LYDIA MARIA CHILD (Text-
     fiche, edited with Patricia Holland) (1980)
THE HUMAN RIGHTS BOOK (1979)
DOROTHEA LANGE: A PHOTOGRAPHER'S LIFE (1978)
NEVER TO FORGET: THE JEWS OF THE HOLOCAUST (1976)
TAKING ROOT: JEWISH IMMIGRANTS IN AMERICA (1976)
VIOLINS AND SHOVELS: THE WPA ARTS PROJECTS (1976)
BOUND FOR THE RIO GRANDE: THE MEXICAN STRUGGLE, 1845–1850
     (1974)
THE EYE OF CONSCIENCE: PHOTOGRAPHERS AND SOCIAL CHANGE
     (with Bernard Cole) (1974)
REMEMBER THE DAYS: A SHORT HISTORY OF THE JEWISH AMERICAN
     (1974)
WORLD OF OUR FATHERS: THE JEWS OF EASTERN EUROPE (1974)
HUNTED LIKE A WOLF: THE STORY OF THE SEMINOLE WAR (1972)
THE RIGHT TO REMAIN SILENT (1972)
UNDERGROUND MAN (1972)
SLAVERY: A WORLD HISTORY (1971, 1972)
TO CHANGE THE WORLD: A PICTURE HISTORY OF RECONSTRUC-
     TION (1971)
FREEDOM COMES TO MISSISSIPPI: THE STORY OF RECONSTRUCTION
     (1970)
BROTHER, CAN YOU SPARE A DIME? THE GREAT DEPRESSION, 1929–
     1933 (1969)
MARGARET SANGER: PIONEER OF BIRTH CONTROL (with Lawrence
     Lader) (1969)
LANGSTON HUGHES: A BIOGRAPHY (1968)
BLACK MAGIC: A PICTORIAL HISTORY OF THE NEGRO IN AMERICAN
     ENTERTAINMENT (with Langston Hughes) (1967)
BREAD—AND ROSES: THE STRUGGLE OF AMERICAN LABOR, 1865–
     1915 (1967)
THADDEUS STEVENS AND THE FIGHT FOR NEGRO RIGHTS (1967)
TIME OF TRIAL, TIME OF HOPE: THE NEGRO IN AMERICA, 1919–1941
     (with August Meier) (1966)

TONGUE OF FLAME: THE LIFE OF LYDIA MARIA CHILD (1965)
IN THEIR OWN WORDS: A HISTORY OF THE AMERICAN NEGRO (3 vols.)
    (1964, 1965, 1967)
A LIGHT IN THE DARK: THE LIFE OF SAMUEL GRIDLEY HOWE (1964)
THOREAU: PEOPLE, PRINCIPLES, AND POLITICS (1963)
A THOREAU PROFILE (with Walter Harding) (1962)
MILESTONES TO AMERICAN LIBERTY (1961)
MARK TWAIN HIMSELF (1960)
A PICTORIAL HISTORY OF AFRICAN-AMERICANS (with Langston
    Hughes, C. Eric Lincoln, and Jon Michael Spencer) (1956; rev. eds.: 1963,
    1968, 1973, 1983, 1995)

Index

About the Author...

Milton Meltzer, a distinguished biographer and historian, is the author of more than 85 books for young people and adults. Born in Worcester, Massachusetts, and educated at Columbia University, he has written or edited for newspapers, magazines, books, radio, television, and films.

Among the many honors his books have won are the Christopher, Jane Addams, Carter G. Woodson, Jefferson Cup, Washington Book Guild, Olive Branch, and Golden Kite Awards, as well as five nominations for the National Book Award. Many of Meltzer's books have been chosen for the honor lists of the American Library Association, the National Council of Teachers of English, and the National Council for the Social Studies.

and the Editor

E. Wendy Saul is an Associate Professor in the Department of Education at the University of Maryland Baltimore County. She writes and teaches about the social construction of children's and adolescent literature and has served for 8 years as the Associate Editor of *The New Advocate*. Currently she works as Principal Investigator for two programs funded by the National Science Foundation—the Elementary Science Integration Project and Computer Access to Science Literature. Her books include *Science Fare* (Harper, 1986), *Vital Connections: Children, Science and Books* (Library of Congress, 1990), and *Science Workshop* (Heinemann, 1993).